HANDFULS *of* SCRAPS

PIECED INTO AMAZING QUILTS

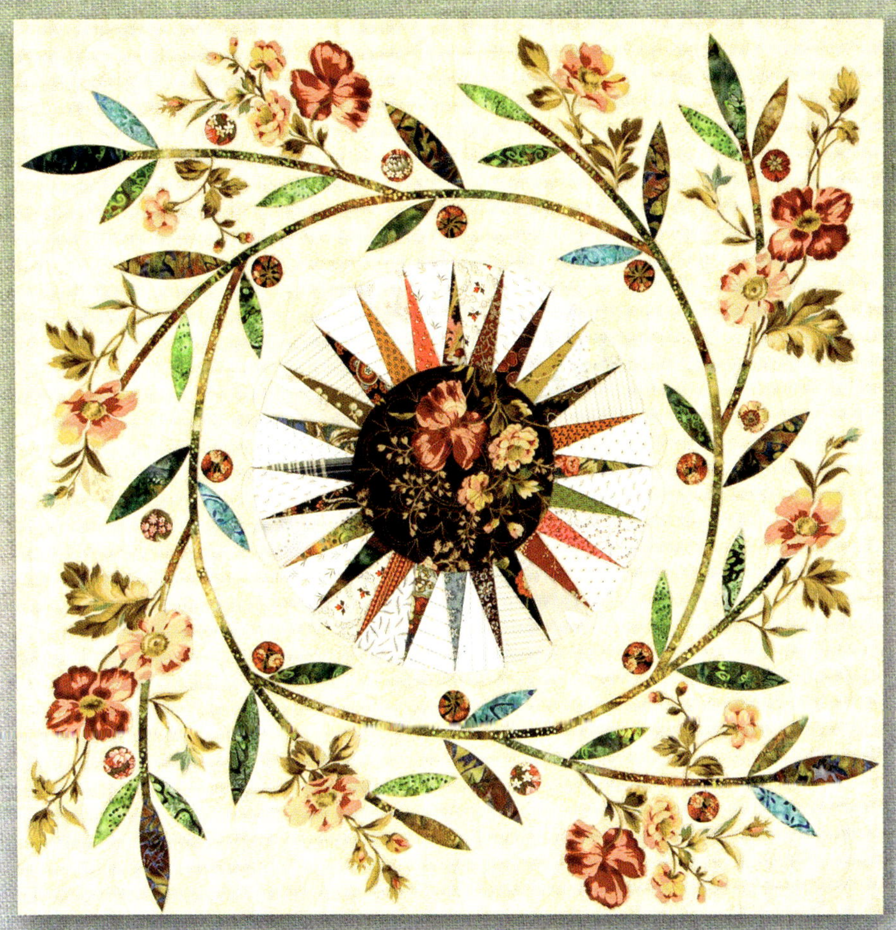

DEDICATED

to my Mama

for noticing my scraps and reminding me
how good it feels to make something out of nothing.

BY EDYTA SITAR *for* LAUNDRY BASKET QUILTS

ACKNOWLEDGMENTS

Like scrappy quilts made of many tiny pieces, this book is the product of many caring hands. Thanks to the following special people for sharing their talent and time to help me create this inspiration for you:

My husband Michael—my closest friend and business partner—encourages my every quilting stitch and allows me to do the work I love. With a steady hand, patience, and resourcefulness, he has captured my quilts in stunning photos for the pages of this book.

My children, as they have grown, have quietly become part of all my quilts: **Delfina** shares with me what colors she likes; **Anna** serves me rejuvenating treats; and in claiming every quilt I make, **Michael** makes me feel like my quilts are perfect.

My Mom put a needle and thread in my hands; **Grandma Anna** showed me how to do patchwork; and in repeatedly reminding me, "You can do this," **my mother-in-law** gave me the confidence to keep trying.

Judy performs magic with words to help tell the stories behind my quilts. I have pulled the wagon to the top of the hill, and she has been my "extra push" of talent, organization, and editing skills to bring this project to these pages.

Kayleen shares my love of color and pattern to document my quilts on these timeless pages. With her eye for artistic opportunities, she has masterfully mixed the words, quilts, and graphics to create this tribute to quilters and their scraps.

Lisa Christensen has applied her personal touch and skill to create technical illustrations from my thoughts, ideas, and models. Her clear and concise sketches make these patterns fun for everyone.

Debbie Campbell and Debbie Meyer, in countless hours of reading and editing of this book, have gently shared their thoughts and input, which are always very much appreciated.

Julie Lillo, my dear friend and quilter extraordinaire, always finds the time — especially during those final hours — to add beautiful quilting stitches to my quilts.

Kim Nimtz, co-owner of Prairie Stitches Quilt Shoppe, has shared her beautiful antique quilt (see page 22) that has inspired me and will surely inspire you.

Martha, my dear friend, has put a final touch on some of my quilts by stitching the binding with her loving hands.

This book was designed, produced, and published by Sitar Family Traditions LLC, DBA: Laundry Basket Quilts, 16860 L Drive North, Marshall, MI 49068
www.laundrybasketquilts.com

Publisher: Sitar Family Traditions LLC, Laundry Basket Quilts
Quilt Design: Edyta Sitar
Sales & Operations: Michael Sitar
Managing Editor: Judith Stern Friedman
Art Director: Kayleen Hardy, Hardy Design Studio
Photography: Michael Sitar, Laundry Basket Quilts
Technical Illustrations: Lisa Christensen

Library of Congress Control Number: 2014912542
ISBN 13: 978-0-9836688-1-7

This book is printed on acid-free paper.
Printed in the United States of America.
10 9 8 7 6 5 4 3 2 1

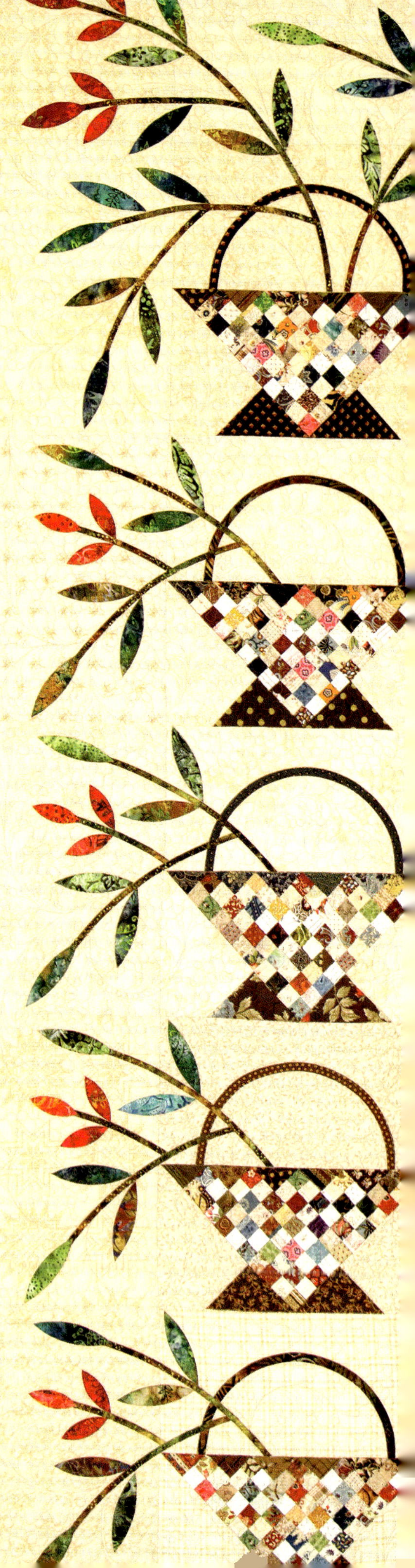

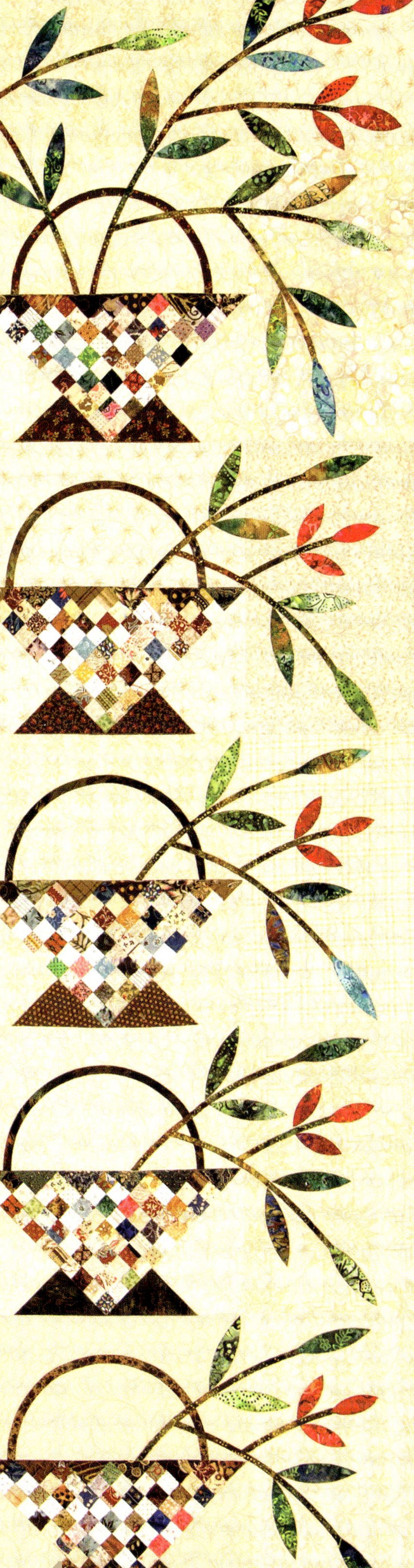

THE START OF SOMETHING SCRAPPY

Table of Contents

FROM *the* AUTHOR

Free your fabrics...

Pull out the boxes from under the bed, reach for the piles in your drawers and baskets, and grab handfuls of scraps that await the limelight. Instead of leaving precious pieces in the dark, you can finally reveal their magic in a quilt!

Handfuls of Scraps is your invitation to turn small, irregular pieces into giant pattern splashes, rainbow-colored waves, and quilted stories on parade. Maybe that muslin will become the playground for a garden full of appliquéd blooms. Or a deep-red remnant will romanticize a log cabin. From scrappy diamonds that make stars shine to postage-stamp squares that take detail to the moon, the most unsuspecting fabrics can make a most impressive impact.

Instead of tucking away your scraps, see them as *opportunities* to quilt something amazing. Imagine the women of earlier times who stitched phenomenal quilts with far more modest remnants. Try your hand at a new technique by fussy-cutting fabric for broderie appliqué. Or get hooked on English paper piecing that simplifies an intricate design.

The antique quilts and quilt patterns here are designed not only to free your fabric but also *to free your quilting spirit.* Journey into your bags full of wishful scraps, and pull out handfuls of possibilities. From simple strips to more challenging projects, each quilting step is a pleasurable journey. You'll see that small, imperfect pieces can ease the pressure to make a perfect quilt. As you whittle down your stockpiles of scraps, you'll stitch new stories into your quilts... and in the end, *you will make something out of nothing.*

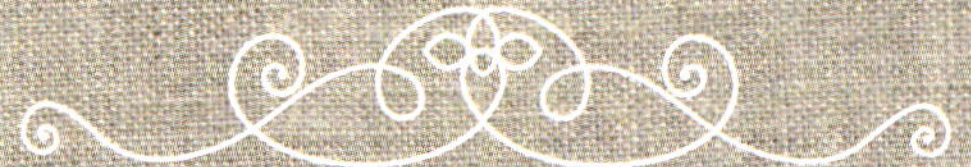

A Special Thanks to the Grand Rapids Public Museum

This western Michigan destination has connected me—and now you—to the past through a collection of scrappy historic quilts. These archived works at the second largest museum in the state offer a rare glimpse into the lives of women, just like you and me, who have shared their experience through extraordinary handwork.

The Grand Rapids Public Museum has generously loaned a sampling of these quilts, which we have included in this book as "eye candy" and inspiration. If you travel to or near Grand Rapids, be sure to stop by to see the antique quilts and other textiles: **Grand Rapids Public Museum I 272 Pearl Street NW, Grand Rapids, MI 49504 I 616.929.1700**

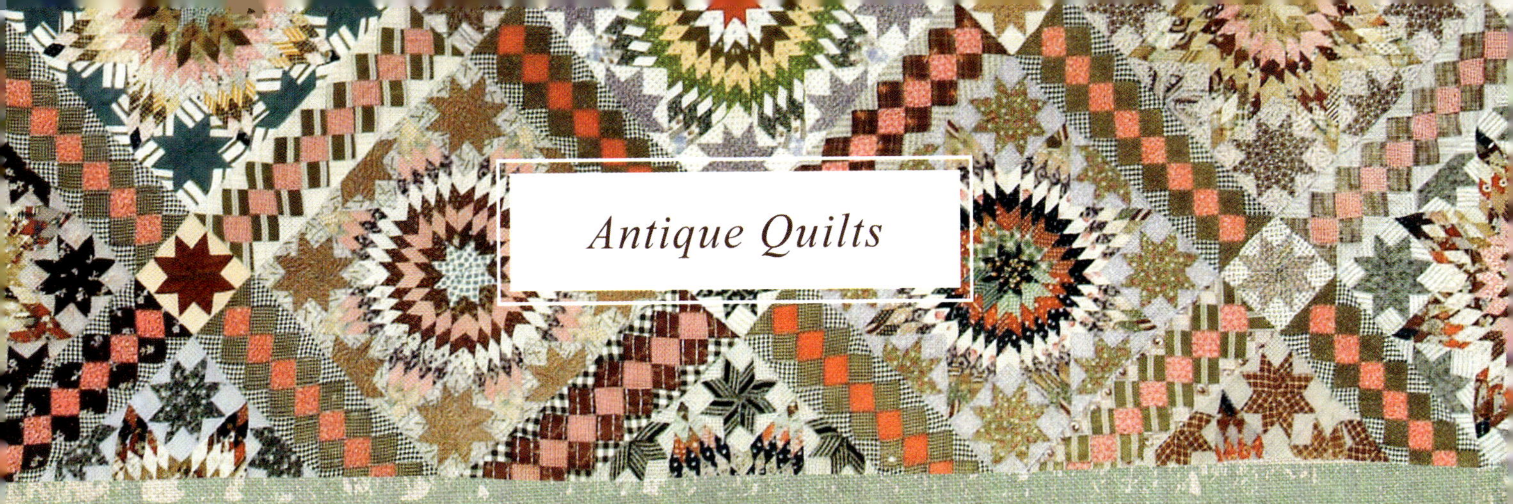

PERMISSION *to* PLAY

Timeless quilts remind us that—no matter what the time and place—their makers endured and celebrated life. The antique quilts that fill this chapter are springboards both for learning and loving. Look closely to see their random stitches, wearing threads, and mismatched colors, and *discover beauty in imperfection.*

Imagine the women of centuries ago who found ways to make quilts from well-worn shirtsleeves, dishtowels, dresses, and random strips they never could or would call scraps. Instead, they relished every piece they scrounged, and stitched to salvage every last woven patch.

As you pore over the striking examples here, you'll see it's okay if the colors don't match, if the stitches aren't straight, and if seams aren't centered. Notice the contrasts between light and dark, the muting effects of muslin squares, and the crazy details in tiny triangles. While alone these pieces appear insignificant, together they create a lasting legacy.

Let this chapter be your go-to permission to play with your scraps, try new stitches, and explore new techniques. Just dig into your bags, loosen those threads, and see where a handful of scraps will take you!

The antique renditions in this chapter include quilts from my personal collection, from the Grand Rapids Public Museum, and a few favorite treasures on loan from dear friends.

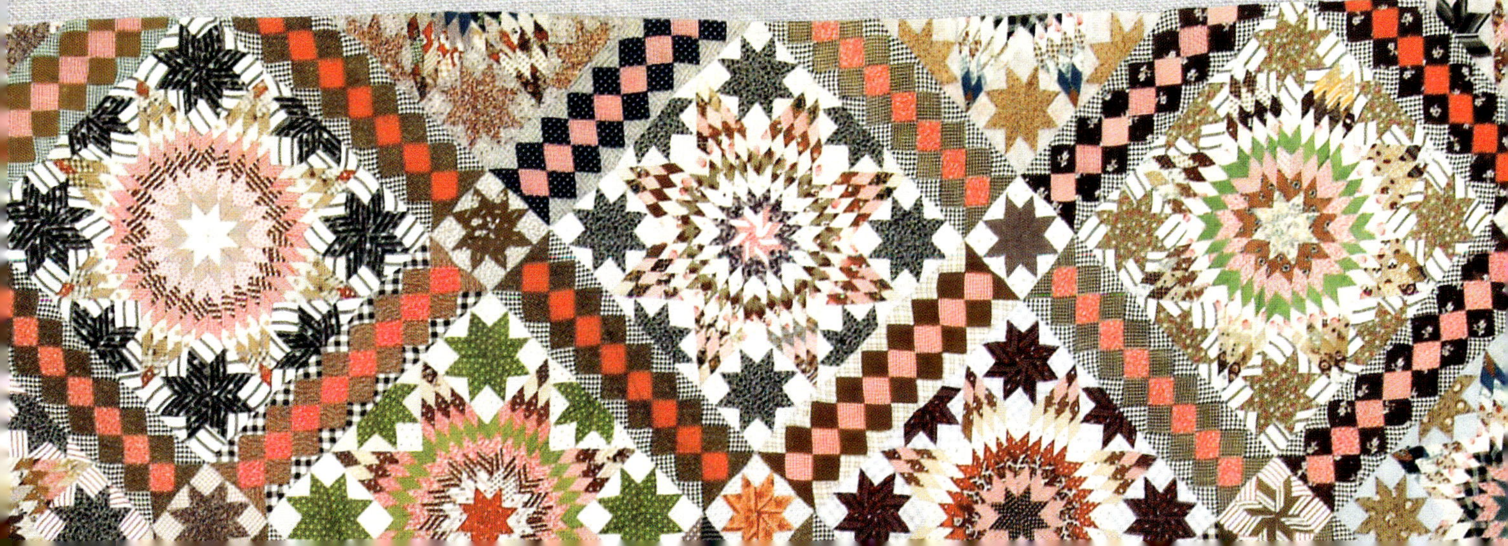

ONE-SHAPE WONDERS

Turn an oh-so-simple shape into an oh-so-splendid scene. Stacked squares become towering walls. Tumbling triangles fall into broken dishes. And diamonds aligned in all directions create a universe of stars. These quilts—all built on a single shape—demonstrate fabric's limitless power to create movement, morph its form, and stir imagination.

Forego the saving and just start sewing to turn your scrappy squares and triangles into captivating color combinations. Just this once, let the fabric and your instincts move you to stitching spontaneously. You'll come to discover something greater at work when the outcome takes you to that "aha" moment.

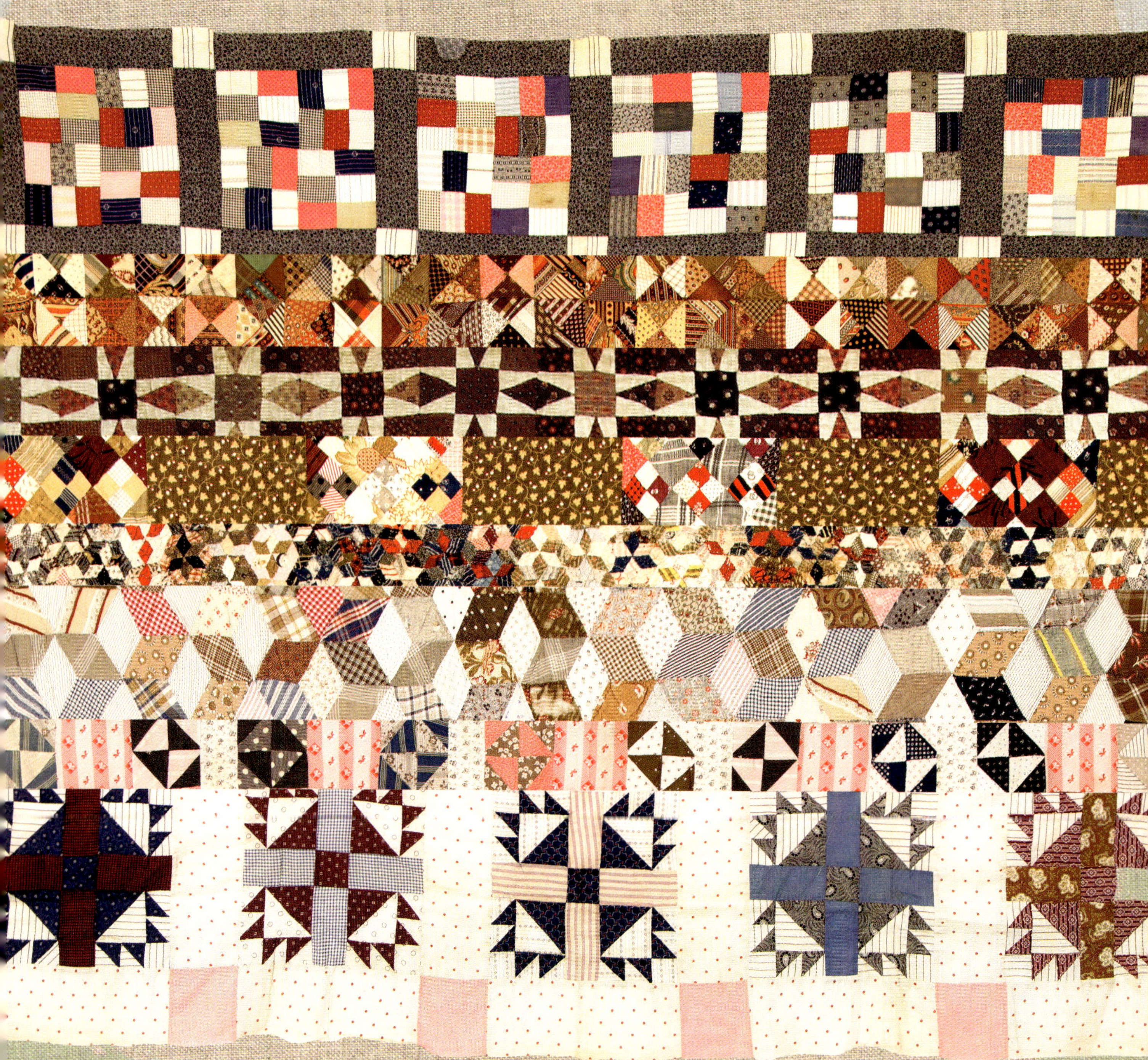

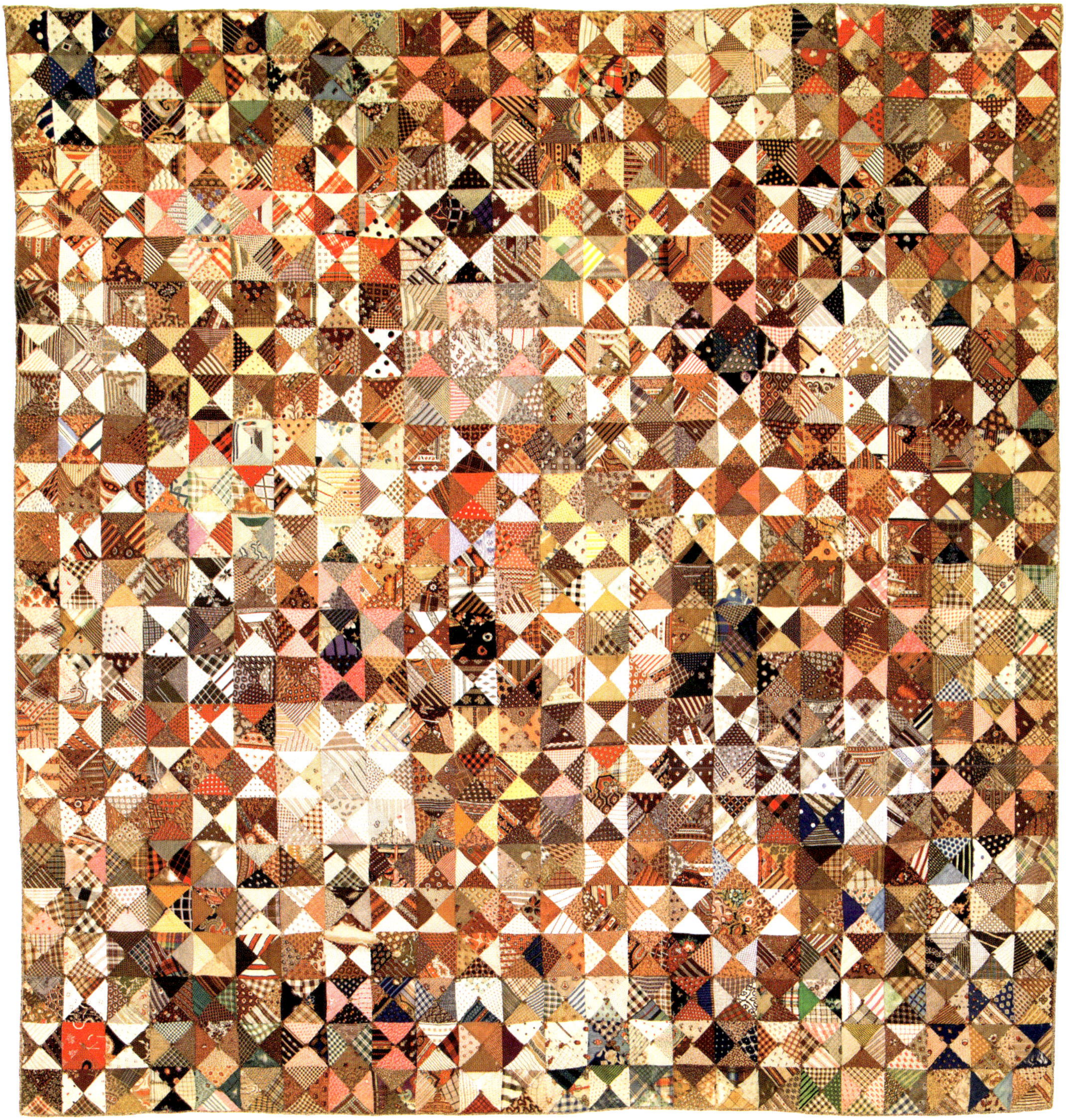

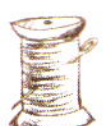
Broken Dish, Sitar Family Collection, antique, *c. 1895*

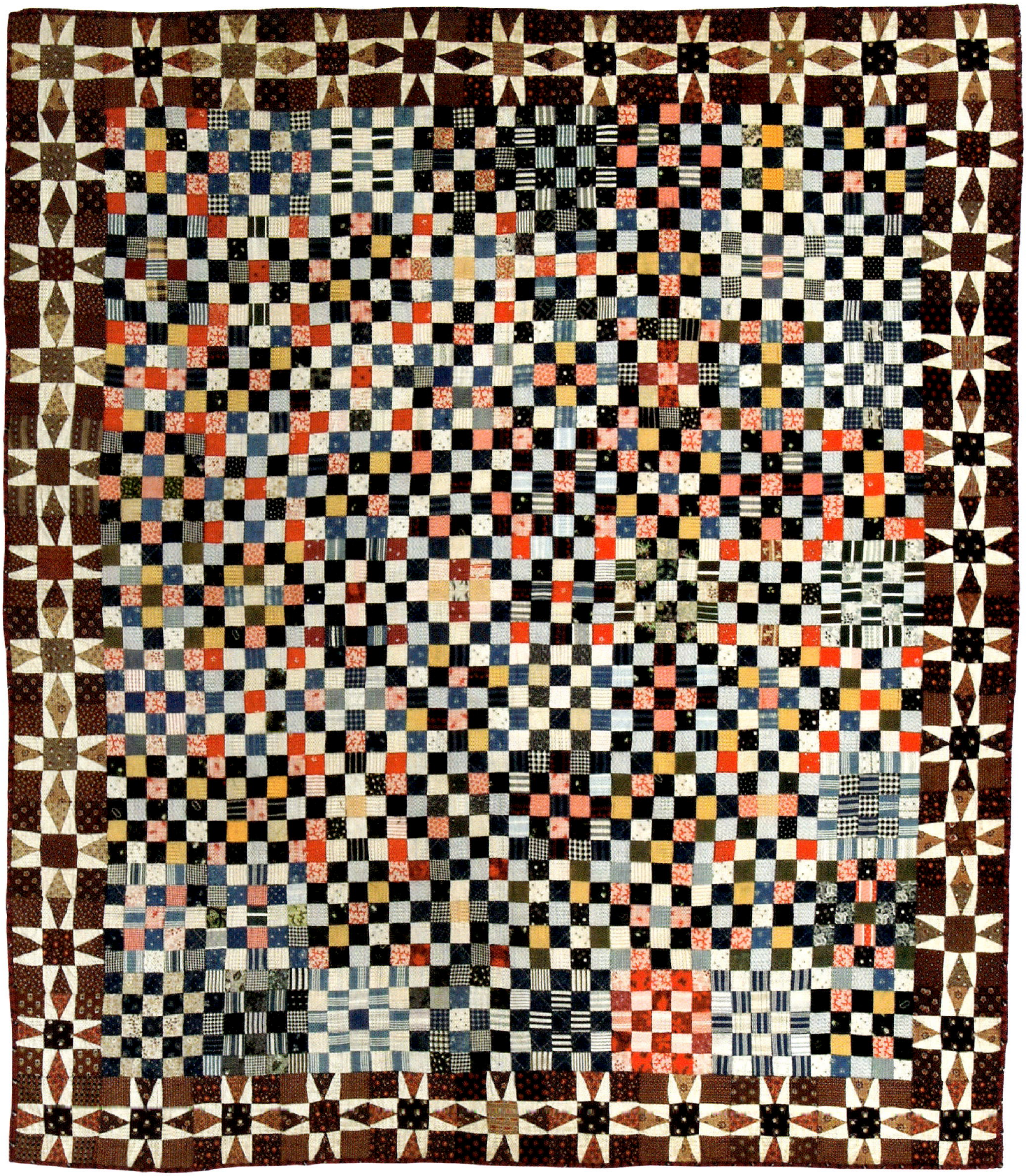

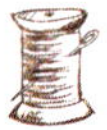
Postage Stamp with Sun Ray Border, Grand Rapids Public Museum, *c. 1860*

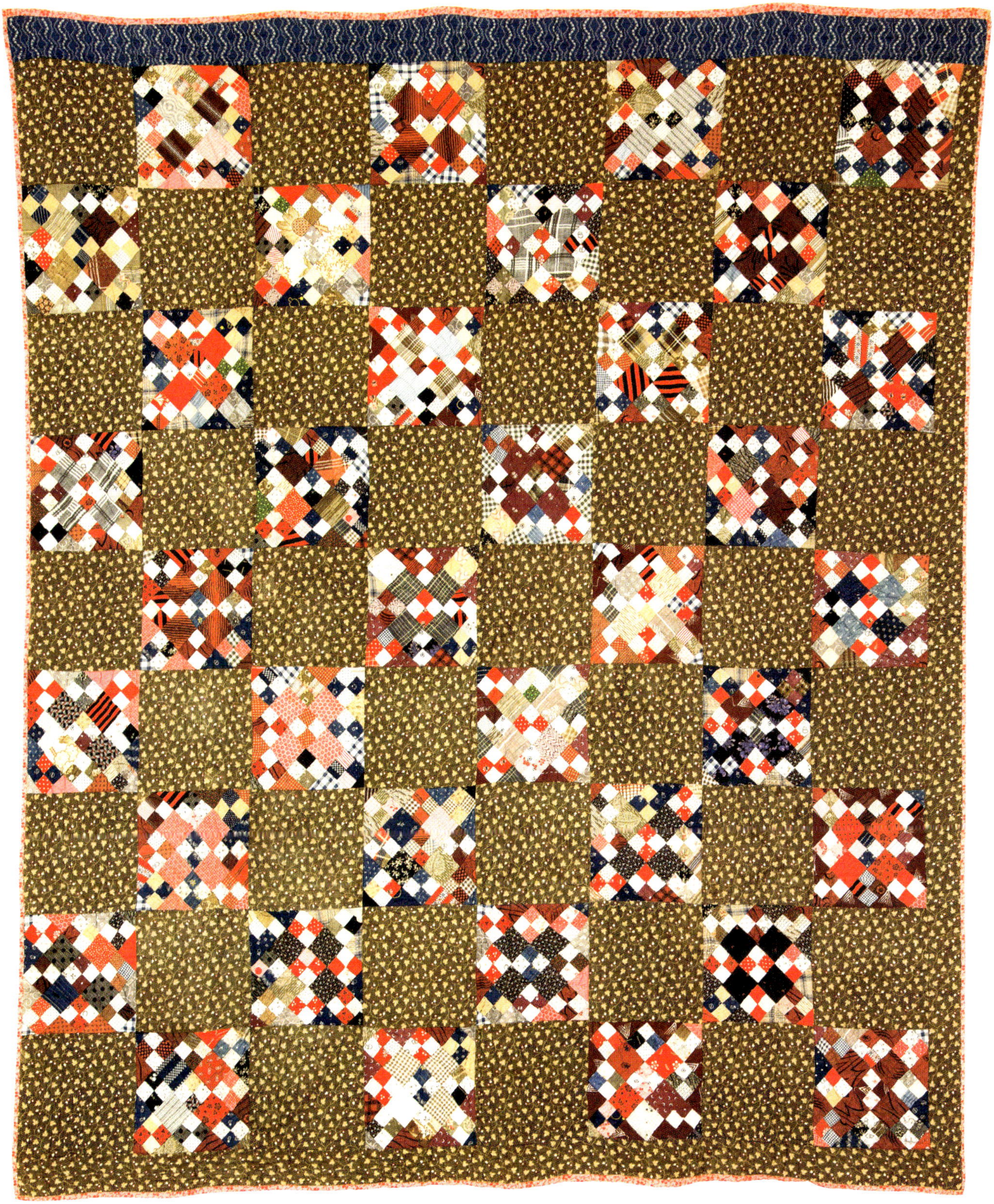

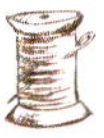 Four Patch, Sitar Family Collection, antique, *c. 1900*

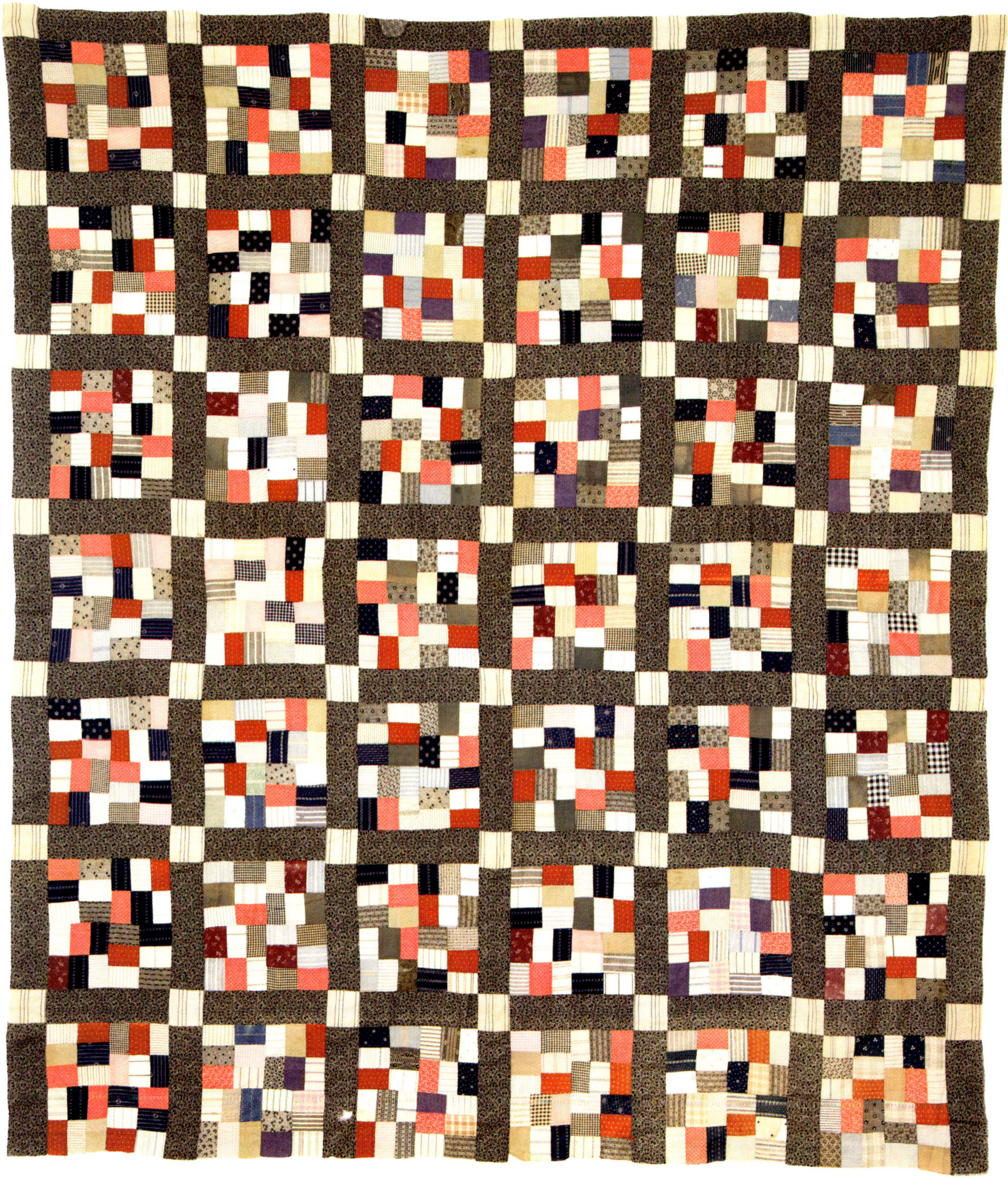

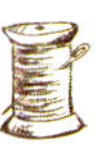 Puzzle Pieces, Sitar Family Collection, antique, *c. 1910*

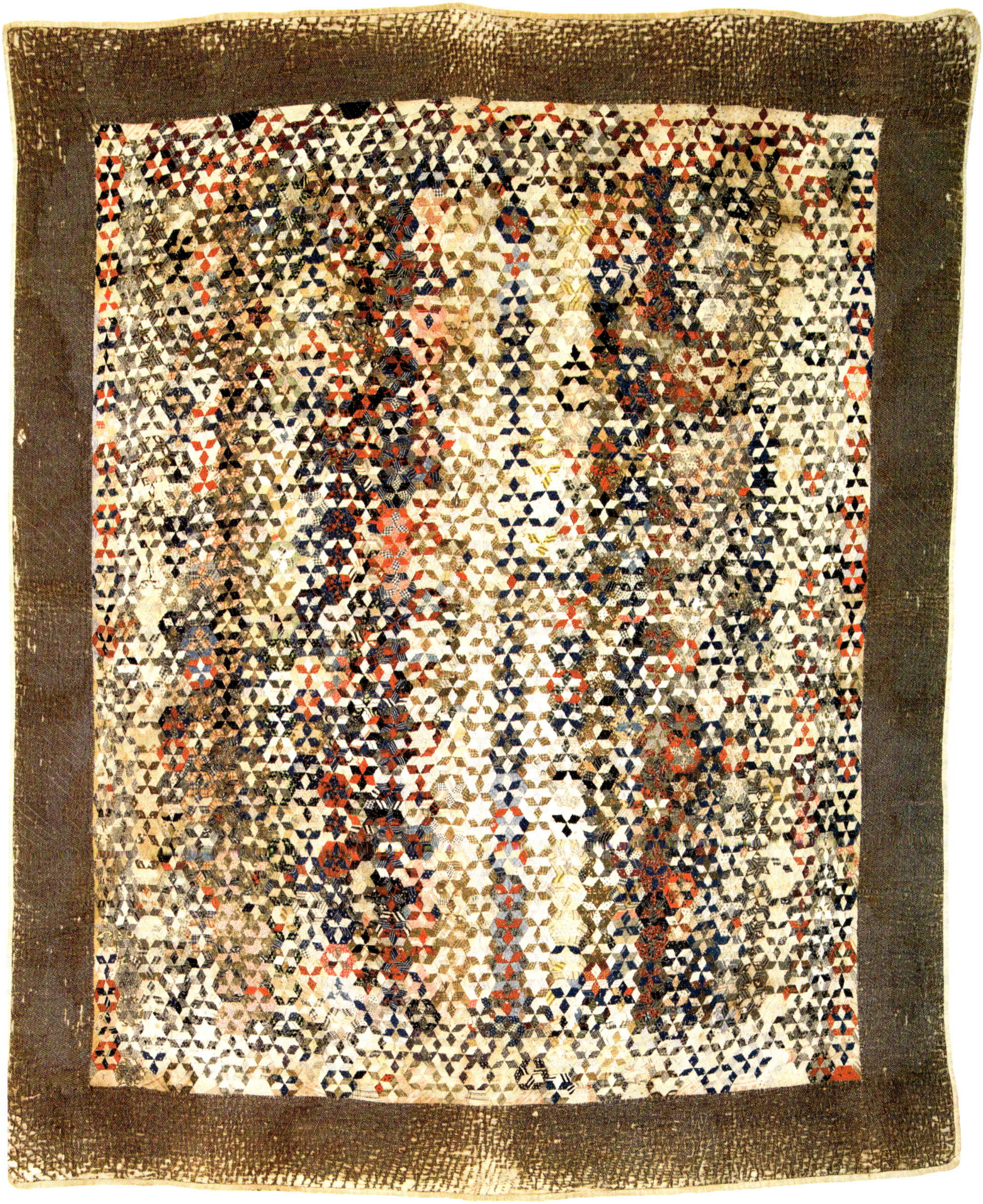

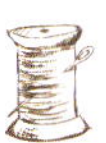 Six-Point Star, Sitar Family Collection, antique, *c. 1880*

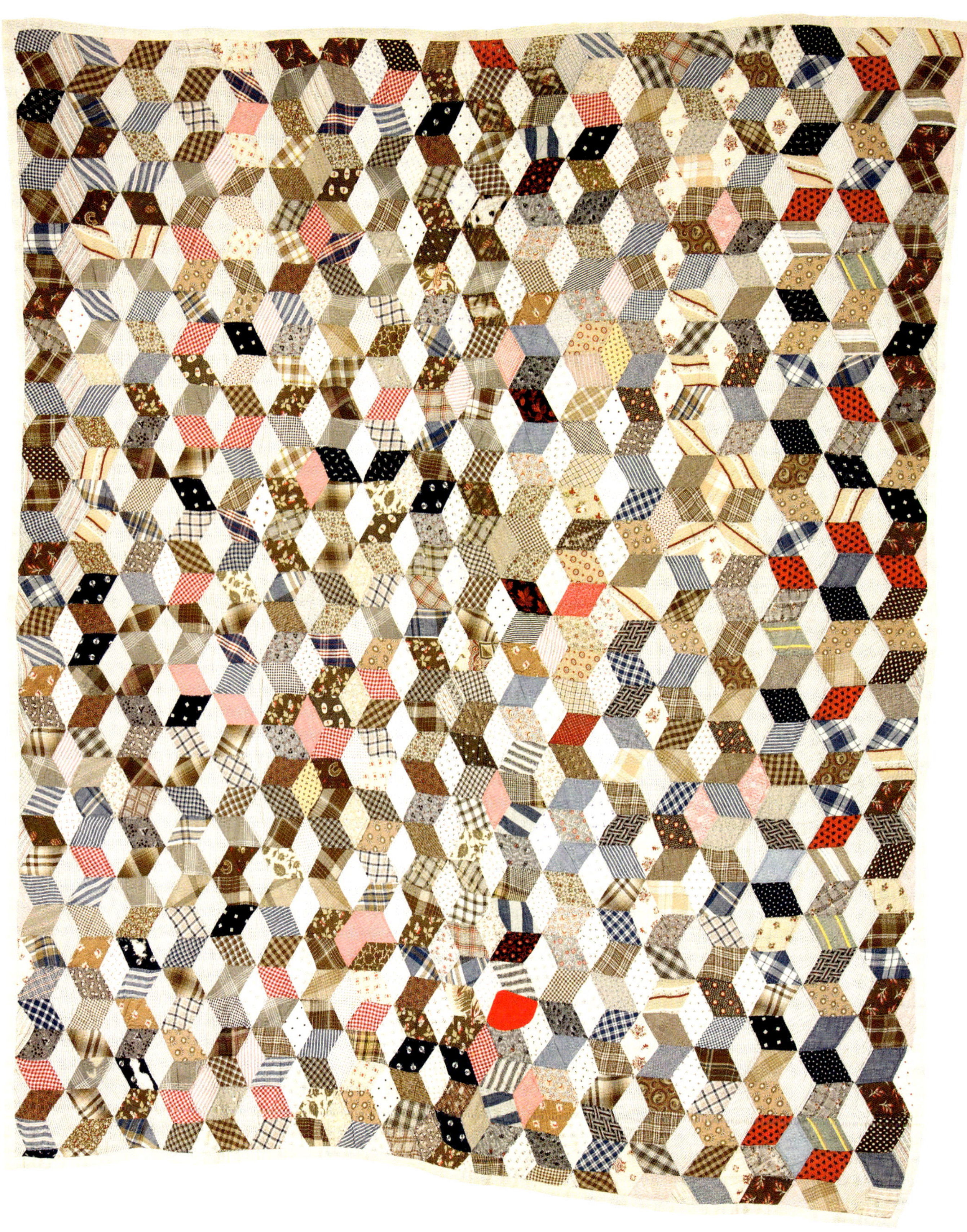

Tumbling Block, Sitar Family Collection, antique, *c. 1912*

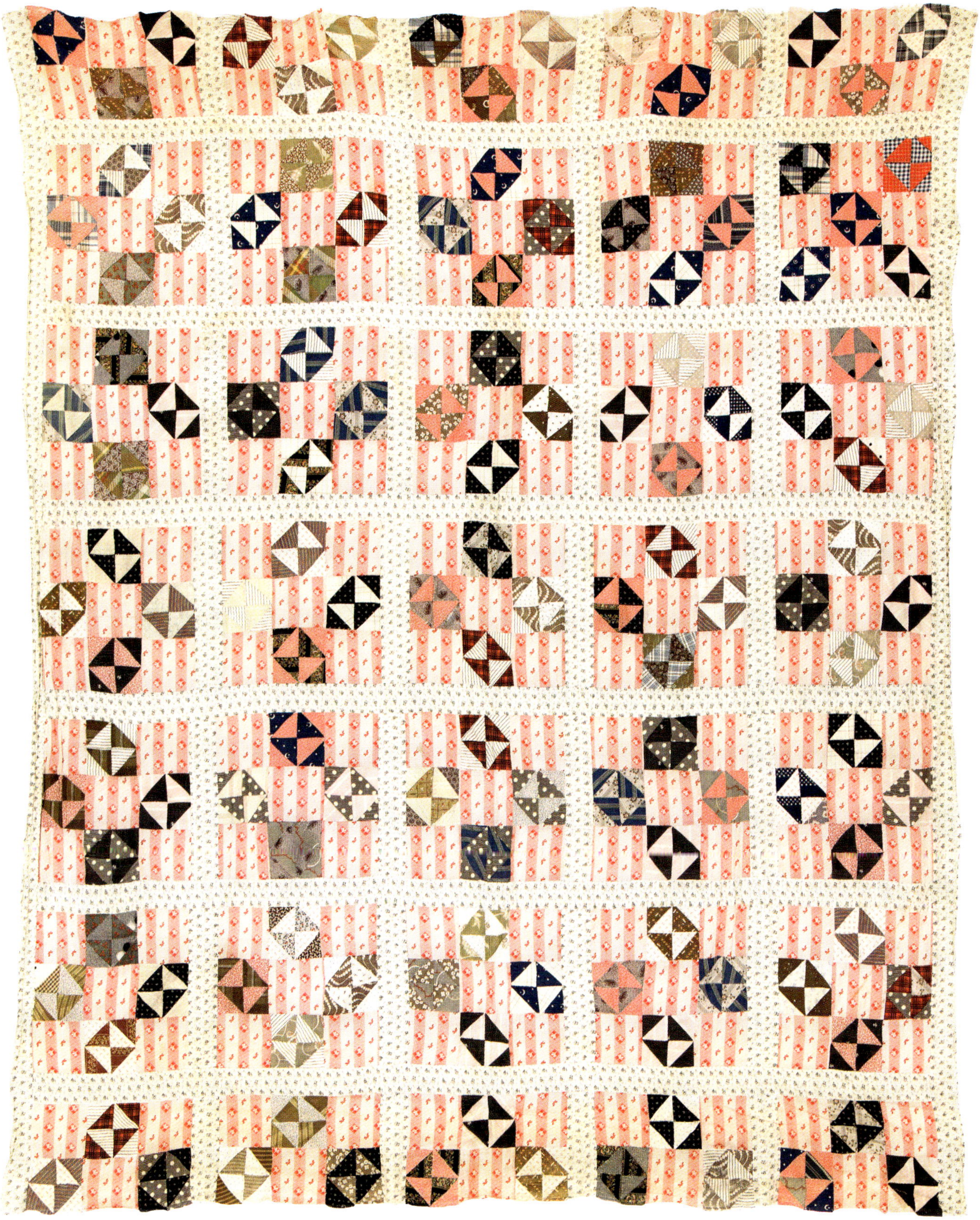

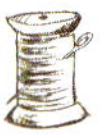 Pink Broken Dish, Sitar Family Collection, antique, *c. 1918*

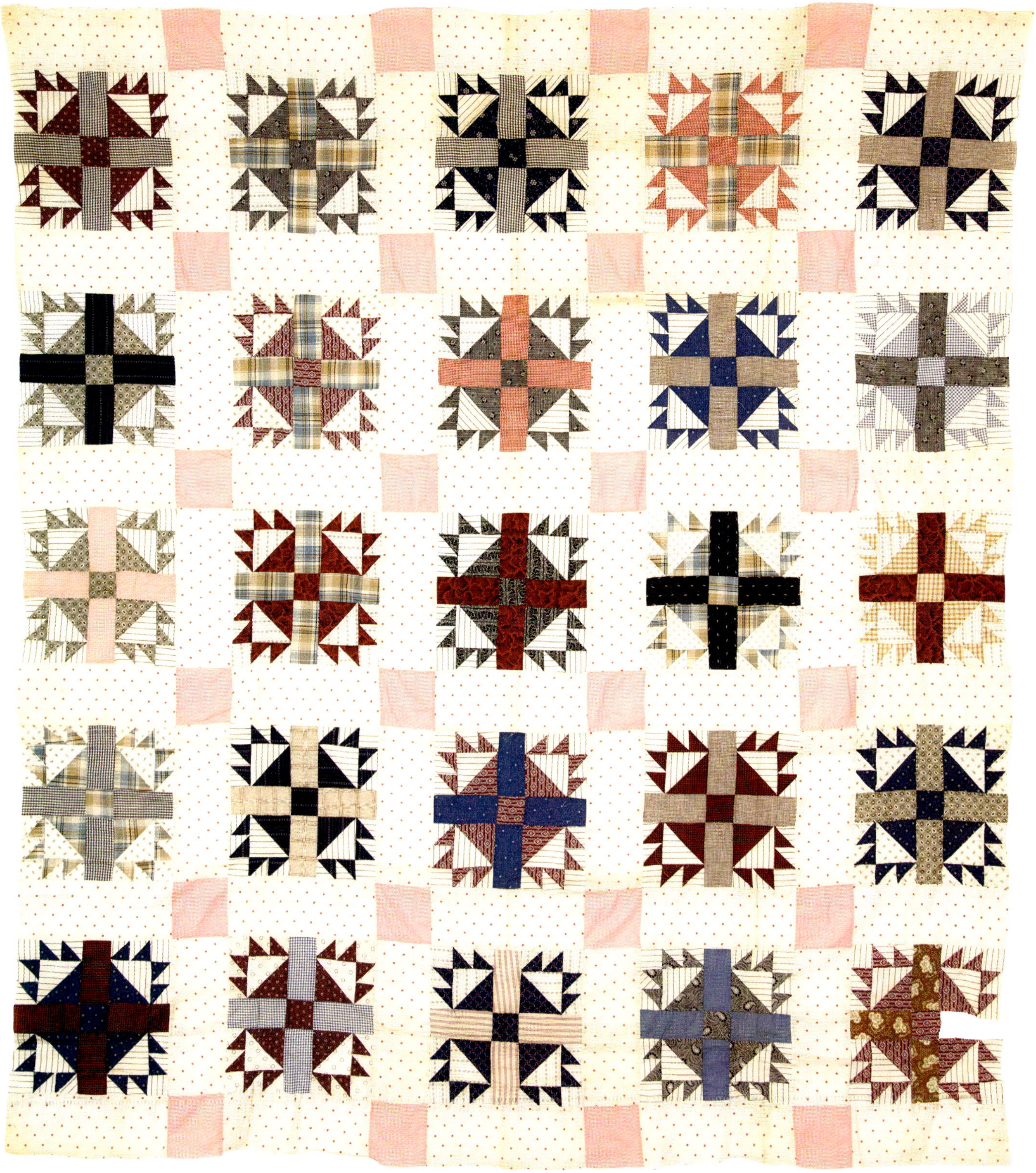

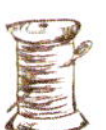
Bear Claw, Sitar Family Collection, antique, *c. 1915*

TOUCH *of* MUSLIN

With limited patterned fabric at hand, resourceful quilters often stretched their supply by adding muslin to the mix. This cream-colored staple became a canvas for creating new quilting patterns and techniques.

Sometimes muslin was a frame for a four patch or a sashing to mediate between loud blocks. It also served as an empty stage upon which the quilter could tout her talents in appliqué, embroidery, and other fine needlework. As a breath for the eye in a busy pattern, muslin also made its own debut weaving through patterns like a necklace chain.

As you examine these masterful quilts, all made with a touch of muslin, consider the impact of white in your designs both in creating pleasing dimension and helping you stretch your own supply of scraps.

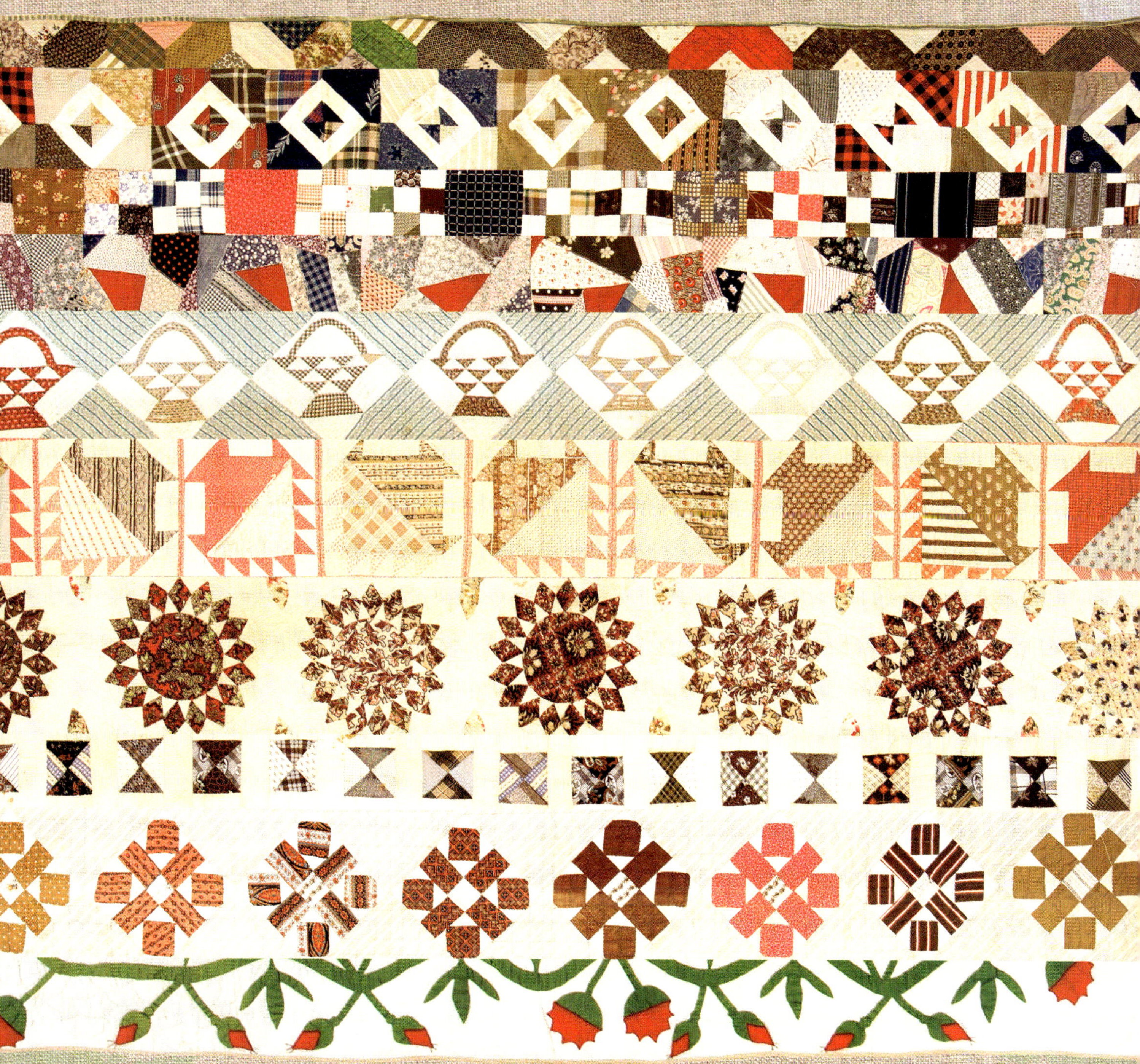

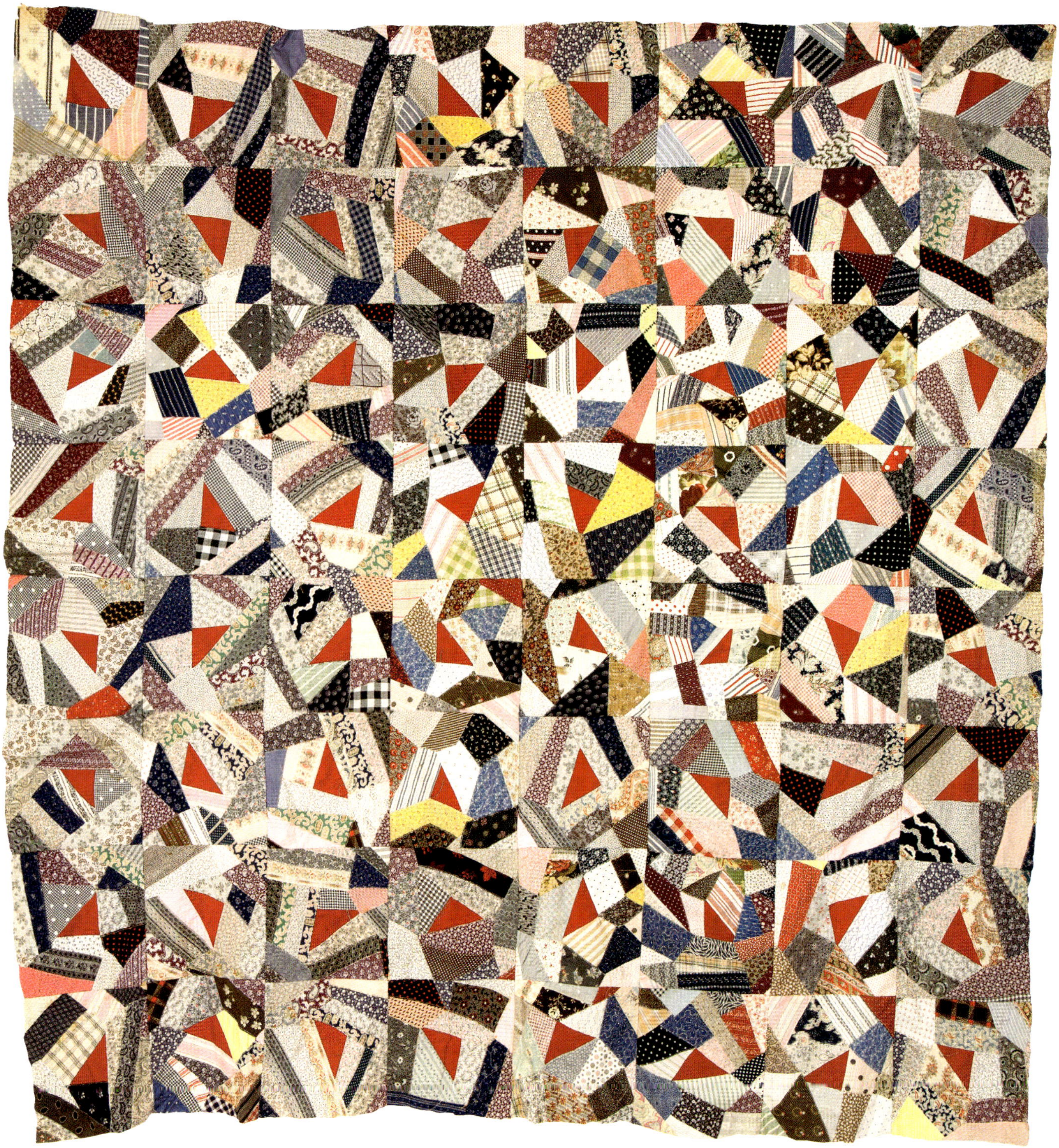

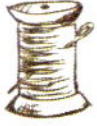 Crazy Quilt, Sitar Family Collection, antique, *c. 1900*

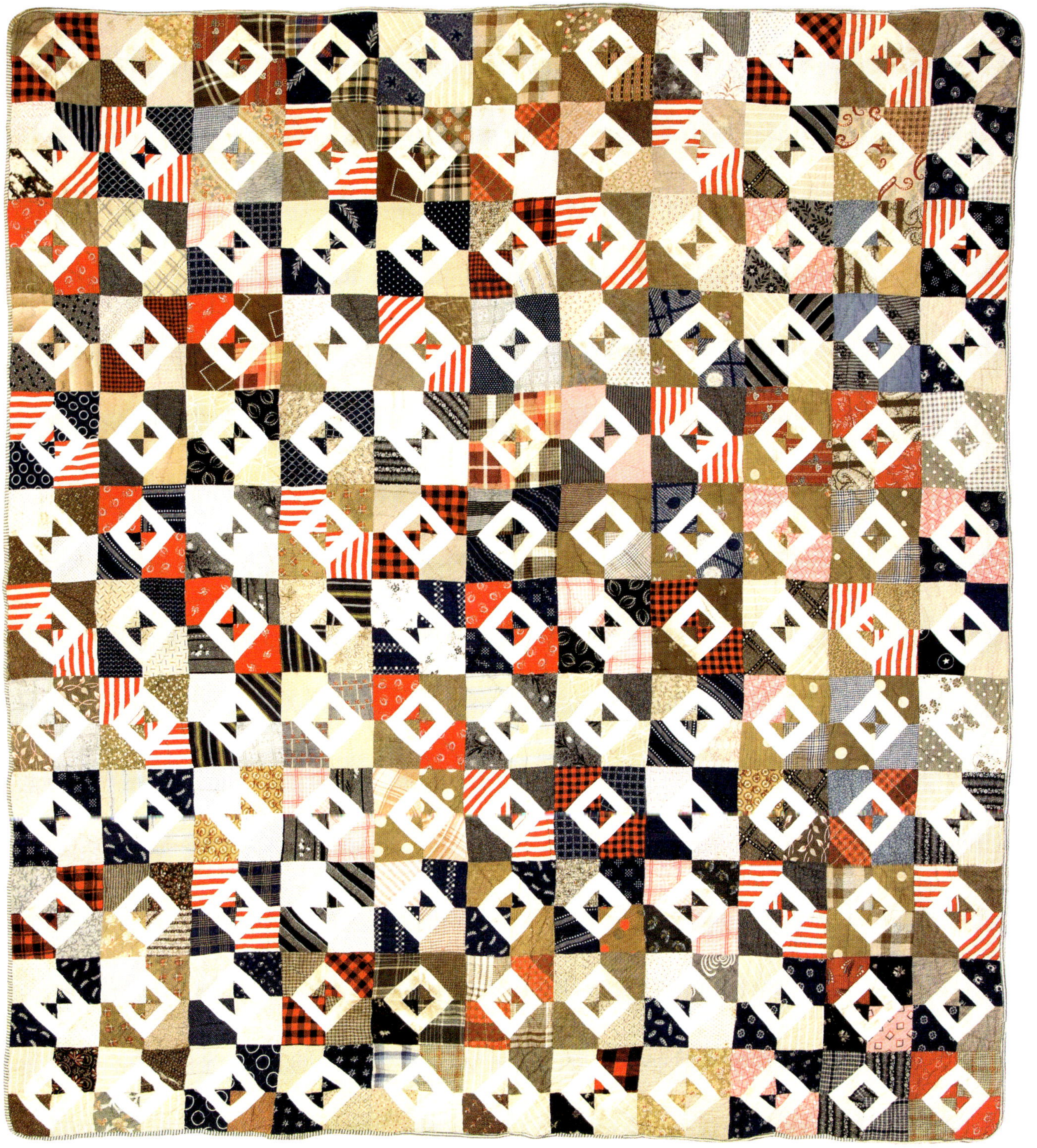

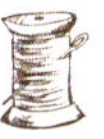 Mailbox, Sitar Family Collection, antique, *c. 1910*

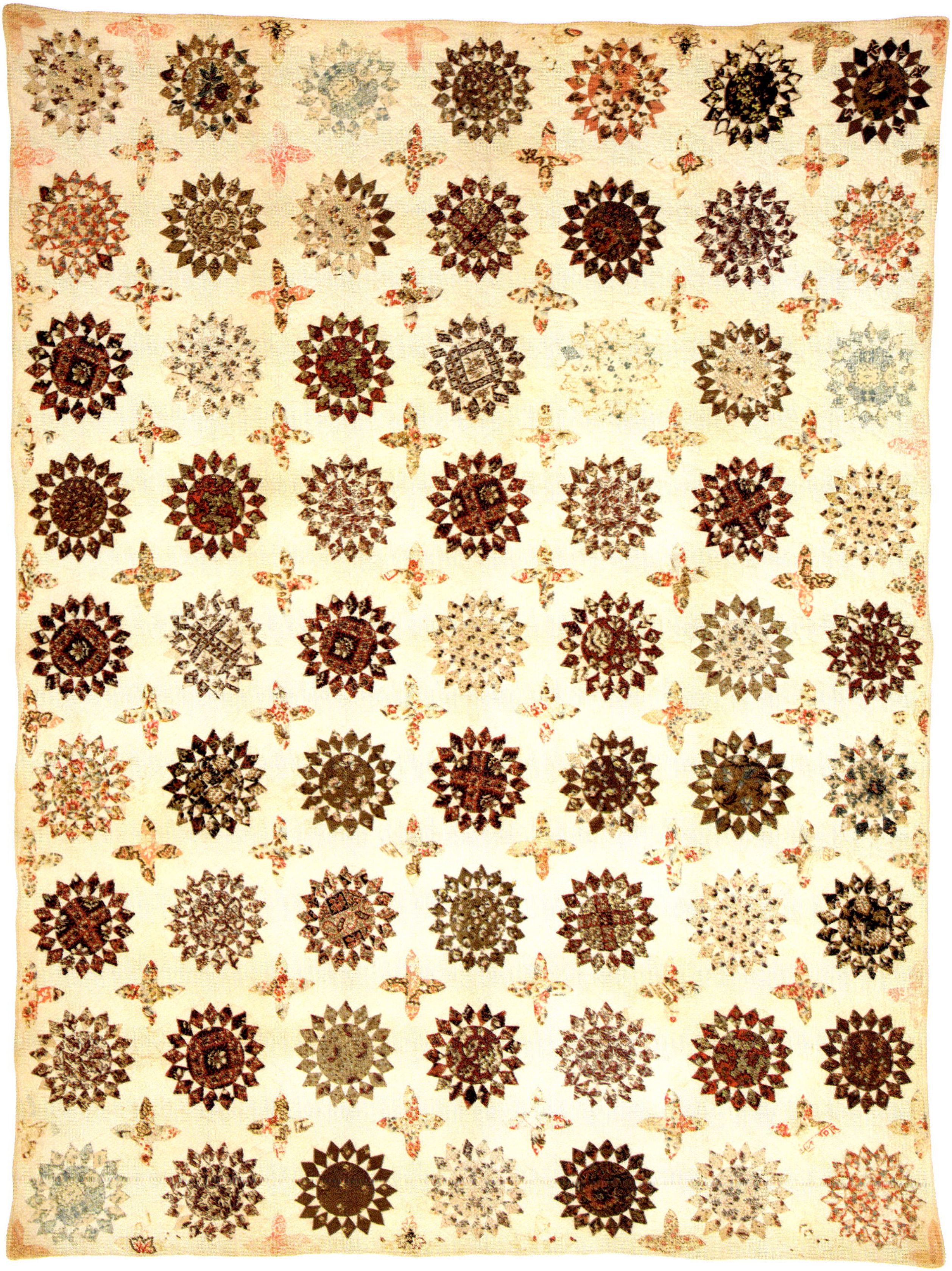

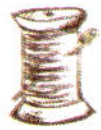 Sunflower, Sitar Family Collection, antique, *c. 1850*

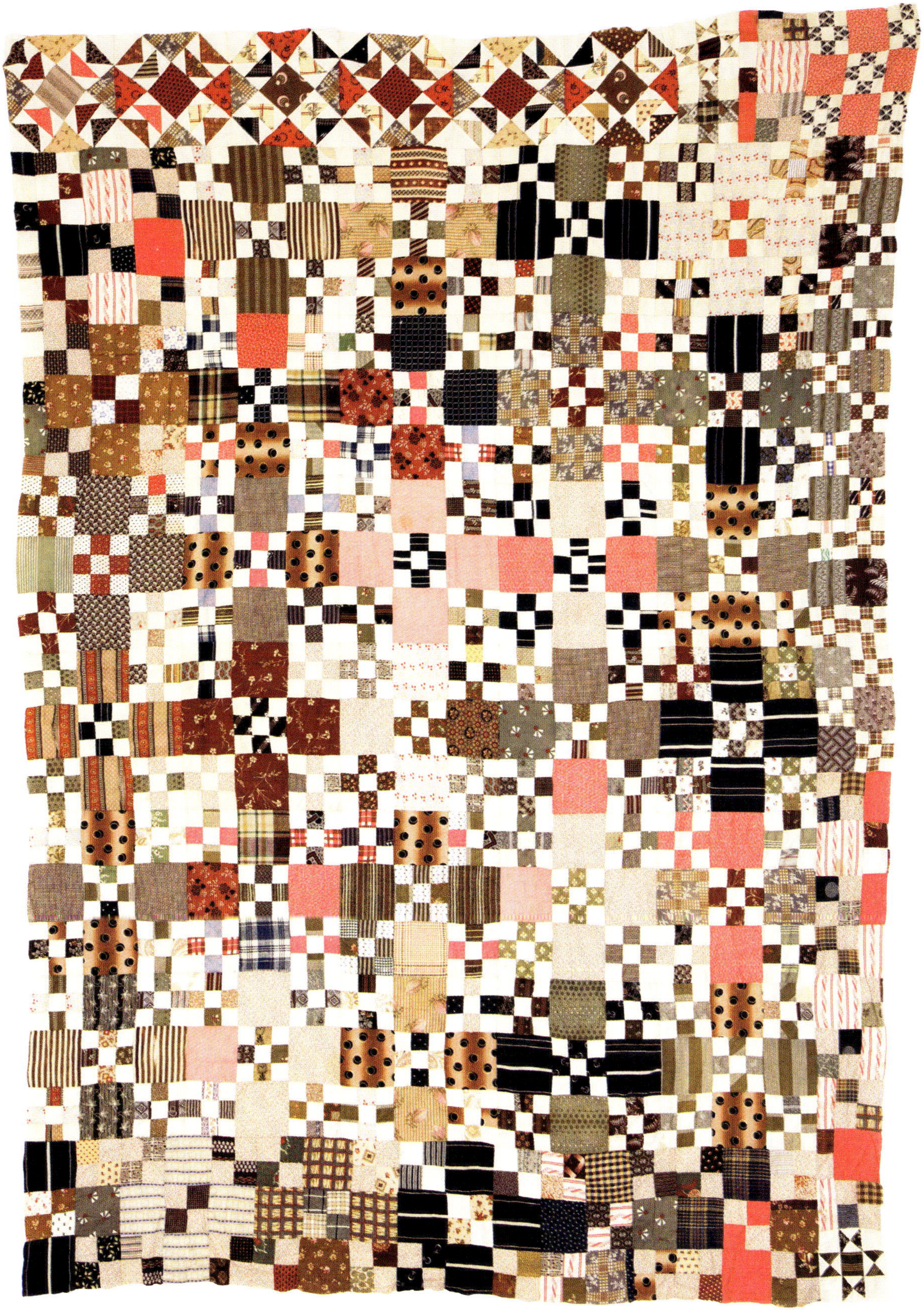

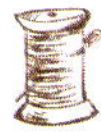

Nine Patch, Sitar Family Collection, antique, *c. 1900*

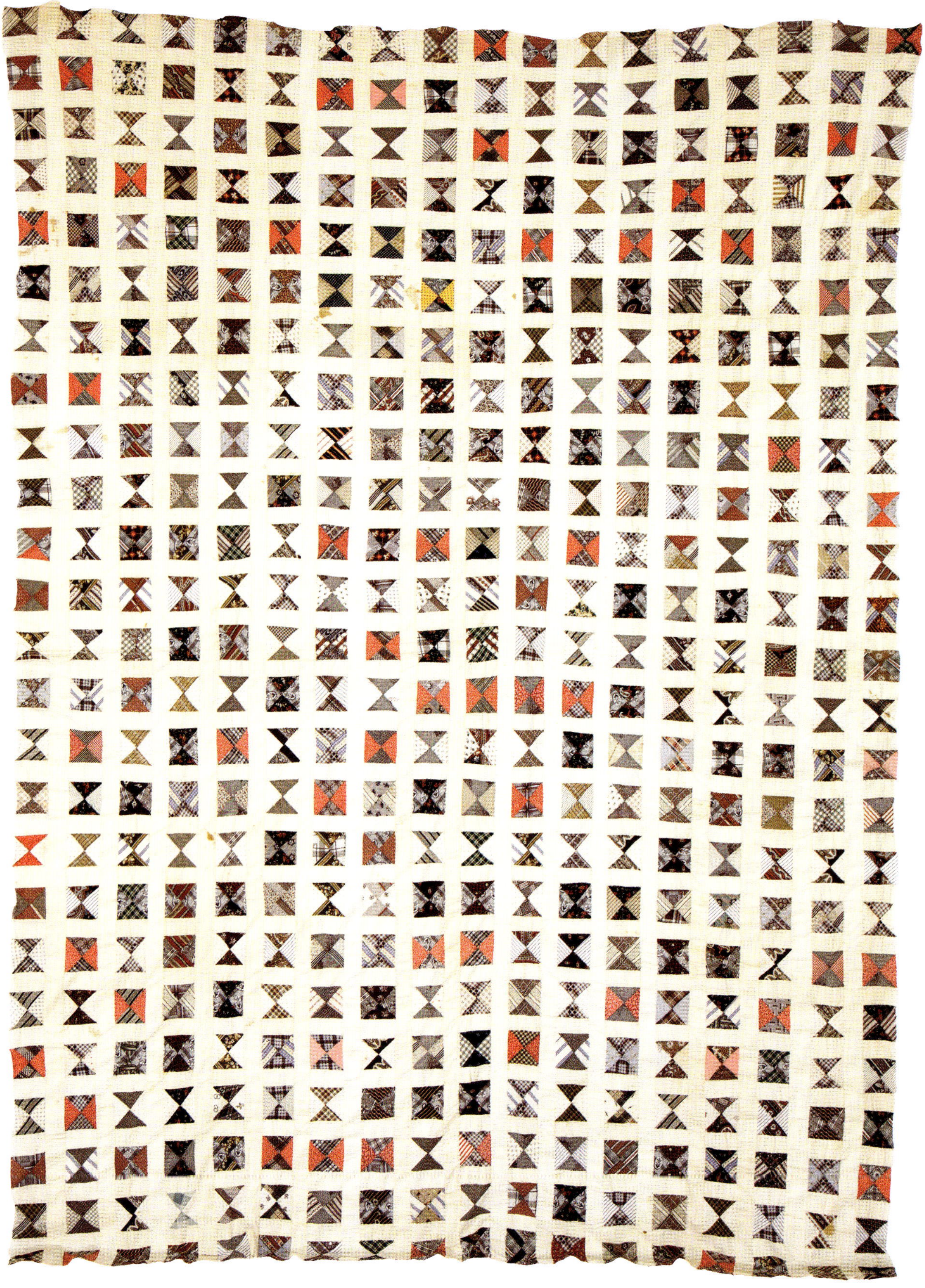

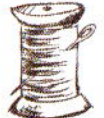 Bow Tie, Sitar Family Collection, antique, *c. 1904*

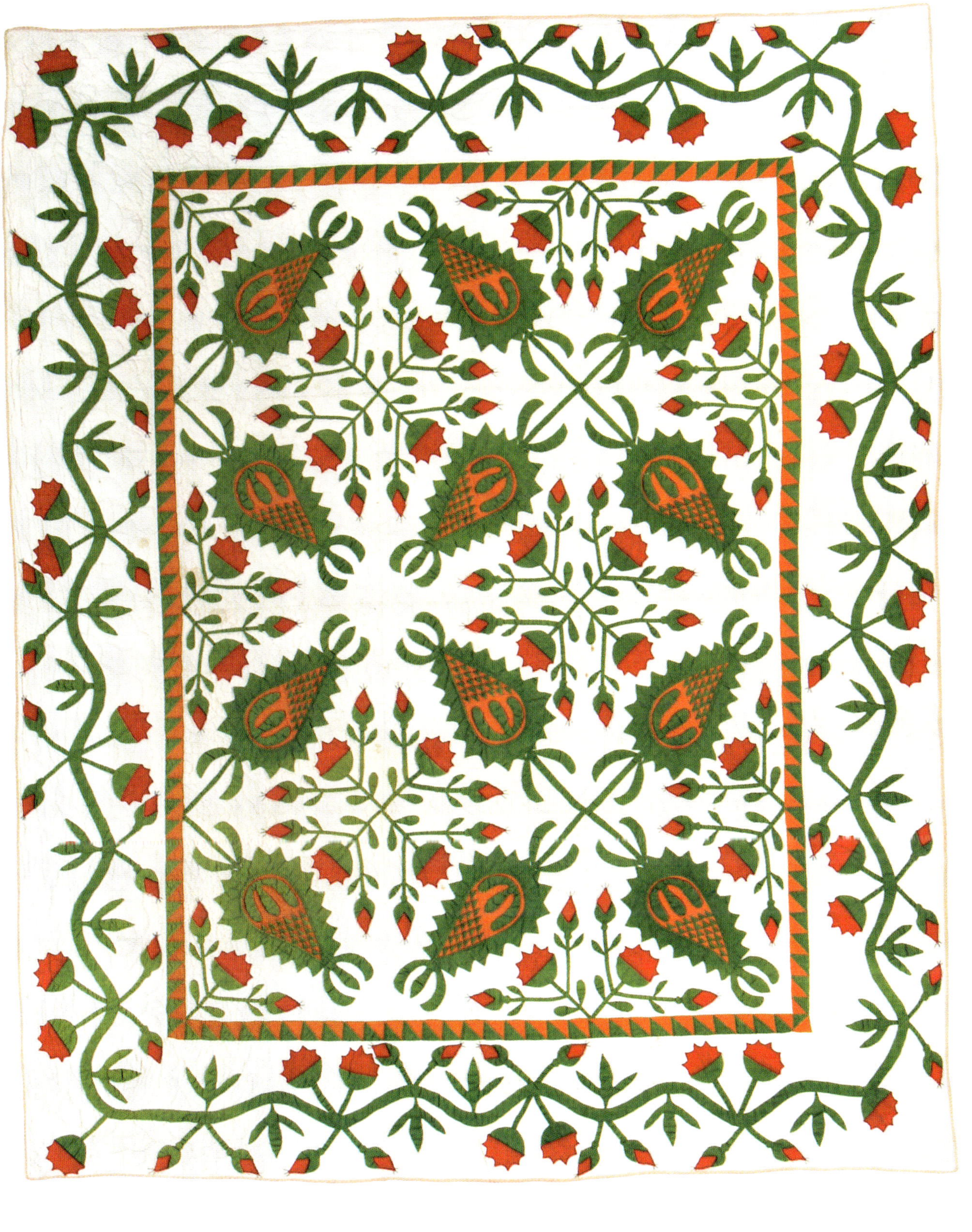

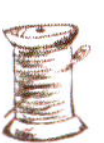 Pineapple and Roses, Grand Rapids Public Museum, *c. 1860*

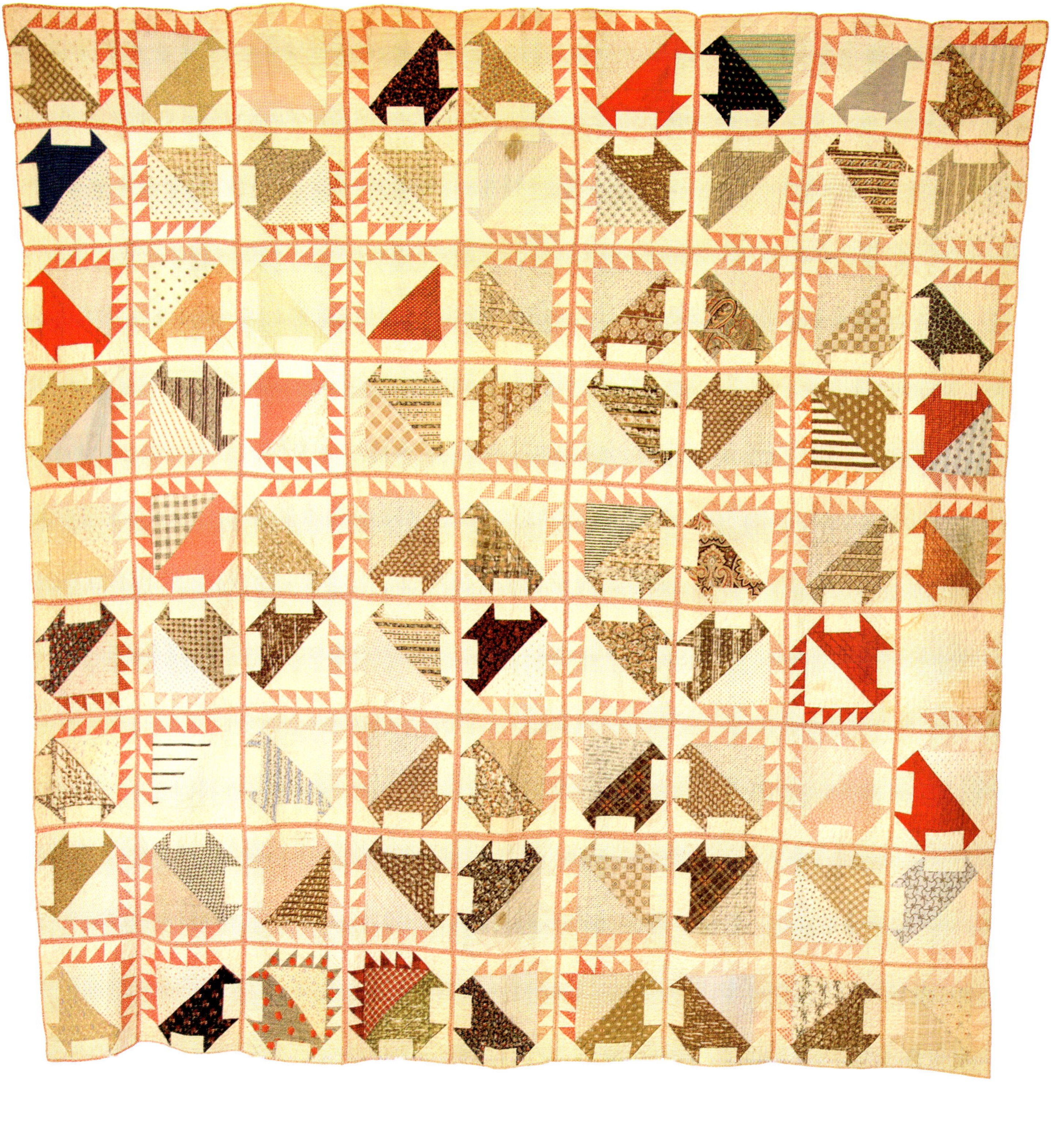

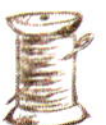 Signature Baskets, owned by Kim Nimtz, antique, *c. 1846*

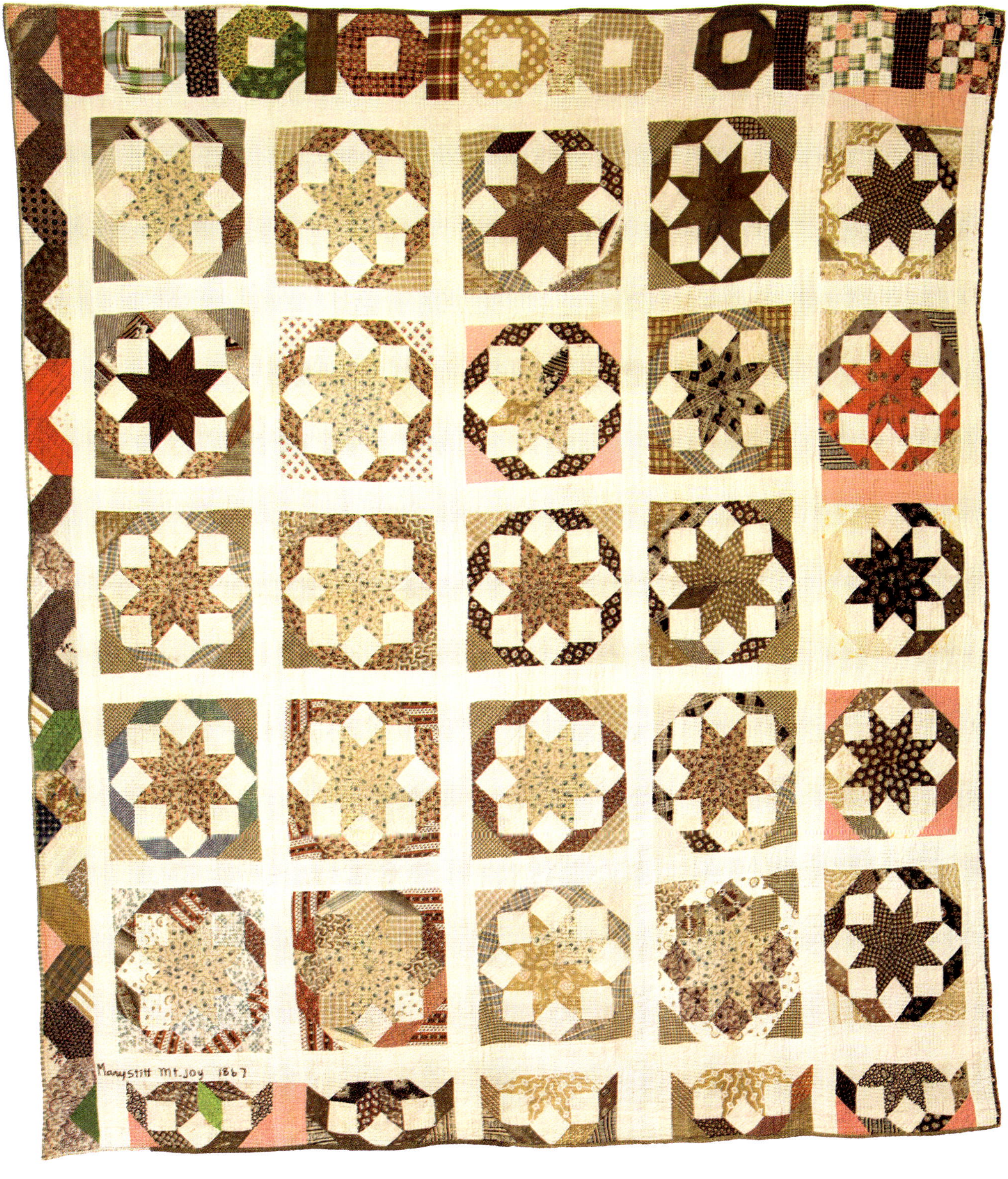

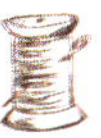 Carpenter Star, Sitar Family Collection, antique, *c. 1867*

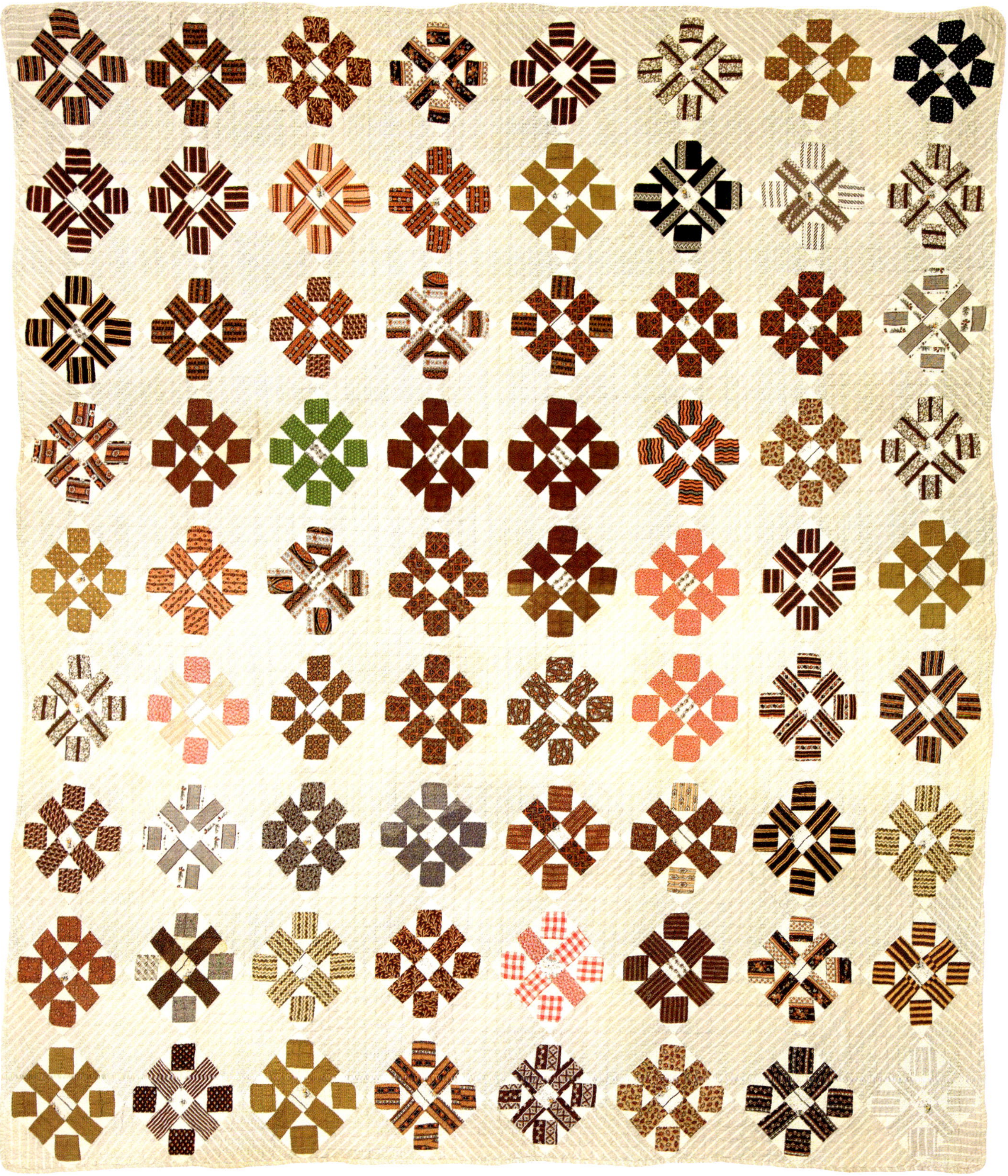

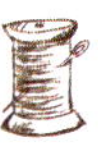 Rolling Stone, Sitar Family Collection, antique, *c. 1880*

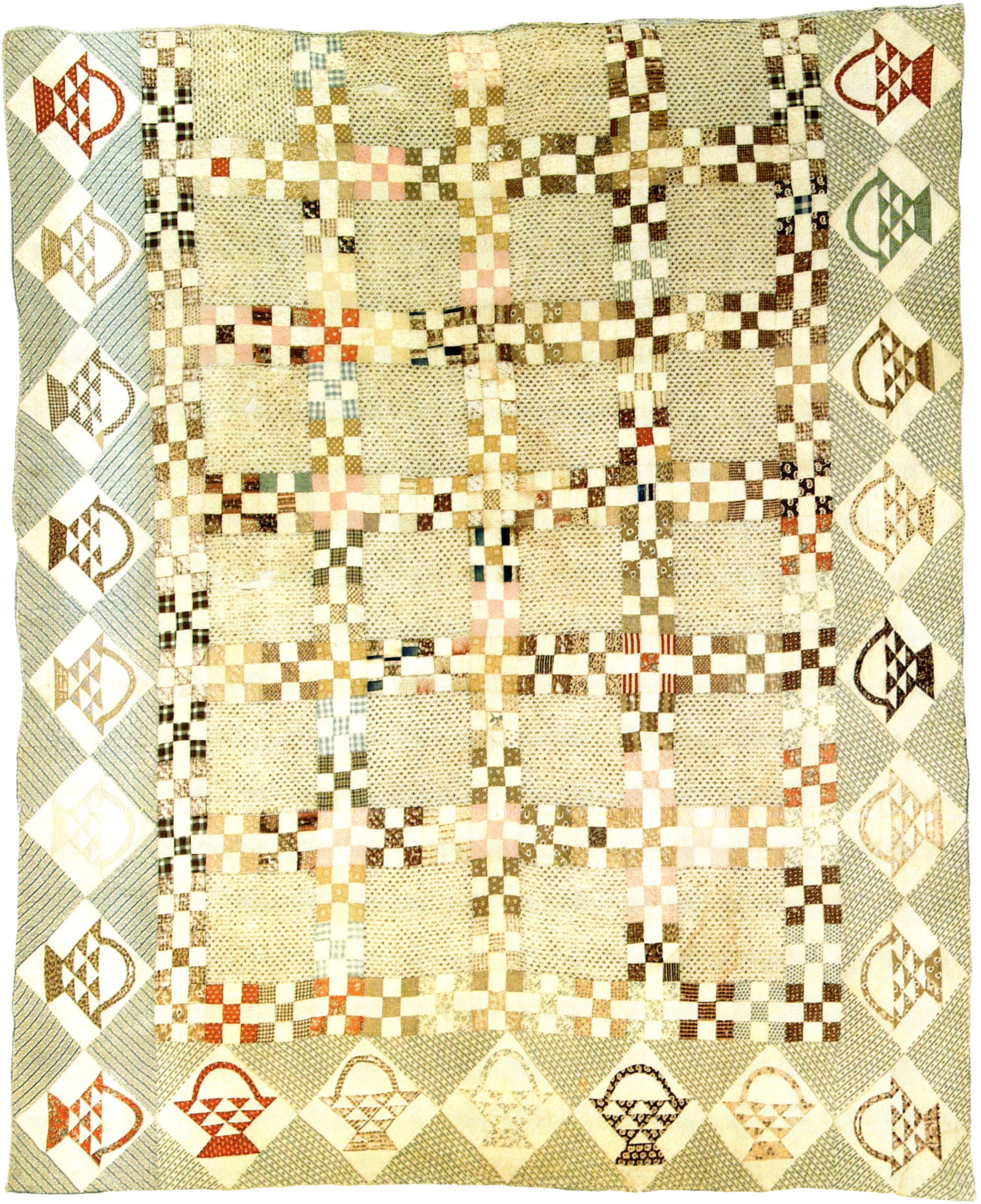

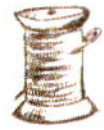 Nine Patch with Flower Basket Border, Grand Rapids Public Museum, *c. 1820 - 1860*

STRIPS *are* IN

Neatly aligned in tin-soldier rows, grouped in quadrants for a courthouse convention, or gathered 'round the hearth of a cozy log cabin, strips are a quilter's quintessential scraps. Versatile in their rectangular form, strips can be cut to almost any other shape or used as sashing between squares and triangles.

Let these vintage versions inspire you to experiment. See how the patterns and colors evolve when you split the values of light and dark; build out from a center of dark to light; or sneak in random strips of white. The more you play, the more you'll love this easy and unpretentious scrappy style.

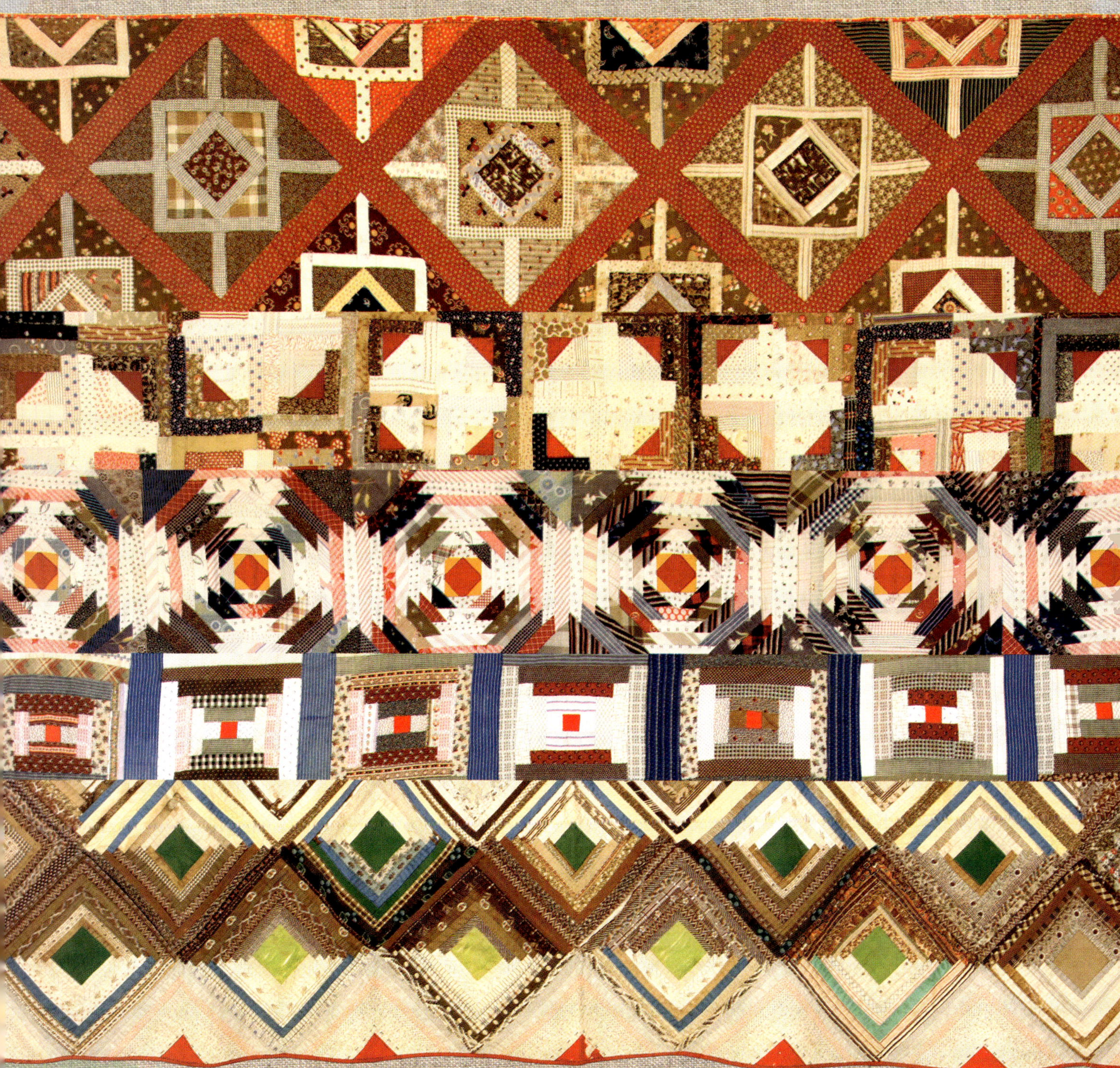

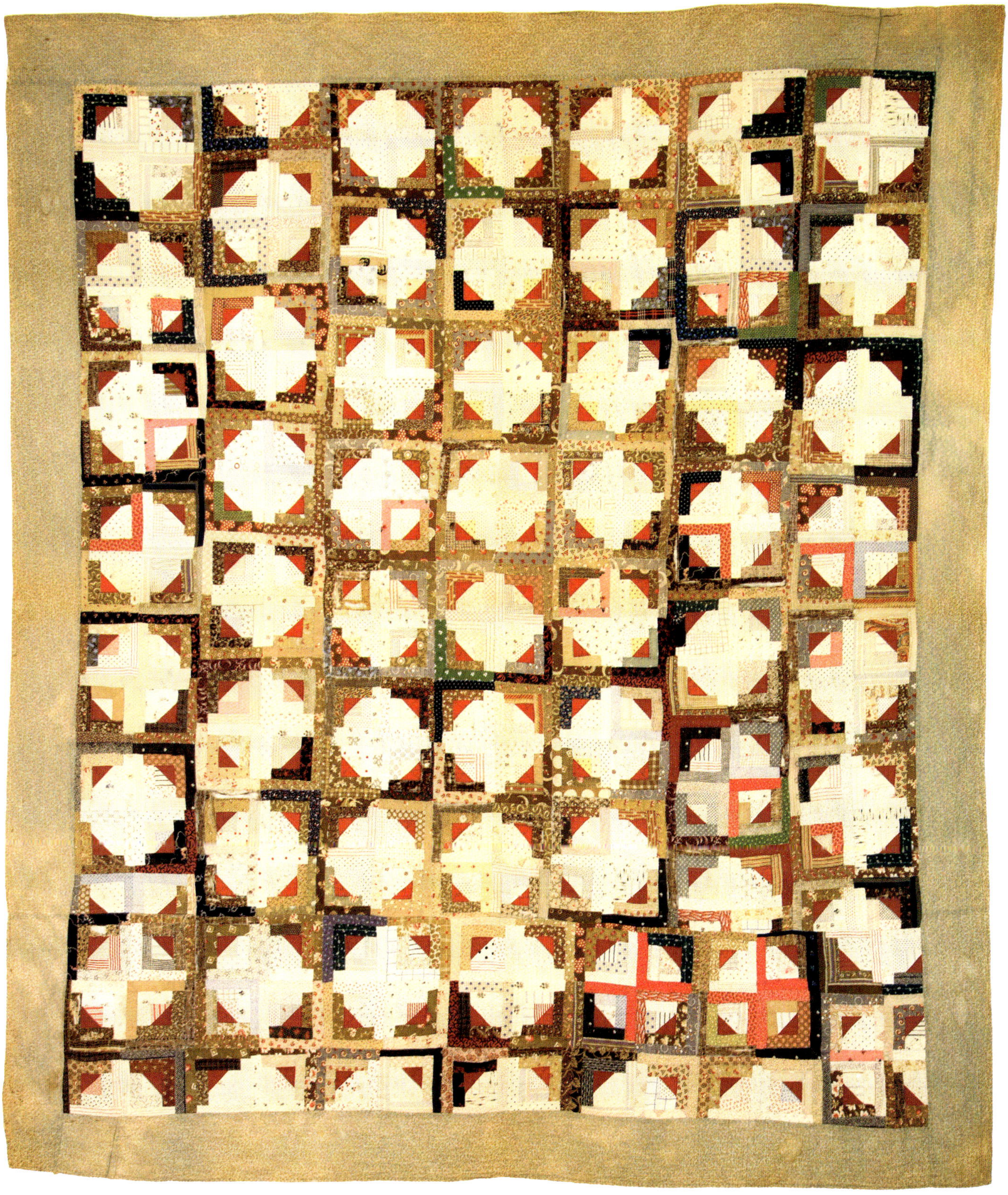

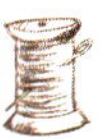 Triangle Log Cabin, Sitar Family Collection, antique, *c. 1870*

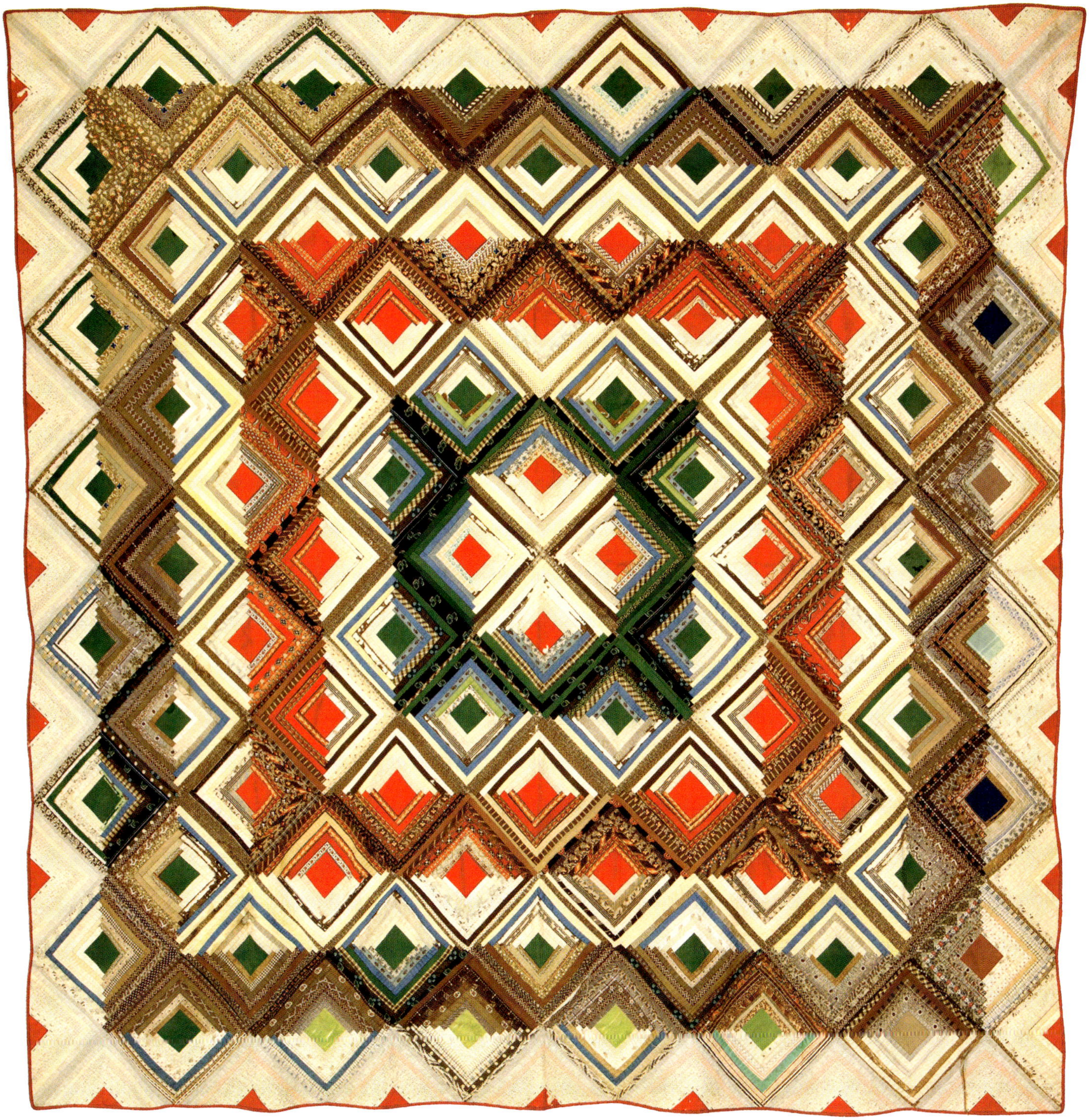

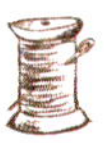 Barn Raising Log Cabin, Sitar Family Collection, antique, *c. 1890*

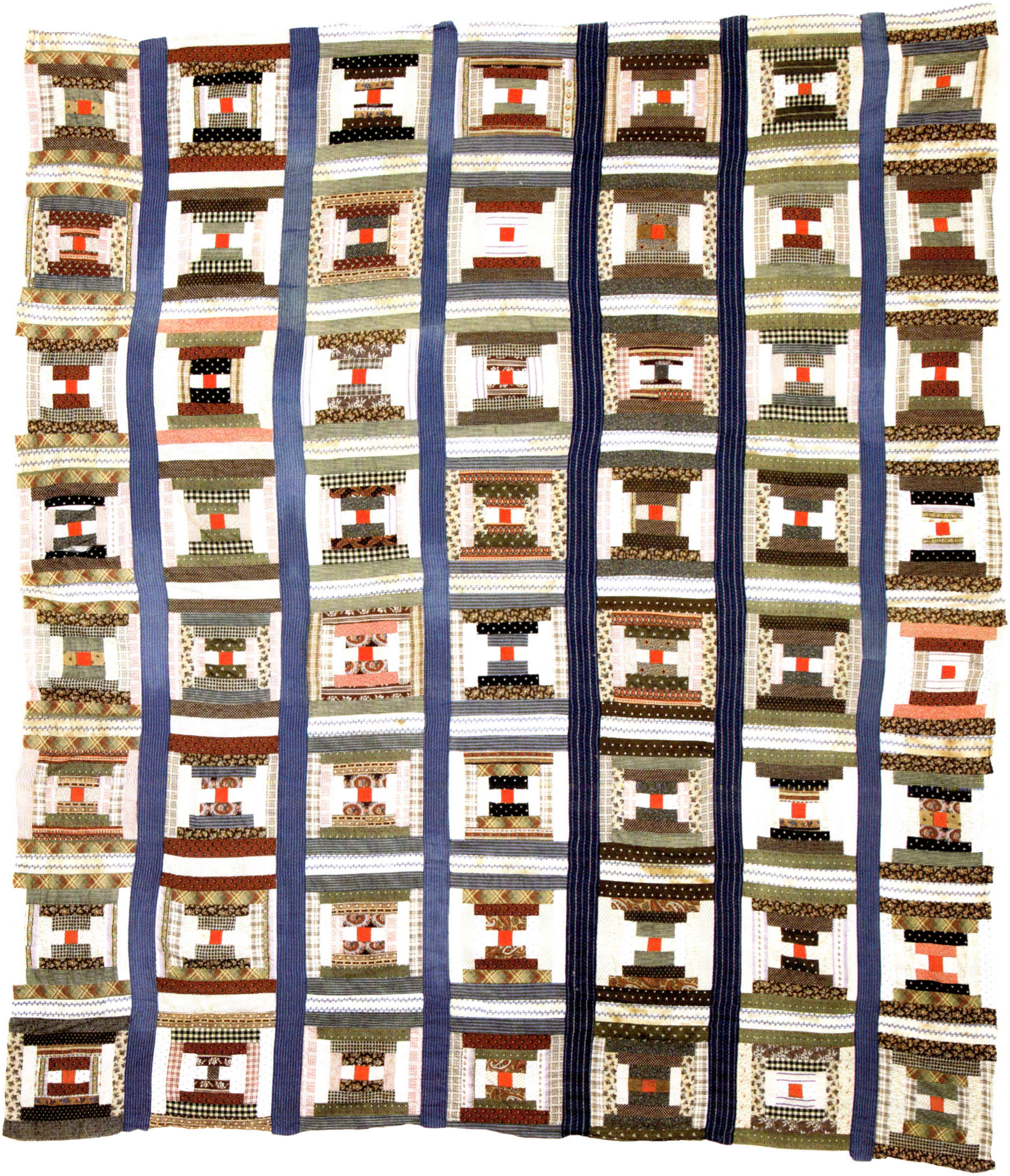

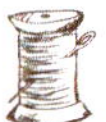 Courthouse Steps, Sitar Family Collection, antique, *c. 1905*

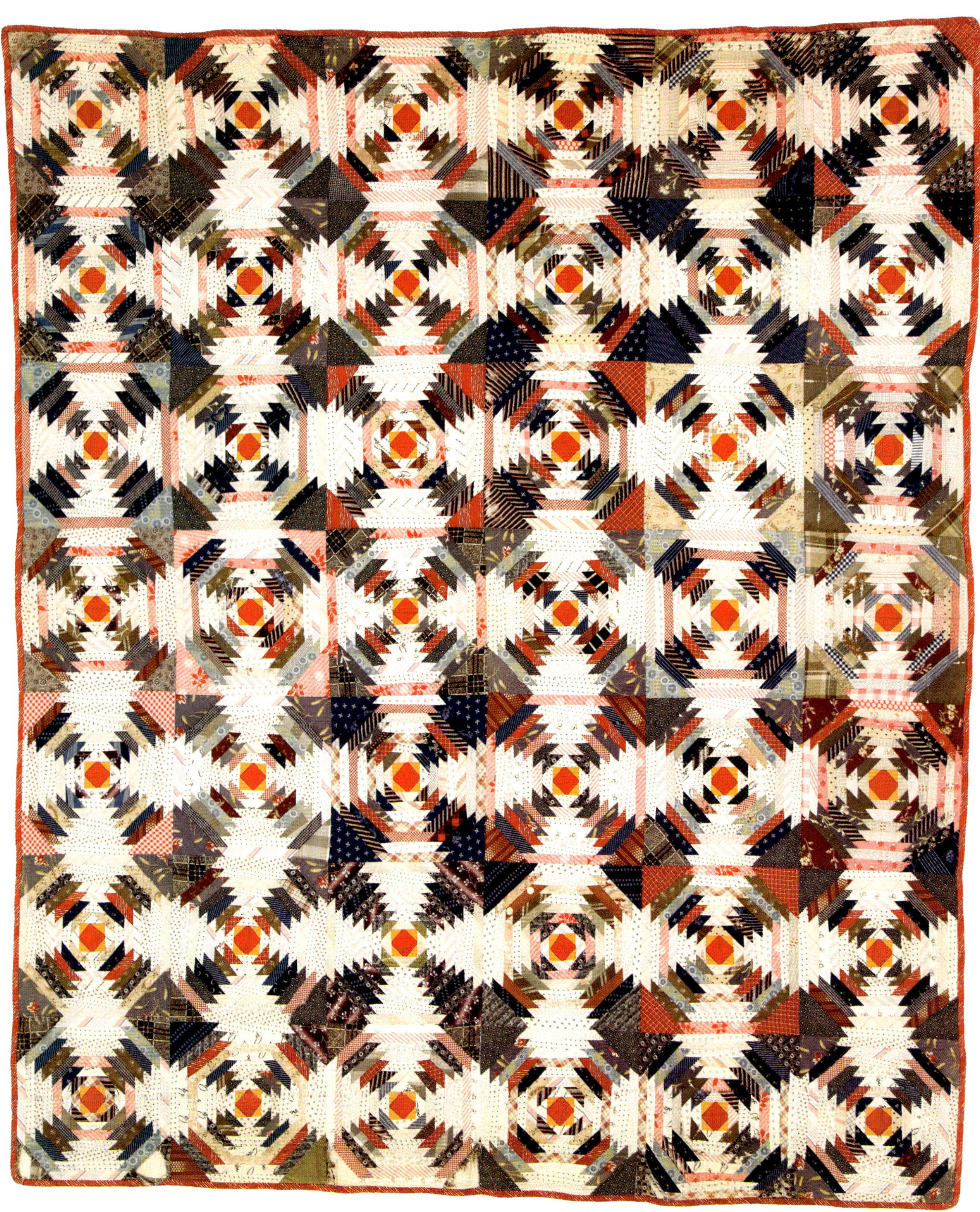

Pineapple Quilt, owned by Patricia Carlton, antique, *c. 1890*

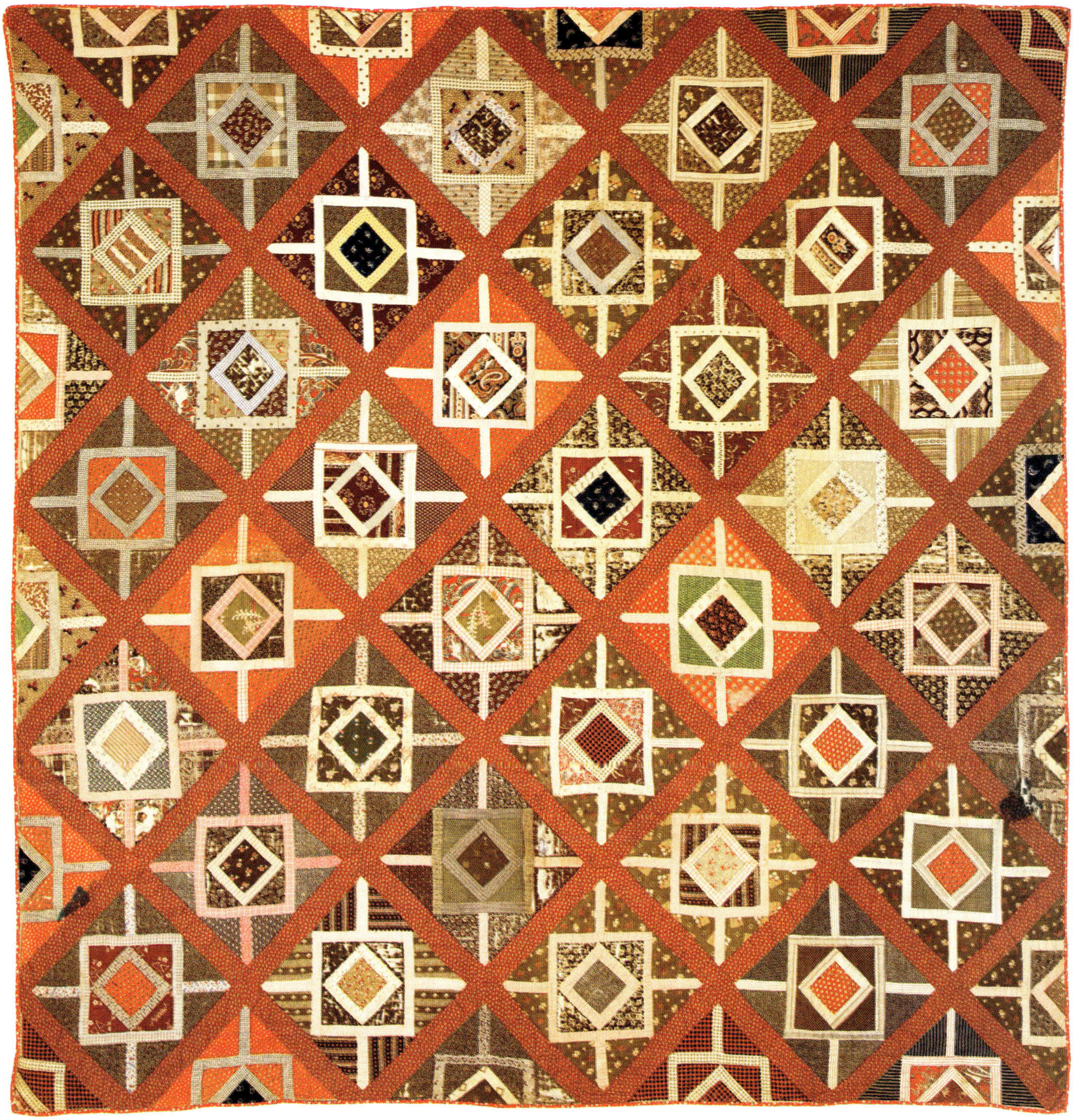

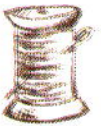 Squared, Sitar Family Collection, antique, *c. 1870*

DIAMONDS *and* STARS

Like precious stones, diamonds are a quilter's best friends. For generations, stitchers have been mesmerized by the multitude of patterns derived from these shapes. Creating drama with their pointed tips, diamonds add edgy details to a quilt, claiming their role as star performers.

Look closely to see how the patterns shift simply by switching the vantage point. Add your tiniest scraps to top the tallest diamond mountain; use color to intensify the rays of a rising sun; or align diamonds side-by-side to zigzag your way to graphic paradise.

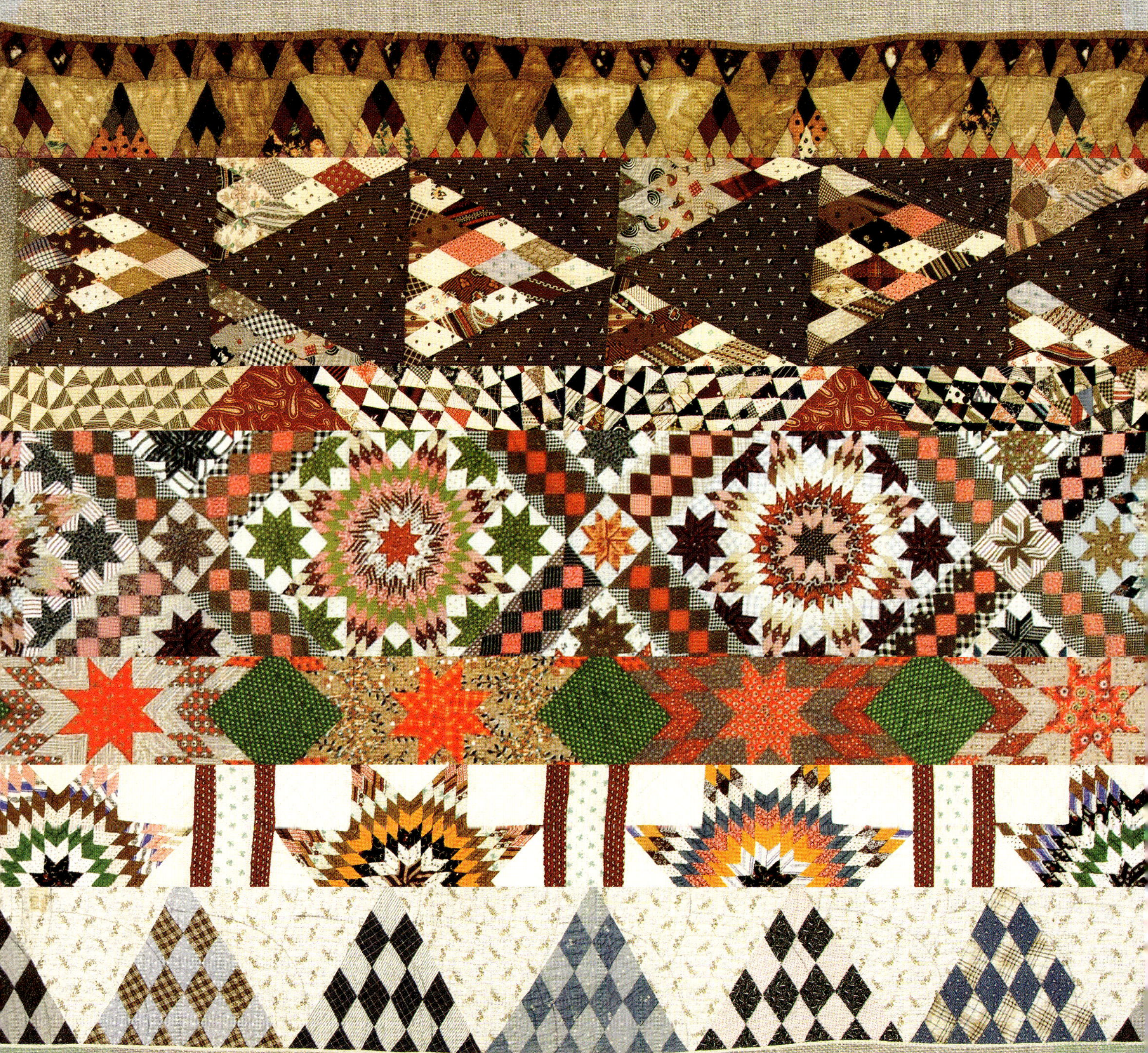

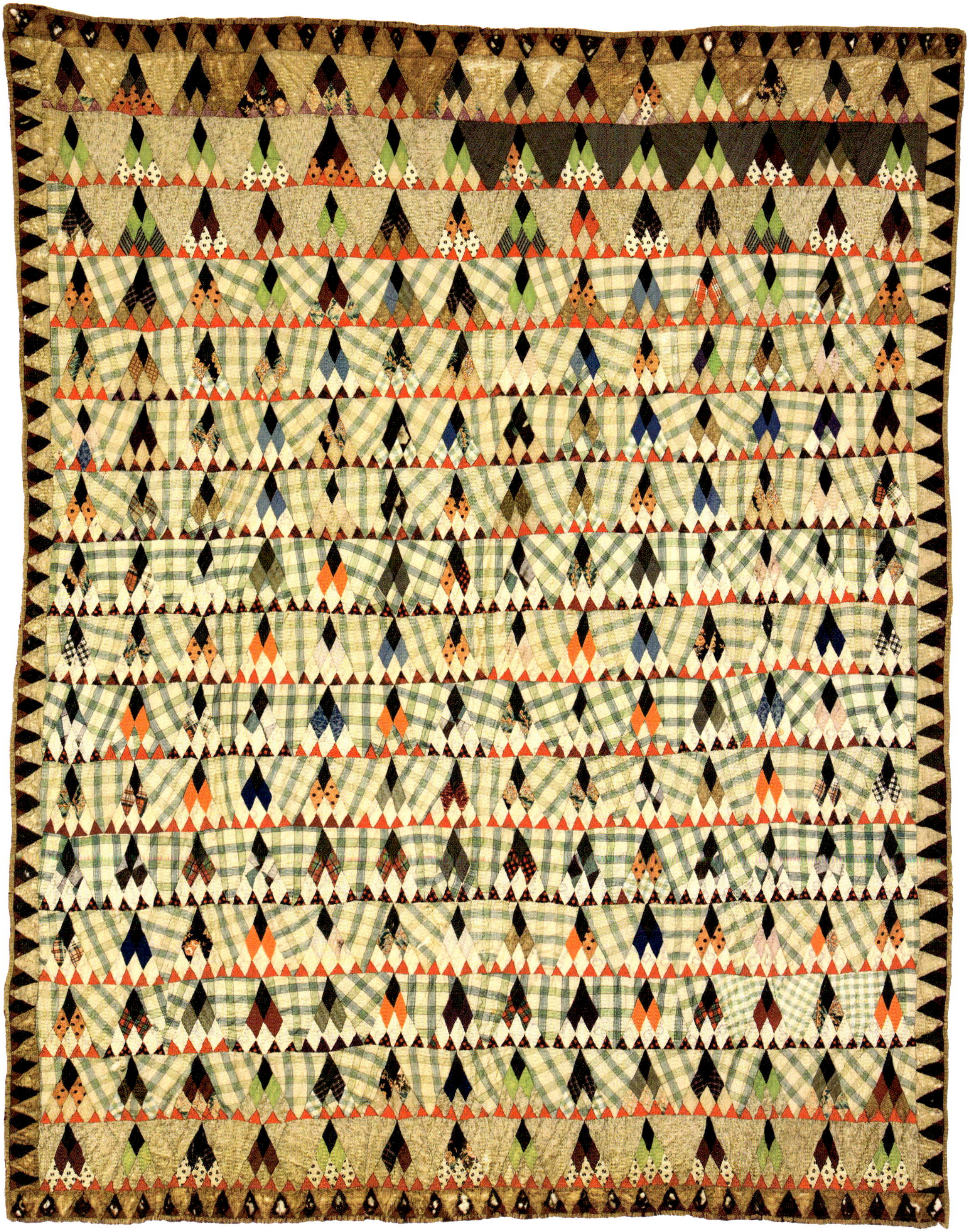

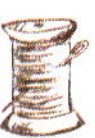 Diamond in Red, Sitar Family Collection, antique, *c. 1890*

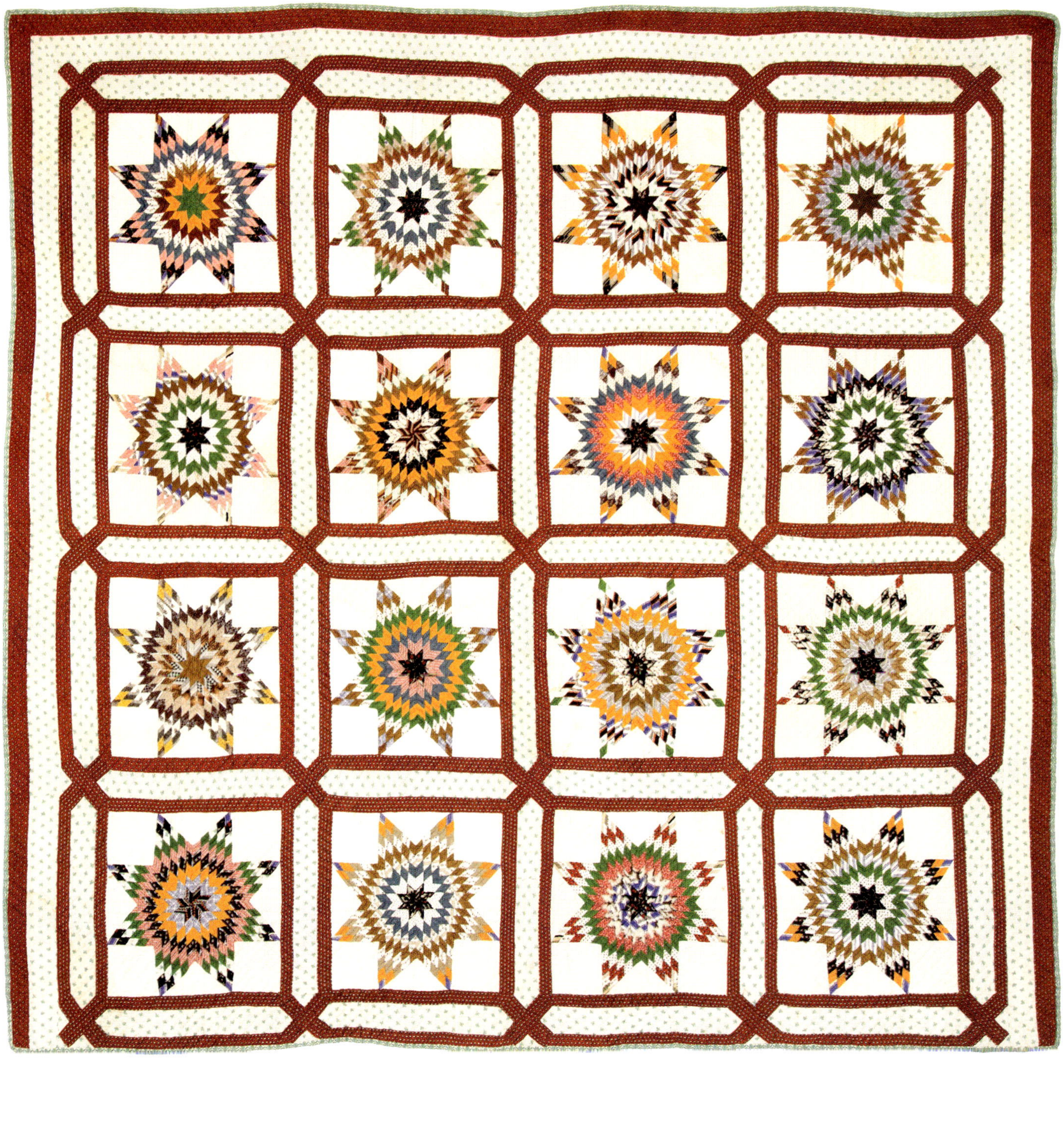

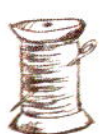

Texas Star, Sitar Family Collection, antique, *c. 1910*

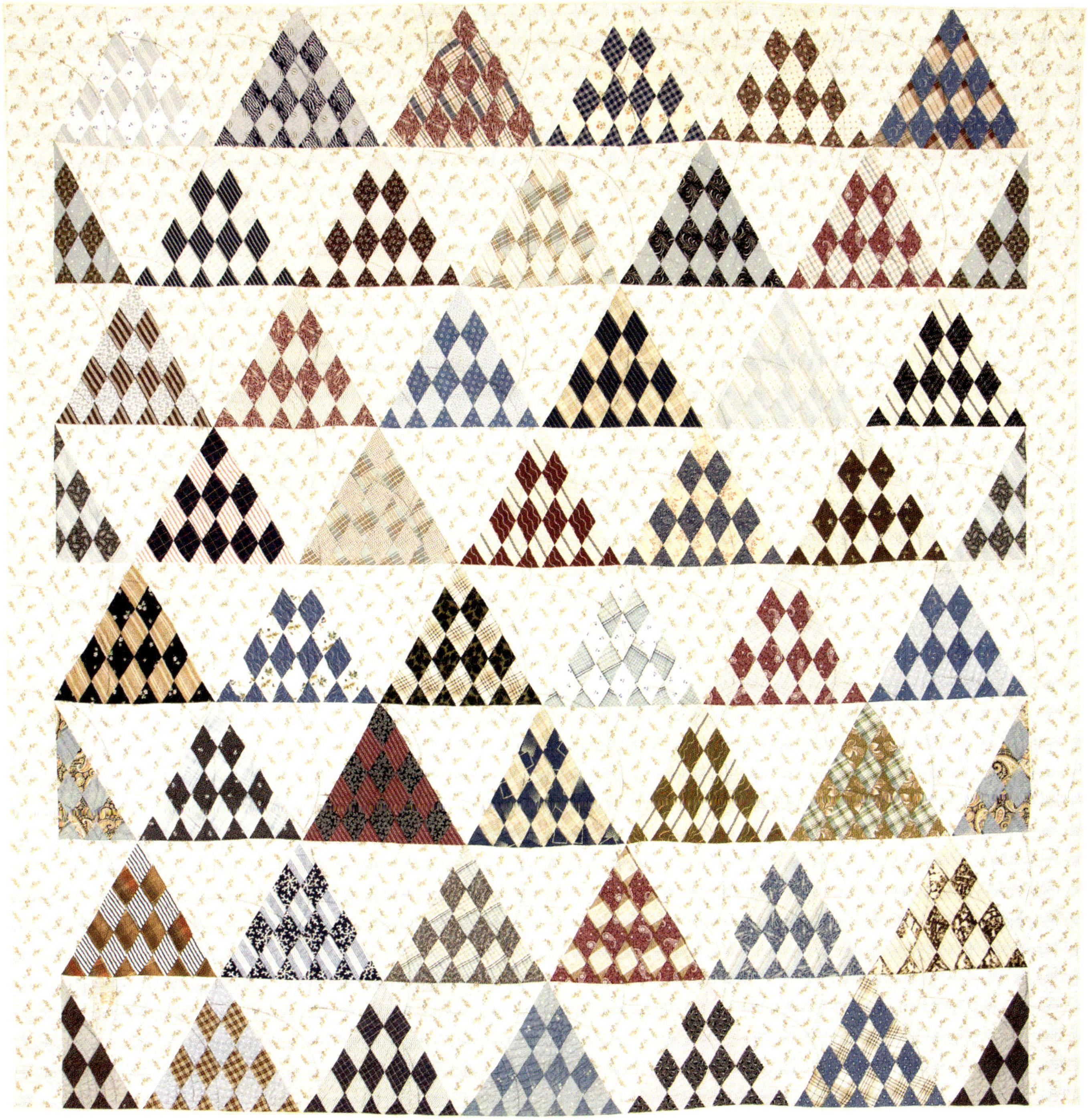

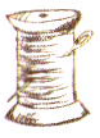 Diamond Delight, Sitar Family Collection, antique, *c. 1900*

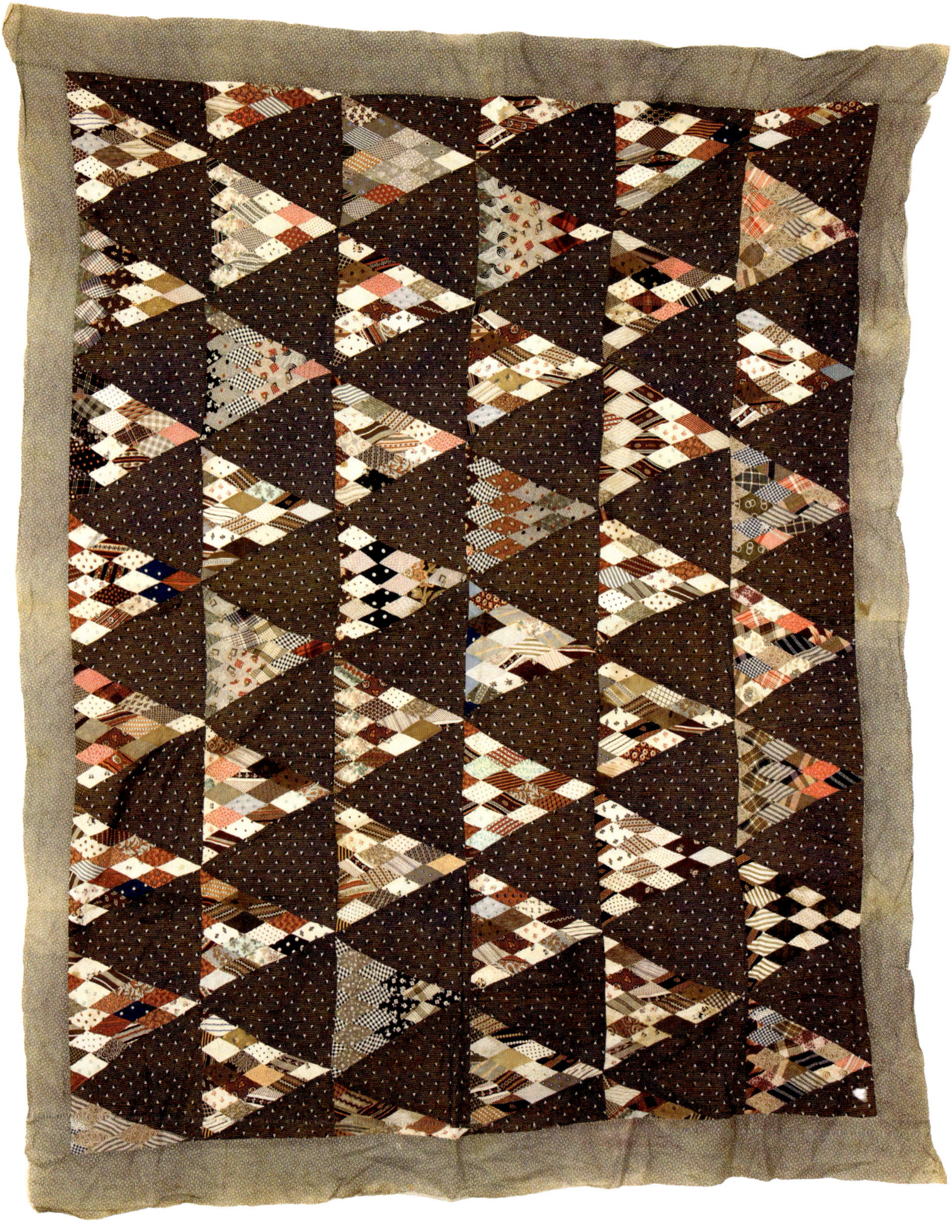

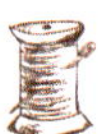

Diamond at Night, Sitar Family Collection, antique, *c. 1880*

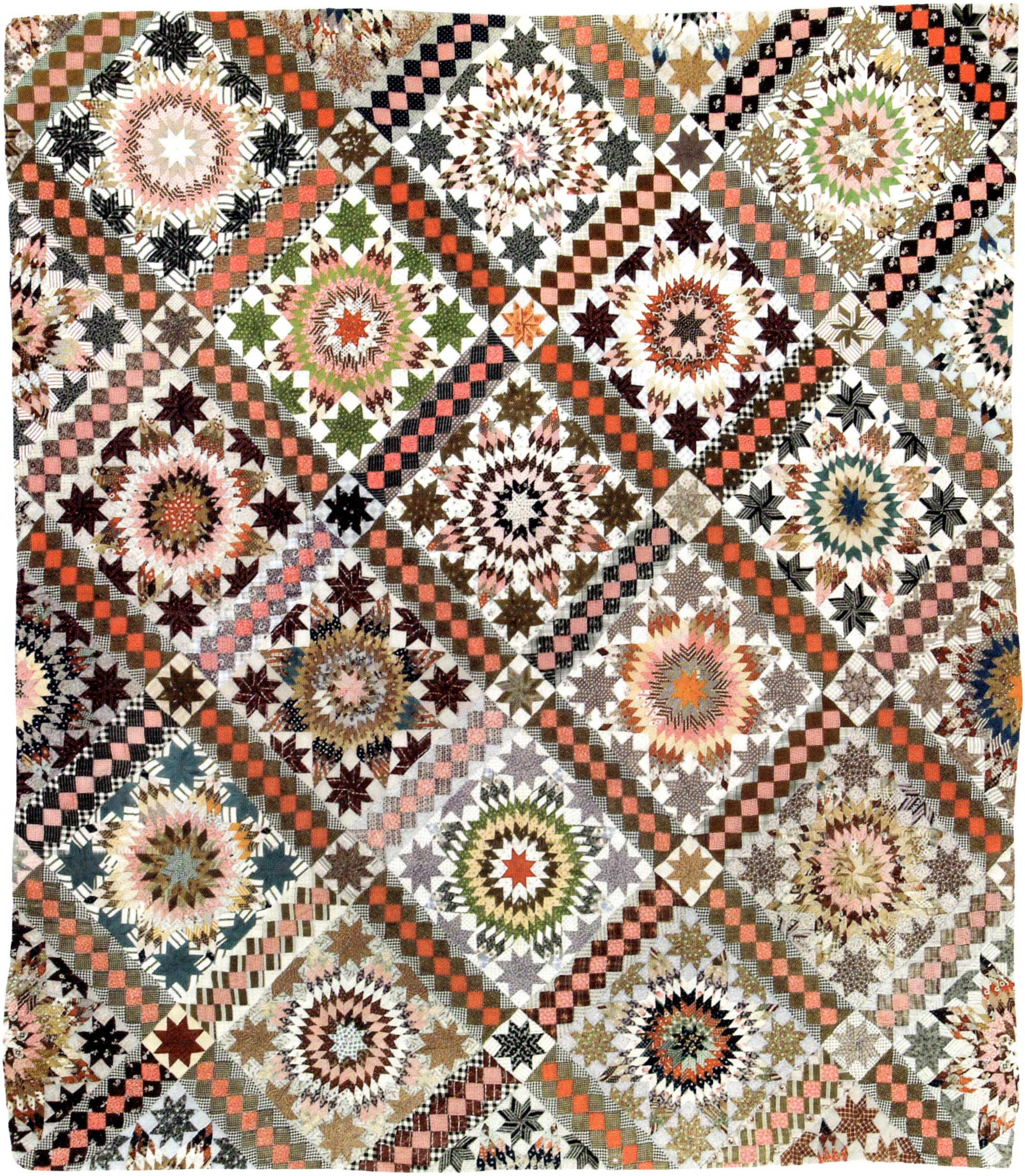

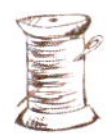 Stars Upon Stars, Grand Rapids Public Museum, *c. 1890–1950*

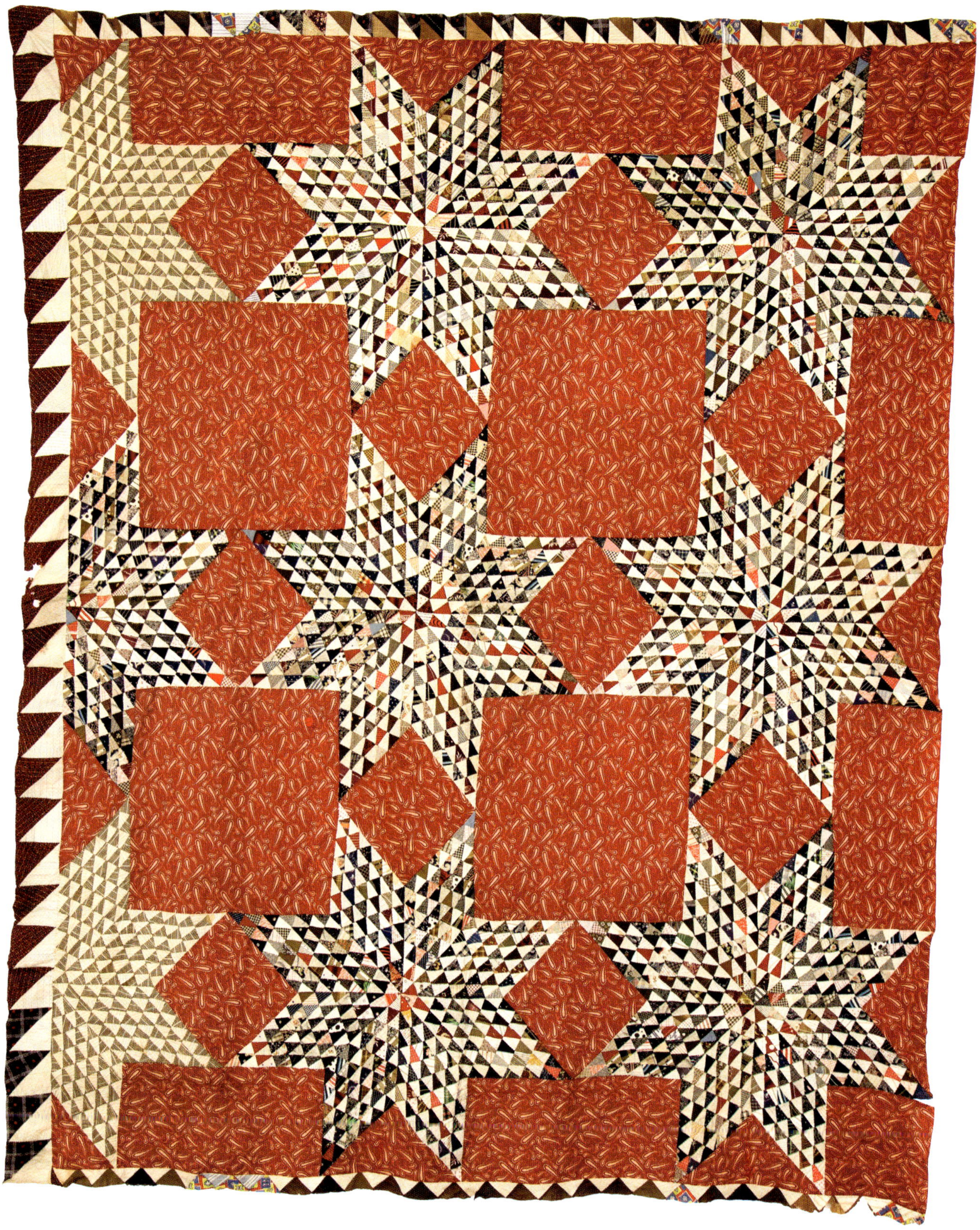

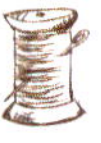
Thimble Star, Sitar Family Collection, antique, *c. 1902*

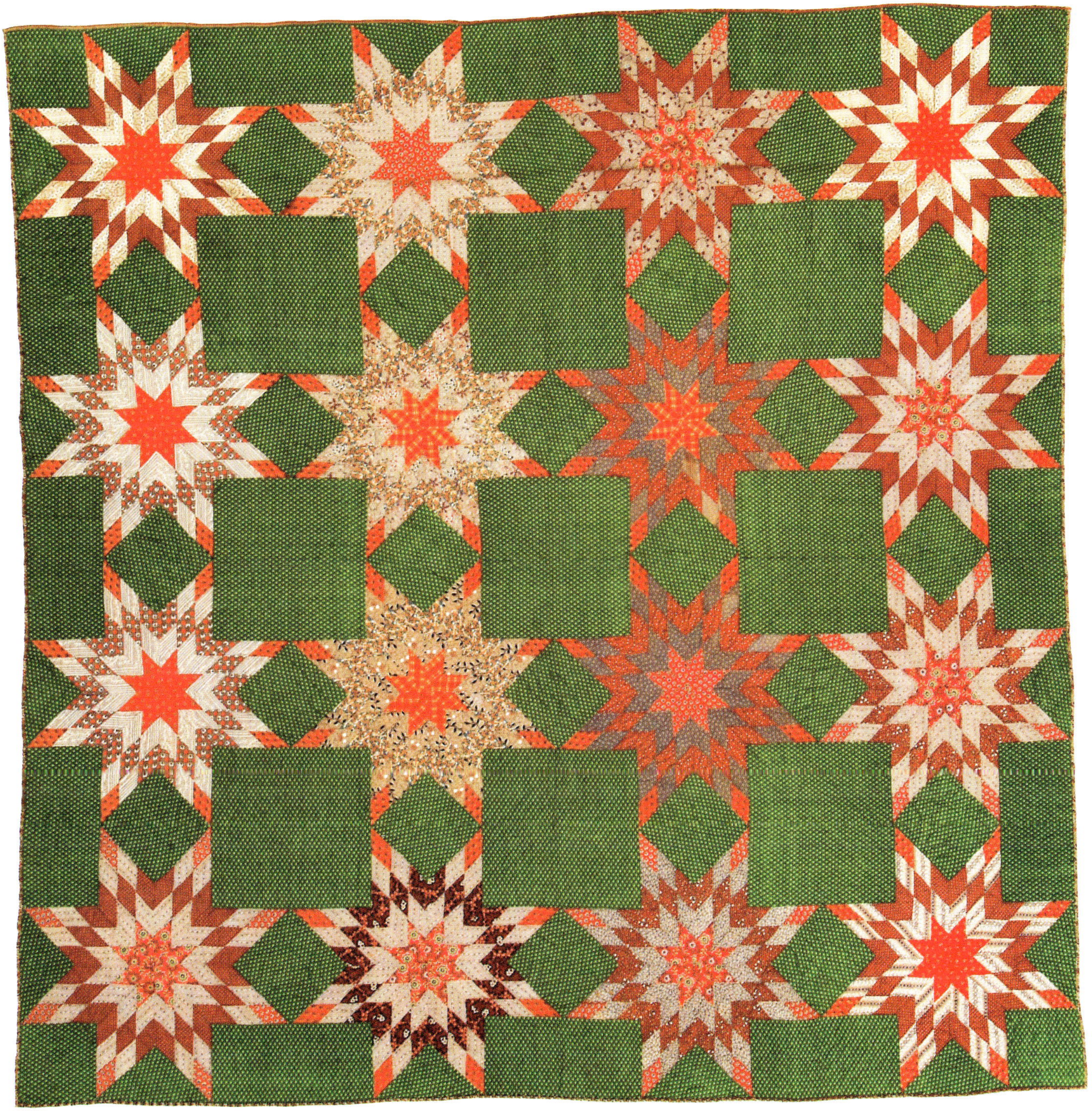

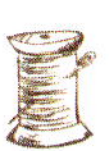 Prairie Star, Grand Rapids Public Museum, *c. 1850*

MEDALLION QUILTS

It's okay to stop and stare: The quilts in this chapter play endless games with scraps. *The smaller, the better* is the motto for these designs that earn their reputation for remarkable details. Building on a fabric focal point, tiny pieces of every color and size lend to the lure of medallion quilts—and because each piece is one-of-a-kind, the resulting quilt is a stand-alone keeper.

To give your medallion quilt a burst of extra joy, sort through your handfuls of fabric scraps, and start with the piece that speaks to you most strongly. Use this fabric as your center, and then add your other fabrics to it. Piece by piece, you'll breathe life into your stash to see that these fabrics should never have been hidden.

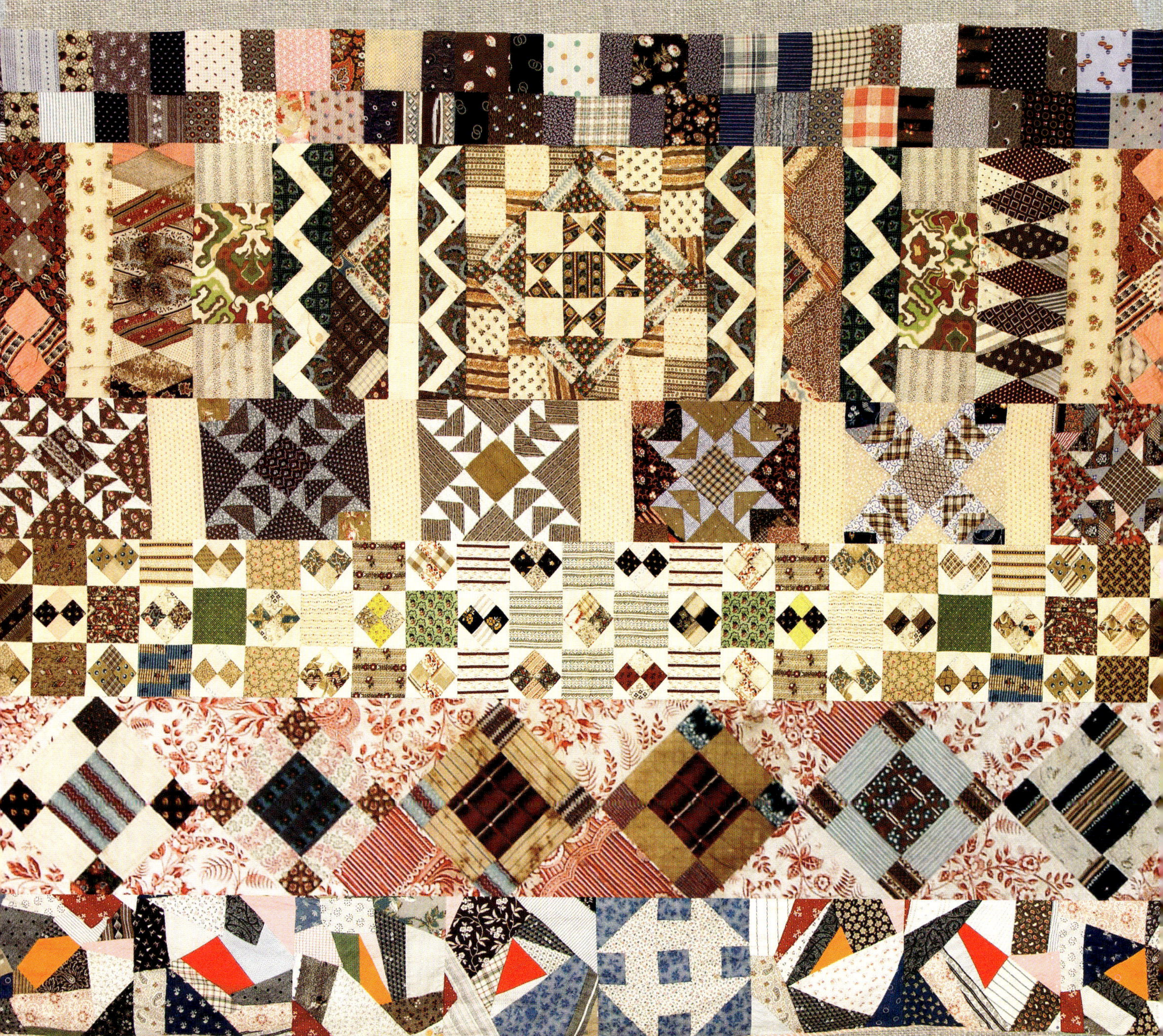

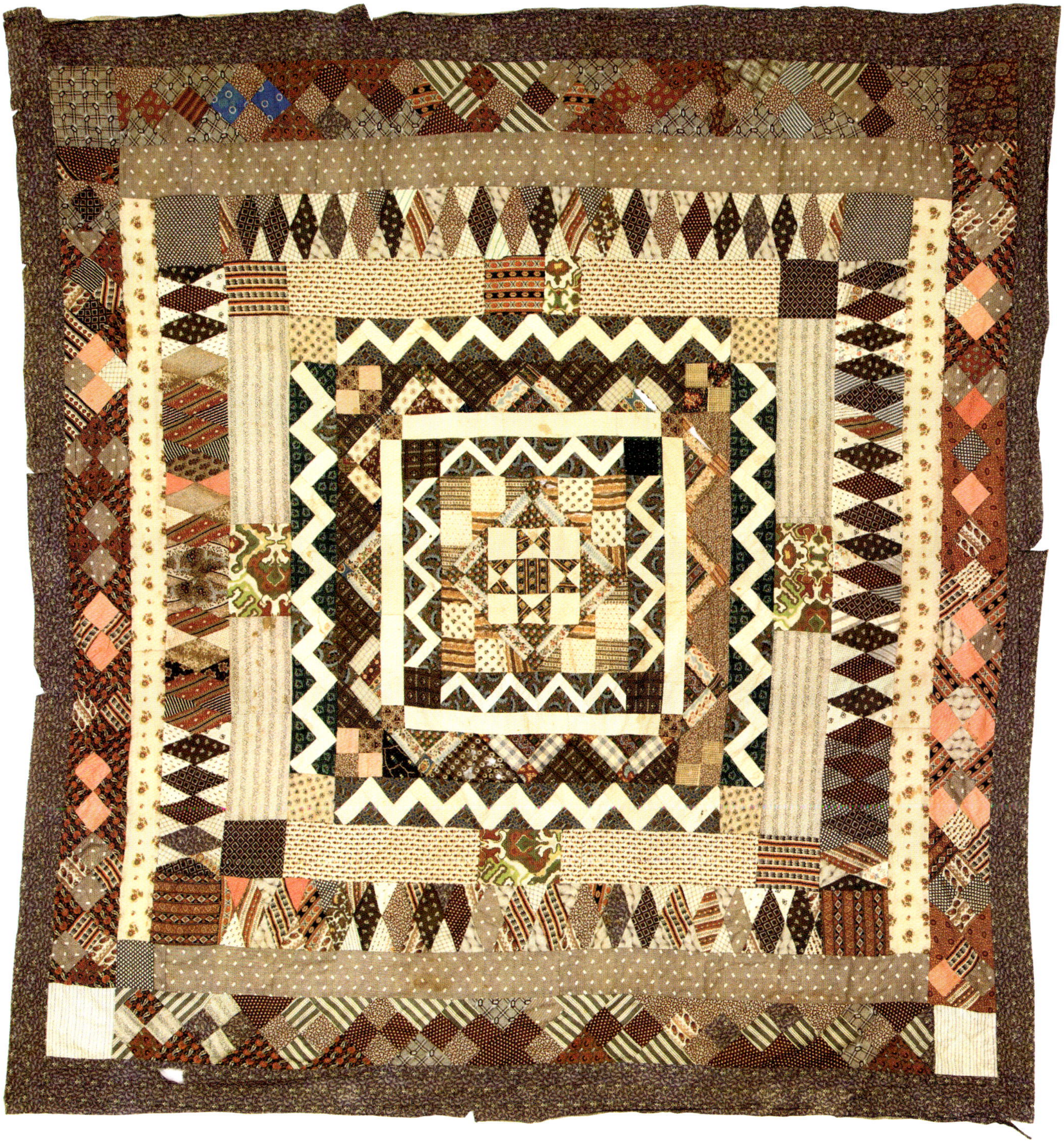

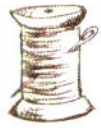 Ohio Star Medallion, Sitar Family Collection, antique, *c. 1840*

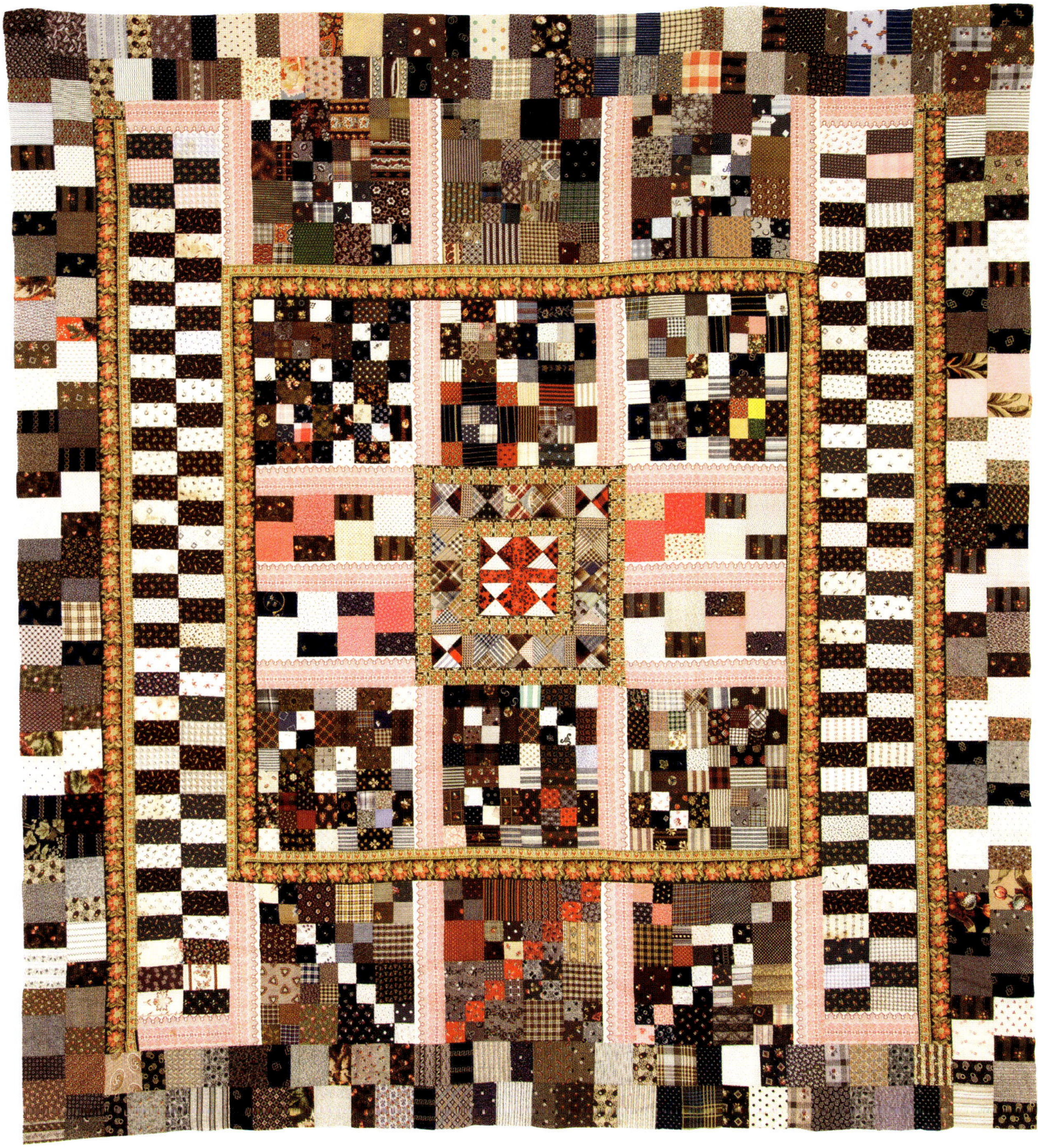

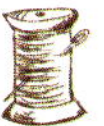 Piano Key Medallion, Sitar Family Collection, antique, *c. 1900*

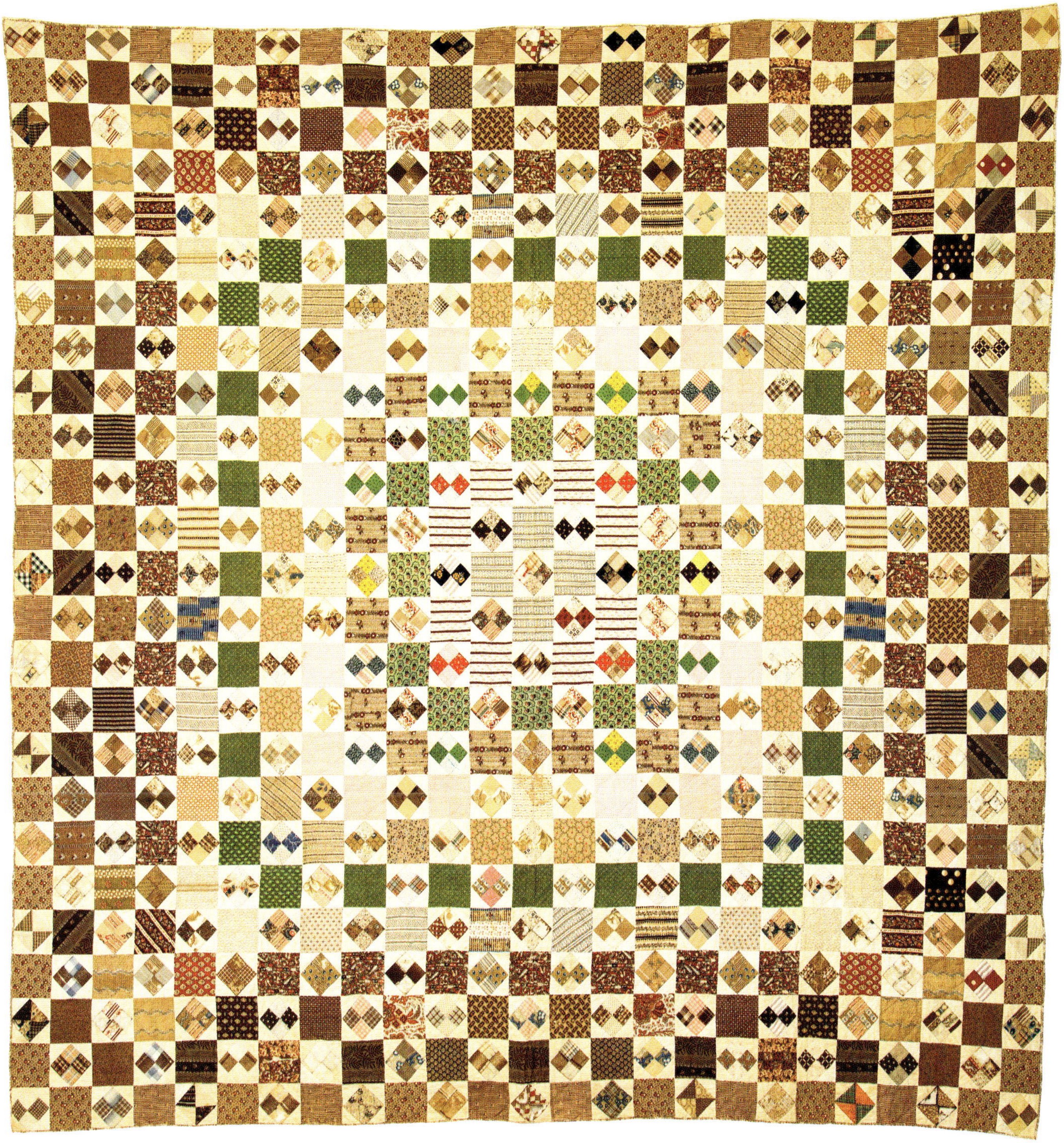

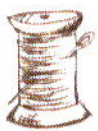 Four Patch Trip Around the World, Sitar Family Collection, antique, *c. 1880*

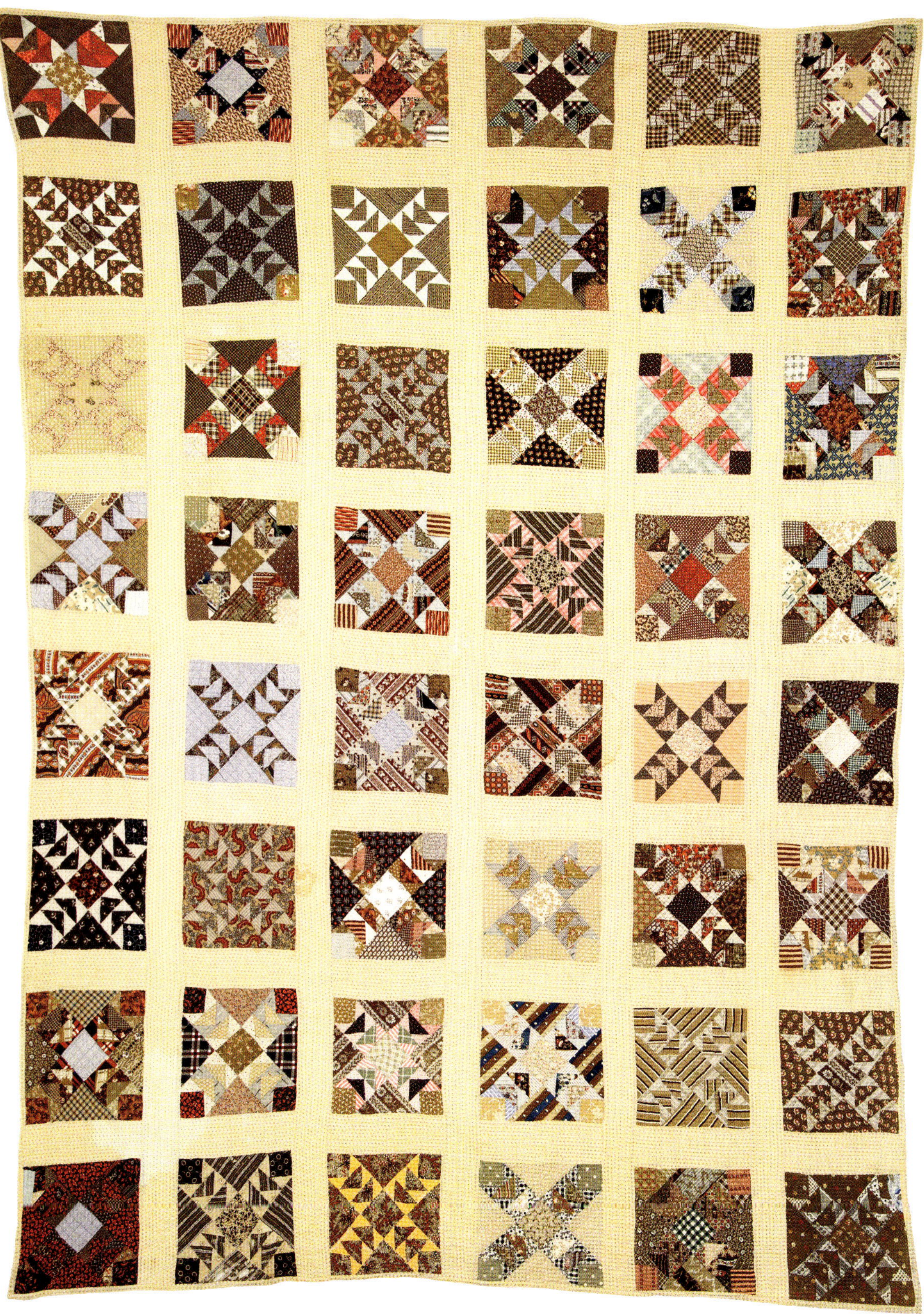

Flying Geese, Sitar Family Collection, antique, *c. 1870*

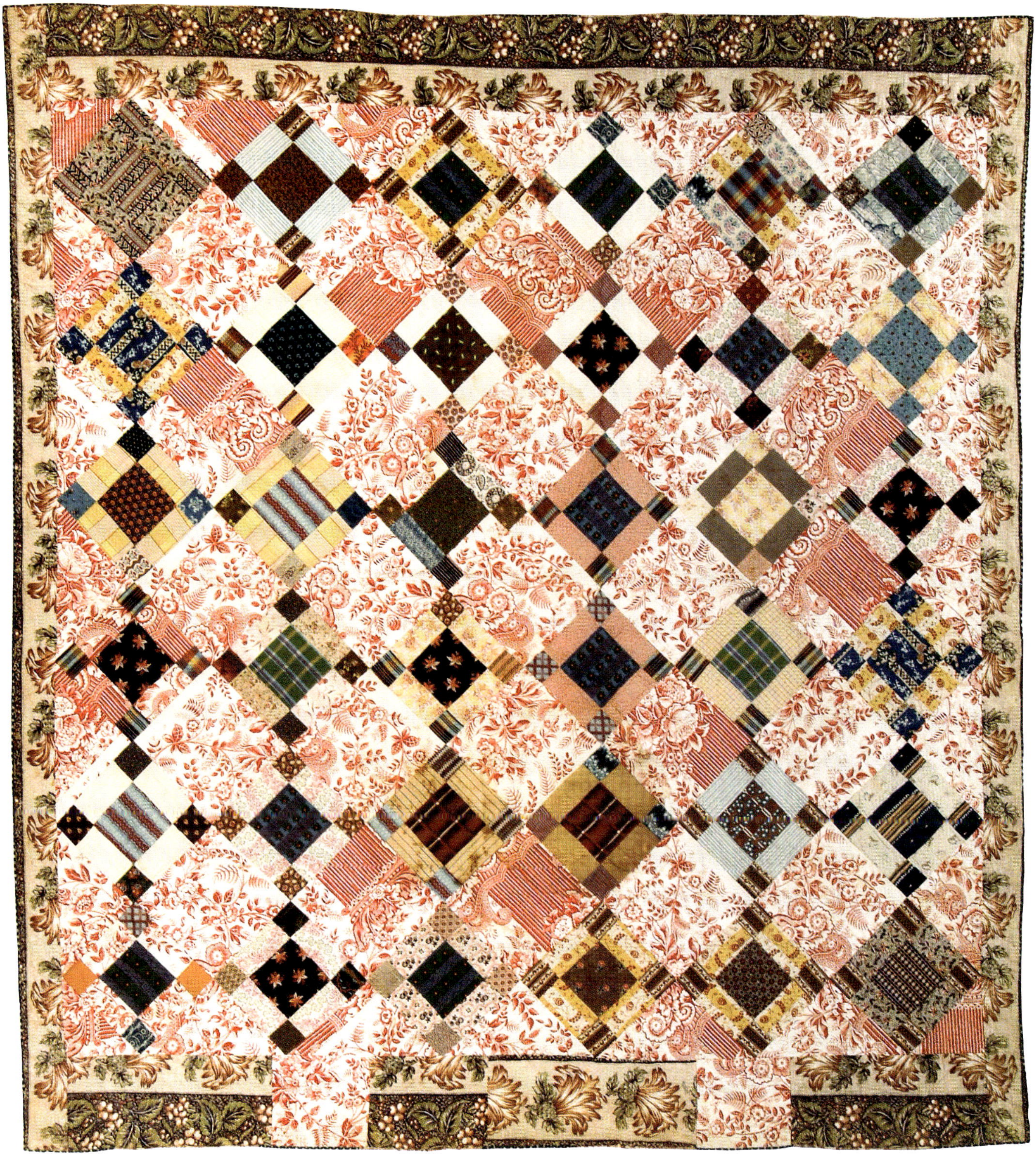

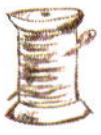 Nine Patch Variation, Grand Rapids Public Museum, *c. 1820*

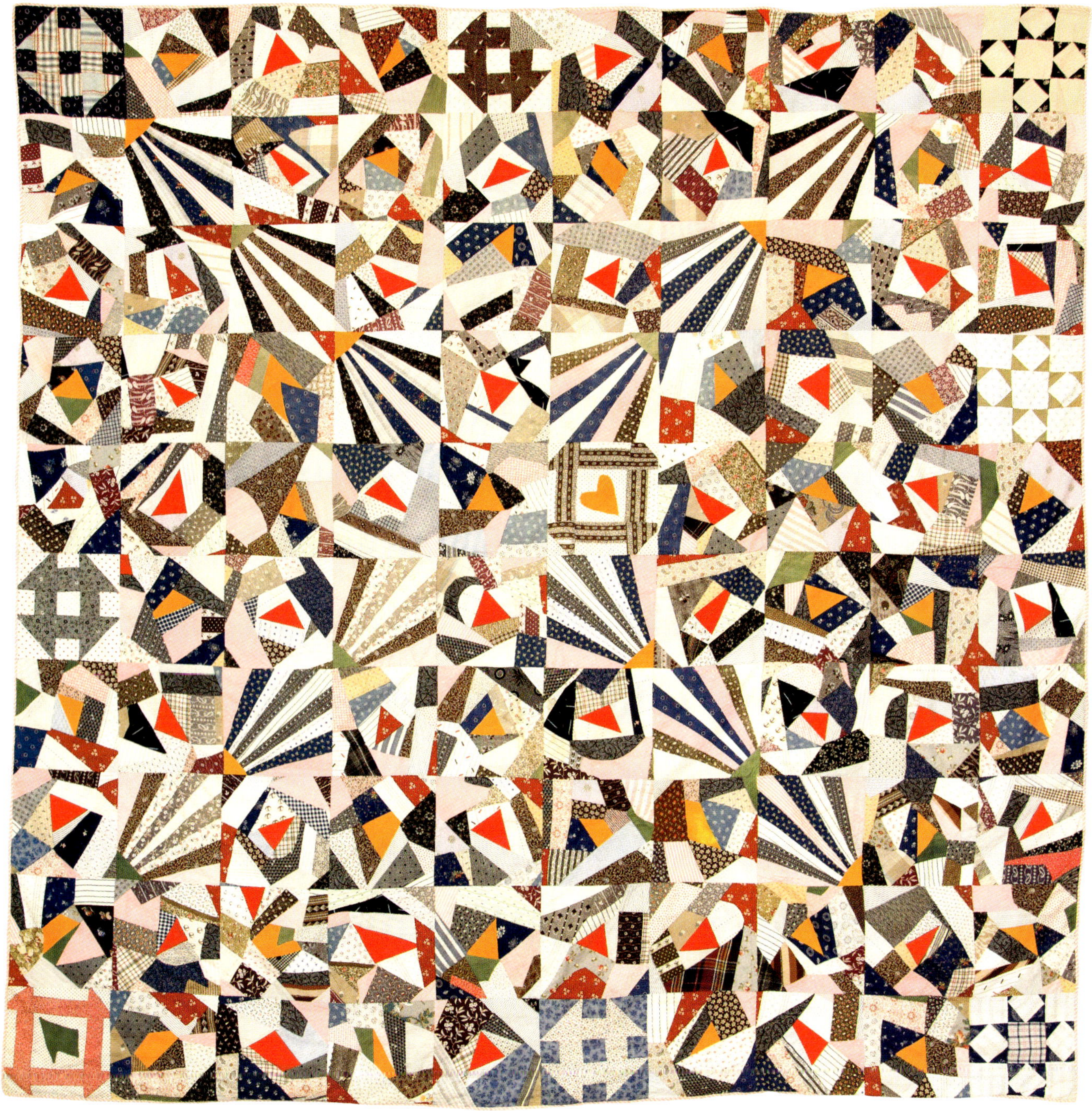

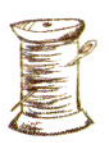 Crazy in Love Medallion, Sitar Family Collection, antique, *c. 1880*

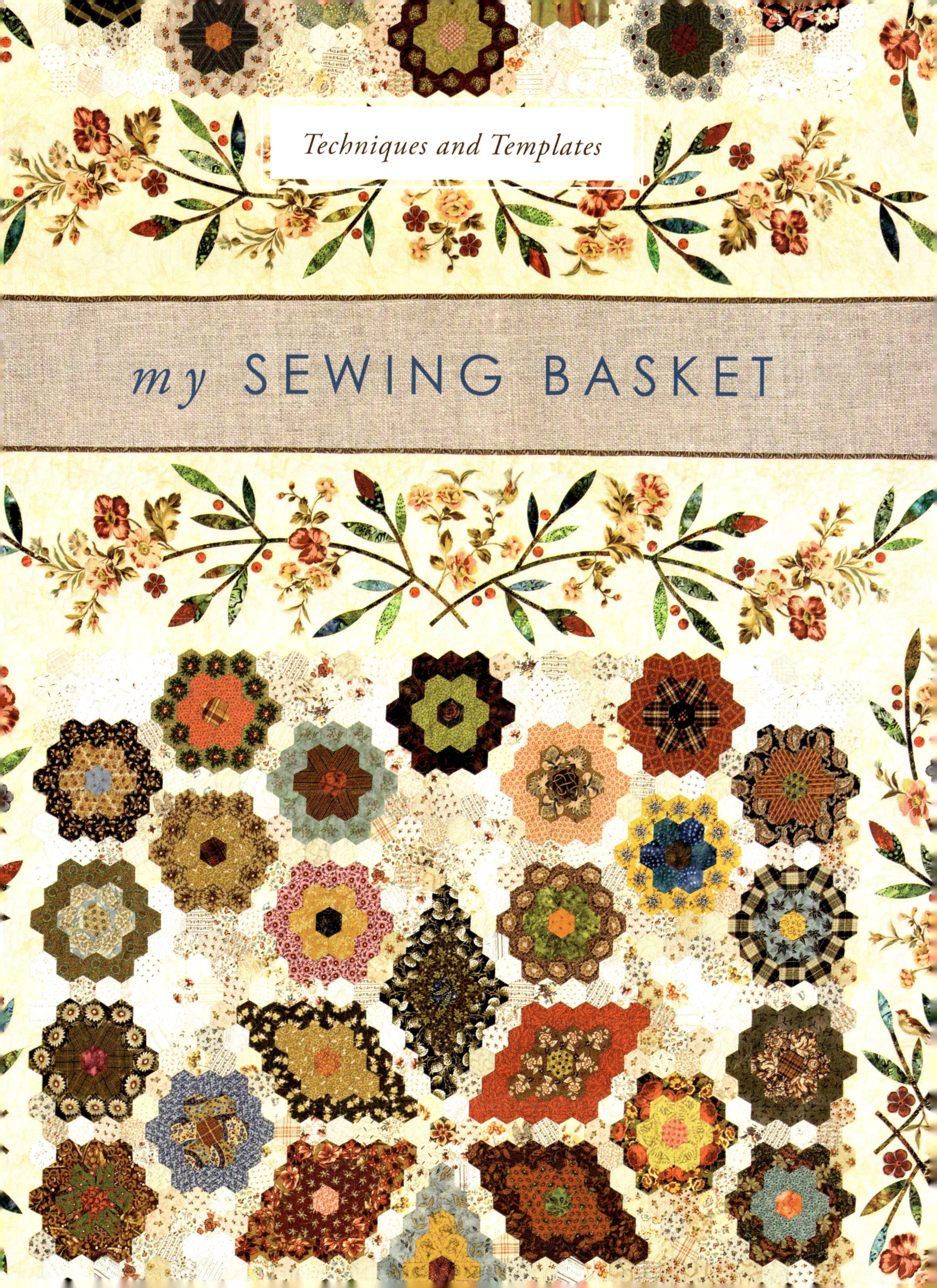

my SEWING BASKET

With every project you create, stretch your scraps and imagination. Refer to these quilting tips and techniques to help you create time-tested heirlooms that reflect your aesthetic and your stitching talents.

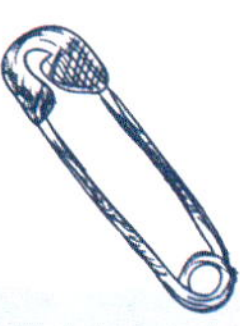

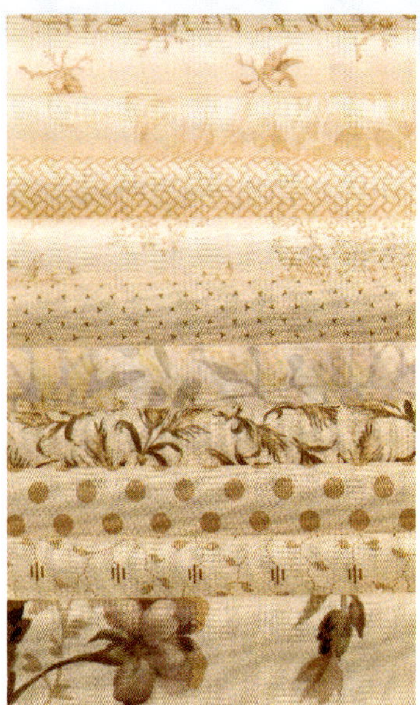

Touch of Muslin

A nice group of light fabrics is essential to your stash and the quilting projects in this book. Often I admire antique quilts in which muslin has been used as a canvas or as an accent between scraps. I like to use tone-on-tone backgrounds in my quilts; they give a vintage look of tea-dyed muslin with a warmer tint.

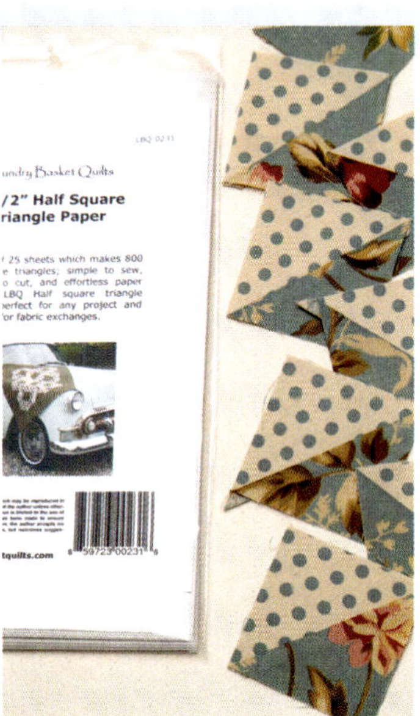

Triangles

Many quilts in this book use a very popular quilting shape: triangles. In the pattern directions, I have provided two methods for creating these wonderful shapes. My favorite is to make them with LBQ Triangle Paper. With this method, the triangles are accurate and fast. You get quite a few of them at once, so you can use them in multiple projects.

Binding: The Finishing Touch

1. Trim the batting and backing even with the quilt top.
2. Sew precut 2½" binding strips together end-to-end or using a 45-degree seam to create a long strip.
3. After folding strip in half wrong sides together, place binding strip on top of quilt top so that all raw edges align on the outside edge of the quilt. Raw edges include 2 binding strip edges, quilt top, batting edge, and quilt back edge.
4. Sew along the edge of the entire quilt to attach the binding to the quilt.
5. When sewing, stop ¼" away from the corner, reposition the binding to align with the next quilt side, and continue sewing.
6. Fold binding around the outer edge of the quilt, and hem it to the back of the quilt.

Fusible Appliqué

1. Trace your pieces to lightweight fusible webbing.
2. Cut out shapes, leaving at least 1/8" fusible webbing around the outside of the shapes.
3. Press each shape piece to the wrong side of fabric, following manufacturer's directions. DO NOT OVERHEAT FUSIBLE WEBBING!
4. Cut the fabric shapes following the traced line exactly.
5. Peel the paper from the back of the fabric shapes, and place your pieces on the background, following the layout.
6. Once all your pieces are in place, press them gently with your iron to secure their position.
7. Prepare your sewing machine; setting should be on a small zigzag or blanket stitch with your favorite thread.
8. To secure your appliqué pieces, stitch around all of the edges.
9. Once completed, gently press block from the back.

Machine Appliqué

1. Trace all the shapes for your appliqué onto matte side of freezer paper.
2. Cut out freezer paper shapes exactly on the traced line.
3. Attach matte side of freezer paper shapes to the wrong side of your appliqué fabric with a touch of glue.
4. Cut the fabric around the shape, staying ¼" allowance away from the freezer paper shape.
5. Using the tip of your iron, turn over the ¼" allowance over the edges of the paper shapes. Hold the iron for a few seconds to allow the fabric to adhere to the shiny side of the freezer paper.
6. Iron your shapes onto the background, following the layout. The shiny side of the freezer paper will allow the appliqué pieces to stick to the background. If needed, use a touch of glue.
7. Prepare your sewing machine; setting should be a small zigzag or blanket stitch with your favorite thread.
8. Stitch around all of the edges.
9. Once completed, gently press block from the back.
10. Using sharp scissors, make a small slit in your background fabric under the appliqué pieces, and remove the freezer paper.

Hand Appliqué

1. Prepare appliqué shapes, following Steps 1-6 from Machine Appliqué.
2. Secure the pieces to the background using silk thread, an appliqué needle, and a small whip stitch to sew around the edges of all pieces.
3. Once completed, gently press block from the back.
4. Using sharp scissors, make a small slit in your background fabric under the appliqué pieces, and remove the freezer paper.

Broderie Appliqué

Even when access to fabric was limited, women went out of their way to stitch beautiful things. Broderie appliqué is the technique they invented to stretch the fabrics they wanted to preserve. For example, rather than using an expensive and hard-to-find floral print for one project, they fussy-cut a single motif and appliquéd it to a separate background fabric. Then they could use the remaining fabric for other stitching projects.

Today, although patterned fabric is much more available, broderie appliqué is alive and well. Quilters use it to embellish quilt borders, to carry a print through different areas of a quilt top, or to add dimension to a center medallion.

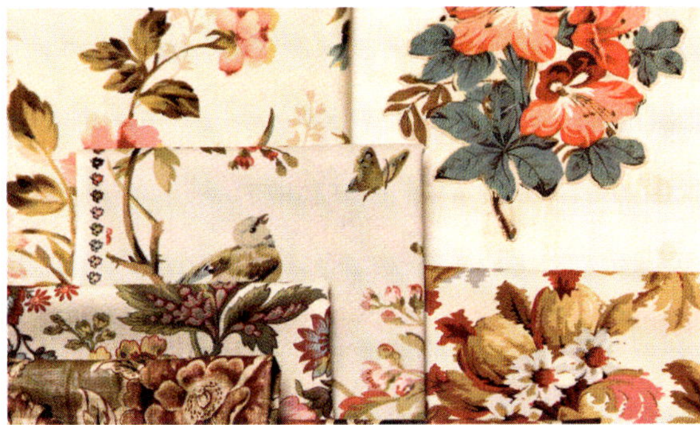

(A) Collecting great fabrics with light background and lovely large flowers is essential to beautiful broderie appliqué. Fabrics with images of birds and butterflies will add something extra to your projects. Many Laundry Basket Quilts big print fabrics are perfect for broderie appliqué.

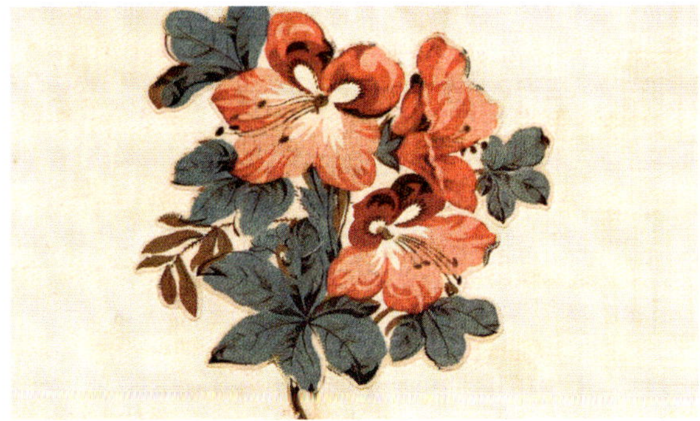

(B) This 1800s antique broderie appliqué block has inspired me to take a closer look at every flower and fussy-cut some beautiful print fabrics to add detail to my appliqué projects.

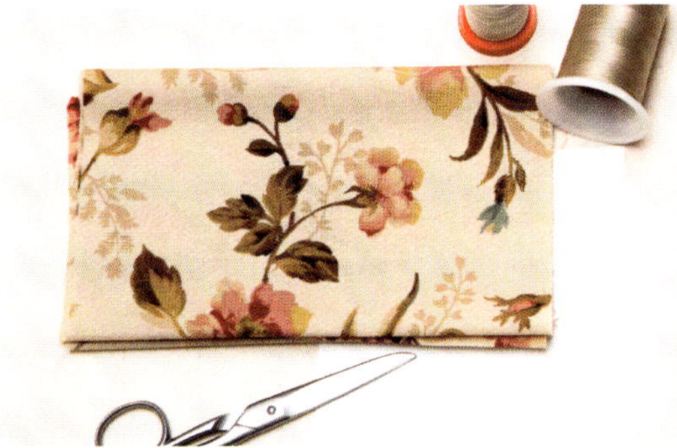

(C) For this technique, you need fabric, scissors, light fusible webbing, thread for your top, and bobbin (I used 2310 50-wt Aurifil). If you want to hide your stitch, use a lighter weight thread on top (100-wt).

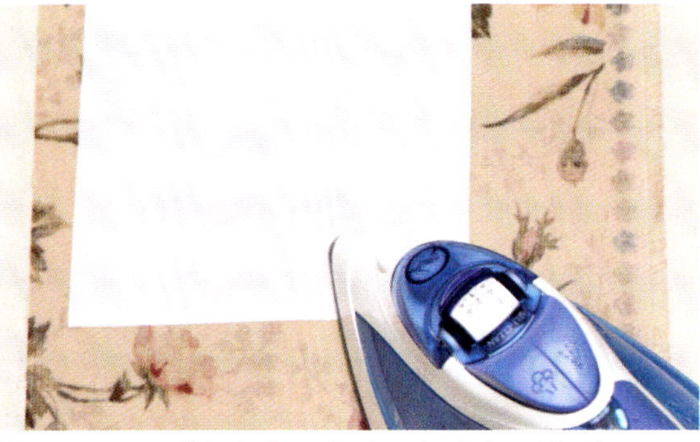

(D) Prepare your fabric by placing it right side down. Press then place fusible webbing to cover the area of the design that you are planning to use. Gently press in place with a dry iron on cotton setting. Do not over-press.

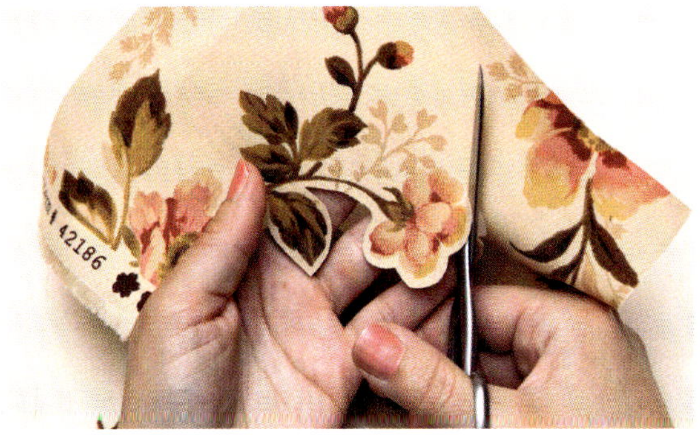

(E) With small sharp scissors, cut out desired flower. Stay approximately ⅛" away from the fabric design, and remember to simplify the edges of the cutout, keeping in mind that you will be stitching around the edges of this shape.

(F) Add the cutouts to your appliqué layout. They will be used to fill empty areas of your traditional appliqué. Press cutouts in place, and then stitch around the edges with a small zigzag or blanket stitch. Your stitch needs to be ⅛" wide to keep your cutouts in place.

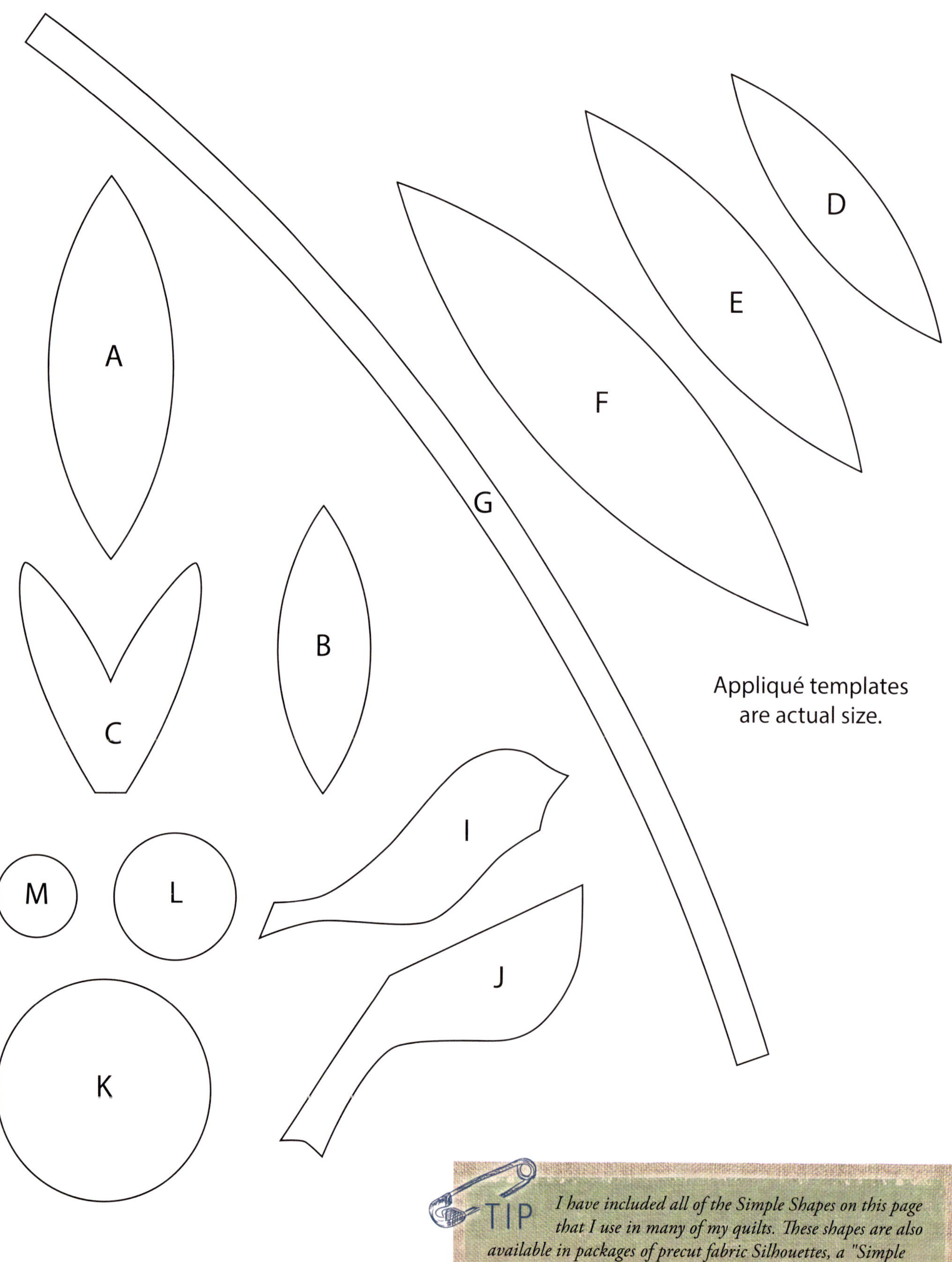

TIP *I have included all of the Simple Shapes on this page that I use in many of my quilts. These shapes are also available in packages of precut fabric Silhouettes, a "Simple Shapes" plastic stencil (LBQ-0428-T), or AccuQuilt Die "GO! Simple Shapes" (item #55177).*

TIME *to* PLAY

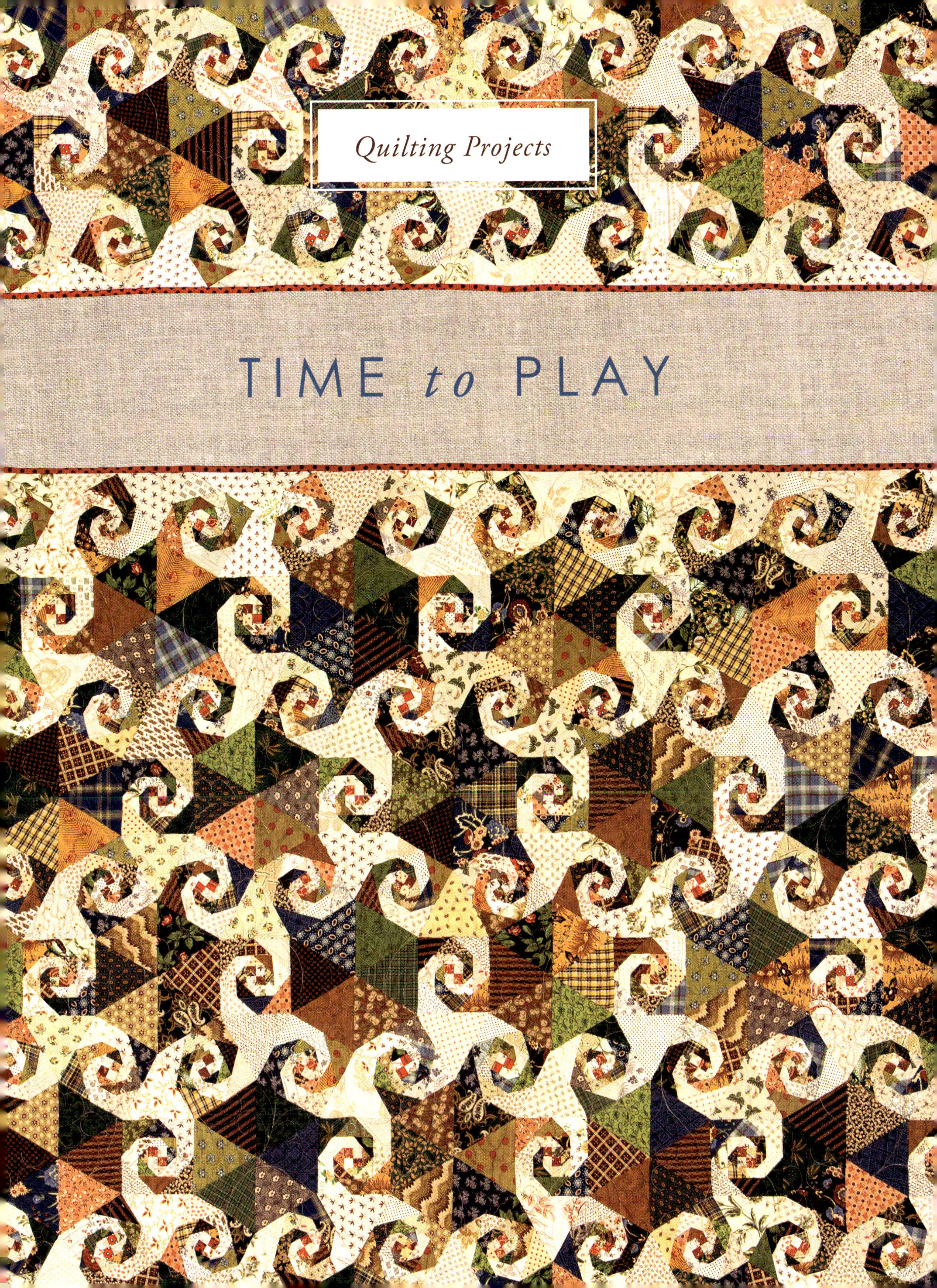

LET *it* SHINE

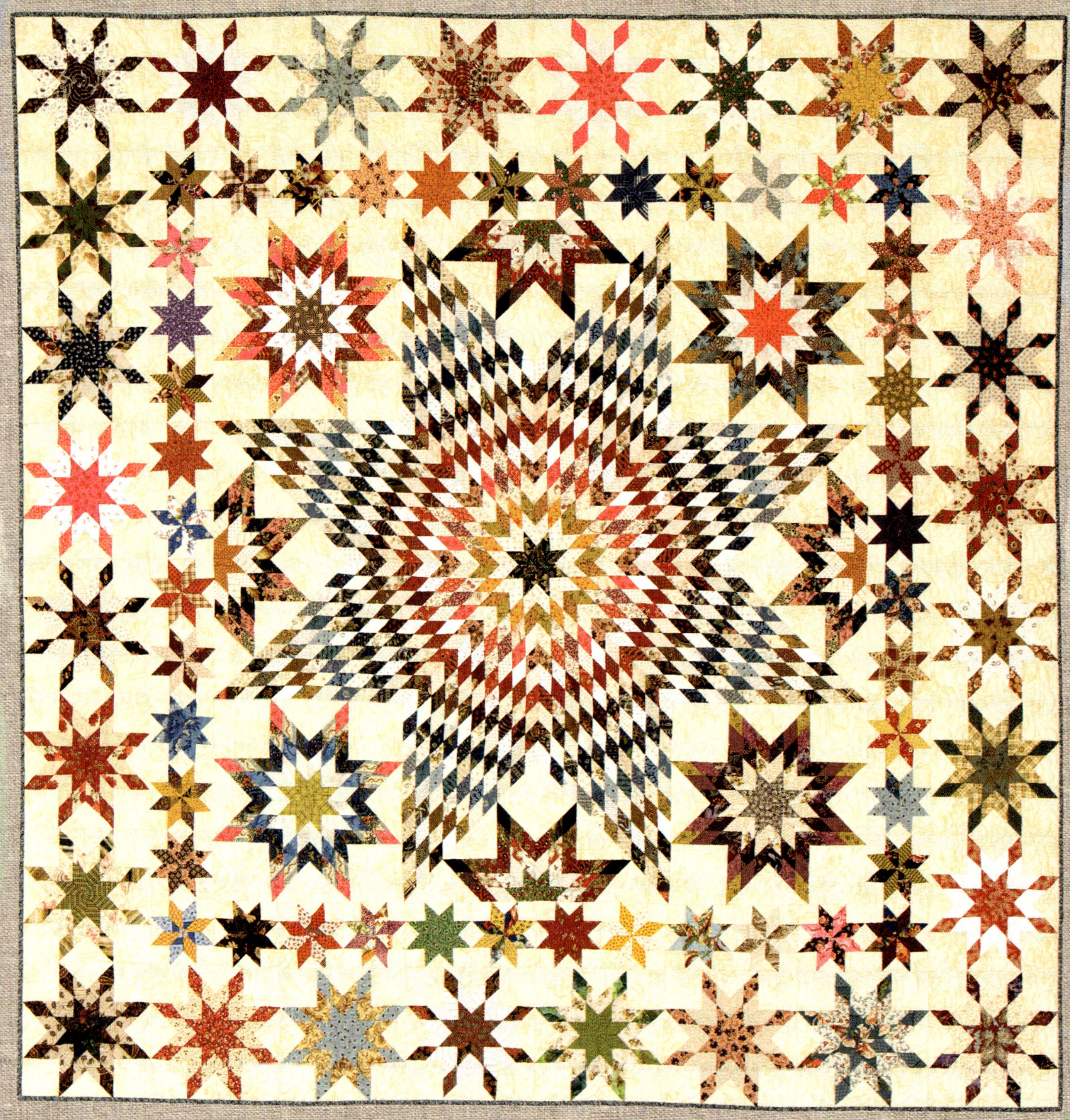

This star-studded sky is actually made from diamonds—all cut from one-and-a-half-inch strips. Scraps of different light, medium, and dark values create a mesmerizing effect as they break away from the center star. A simple eight-pointed shape forms the basis for single-, double-, and triple-layered constellations.

LET IT SHINE

Finished quilt size: 76½" x 76½".

Fabric Requirements

Stars:

26 light fat eighths (9" x 21")
36 dark fat eighths (9" x 21")

Background: 3½ yards light fabric

Binding: ⅔ yard blue fabric

Backing: 4½ yards fabric

Fabric Cutting

Stars:

From 26 light fat eighths, cut:
130 strips 1½" x 21"

From 36 dark fat eighths, cut:
180 strips 1½" x 21"

Background Fabric:

Medium Star and Half Star

3 strips 4⅝" x width of fabric
From the strips, cut 20-4⅝" squares

2 strips 7¼" x width of fabric
From the strips, cut 8-7¼" squares, cut in half twice on the diagonal to make 32 quarter-square triangles

Tiny Star

9 strips 1⅞" x width of fabric
From the strips, cut 176-1⅞" squares

4 strips 3¼" x width of fabric
From the strips, cut 44-3¼" squares, cut in half twice on the diagonal to make 176 quarter-square triangles

Small Star

11 strips 3¼" x width of fabric
From the strips, cut 112-3¼" squares

4 strips 5¼" x width of fabric
From the strips, cut 28-5¼" squares, cut in half twice on the diagonal to make 112 quarter-square triangles

Binding:
8 strips 2½" x width of fabric

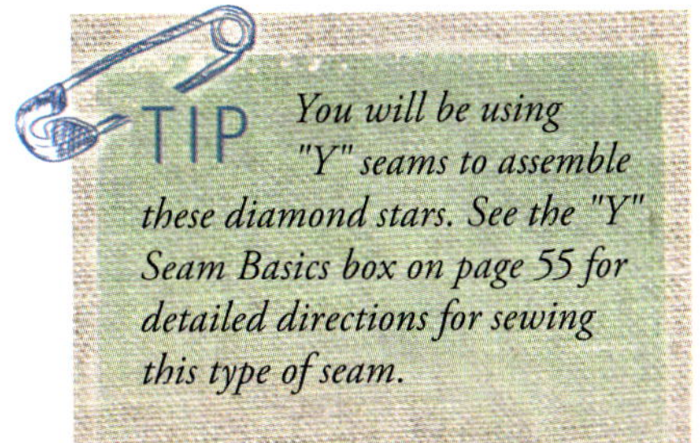

There are five stars: tiny, small, medium, half, and large. The construction is the same for all the stars. The number of strips and measurements for the corner and setting triangles will vary. Step by step instructions are given for the medium stars. Also refer to these steps when constructing the tiny, small, and large stars.

1 **Medium Stars:** *Accurate cutting and sewing is very important. Use "Best Press" or spray starch at each step for fabric that acts more like "cardboard or paper" than fabric, and remember to use a ¼" seam allowance.*

(A) Sew 3–1½" x 21" strips together: dark, light, dark. Stagger the strips about 1". *See diagram below.* Press seams open. Make 12 strip sets. Align the 45° line on the ruler with the strip set edge, and cut a 45° angle on the strip set. Align the 1½" line with this cut edge and the 45° line on the ruler on one of the seams to cut the strips. Cut 96 sections.

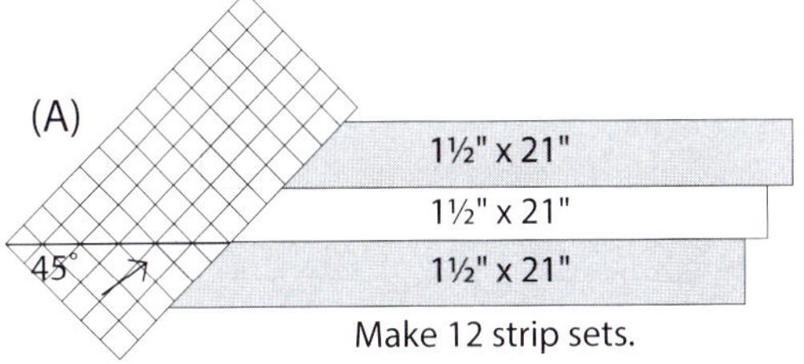

Make 12 strip sets.

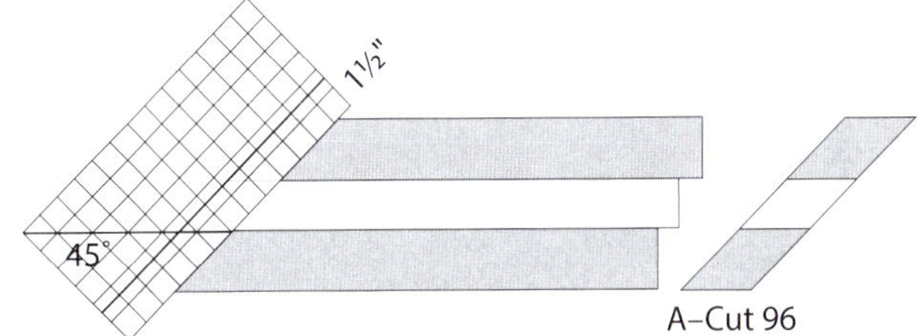

A–Cut 96

(B) Sew 3–1½" x 21" strips together: light, dark, light. Stagger the strips about 1". *See diagram below.* Press seams open. Make 6 strip sets. Align the 45° line on the ruler with the strip set edge, and cut a 45° angle on the strip set. Align the 1½" line with this cut edge and the 45° line on the ruler on one of the seams to cut the strips. Cut 48 sections.

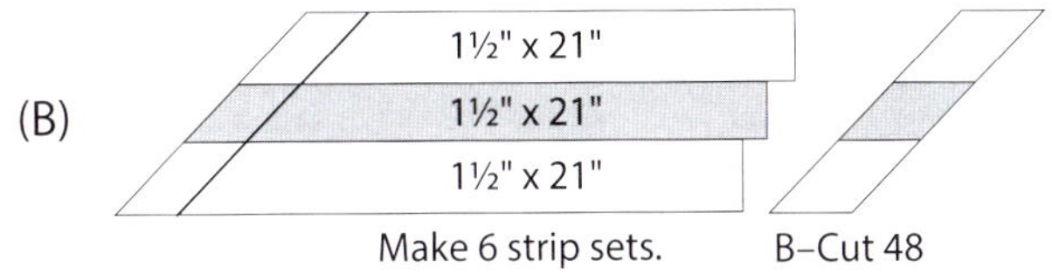

Make 6 strip sets. B–Cut 48

2 Combine 3 strips to make a diamond. Make 48 diamonds. Mark dots ¼" from the points of the diamonds.

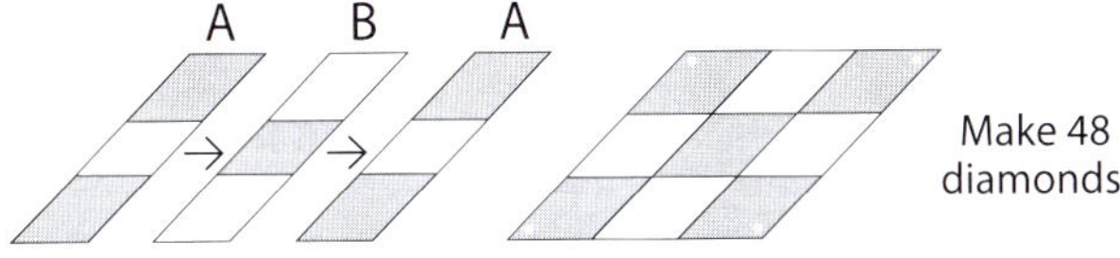

Make 48 diamonds.

3 Combine 8 diamonds, 4–4⅝" x 4⅝" background squares and 4–7¼" background quarter-square triangles to make one Star. Use "Y" seams to add the background squares and triangles. Set in the triangles first and then the squares, pushing the seam allowance toward the Star. Trim the star to measure 14½" x 14½". *Be sure to leave a ¼" seam allowance at the points.* Make 4 stars.

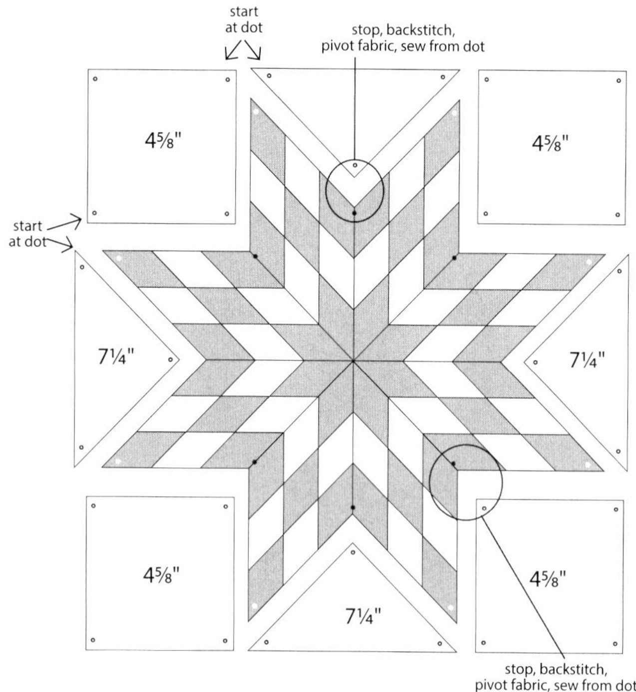

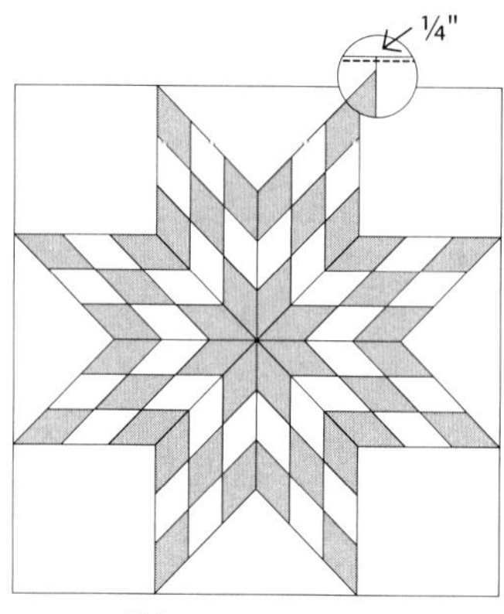

Trim to measure
14½" x 14½" unfinished

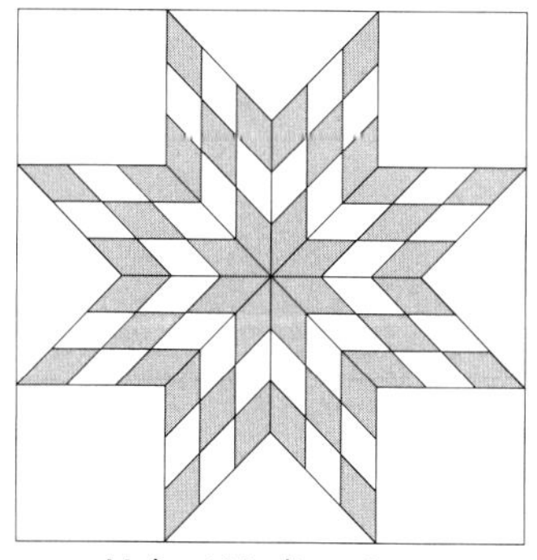
Make 4 Medium Stars:
14½" x 14½" unfinished.

4 **Half Stars:**
Combine 4 diamonds, 1-4⅝" background square, and 4-7¼" background quarter-square triangles to make one Half Star. Make 4.

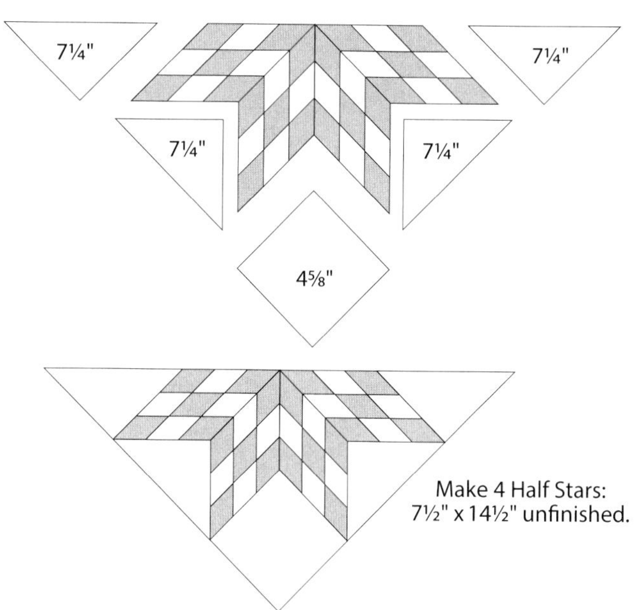

Make 4 Half Stars:
7½" x 14½" unfinished.

5 **Tiny Stars:**
(A) Align the 45° line on the ruler with the edge of a 1½" x 21" dark strip, and cut a 45° angle on the strip. Align the 1½" line with this cut edge and the 45° line on the ruler on the strip edge to cut the strips. Cut 8 diamonds from each of the 44 strips for a total of 352 diamonds. Mark dots ¼" from the points of the diamonds.

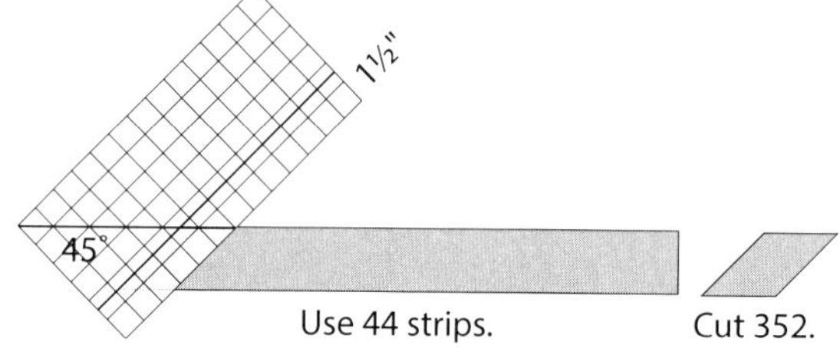

(B) Combine 8 diamonds, 4-1⅞" background squares, and 4-3¼" background quarter-square triangles to make one Tiny Star. Trim to 5¼" x 5¼". Make 44.

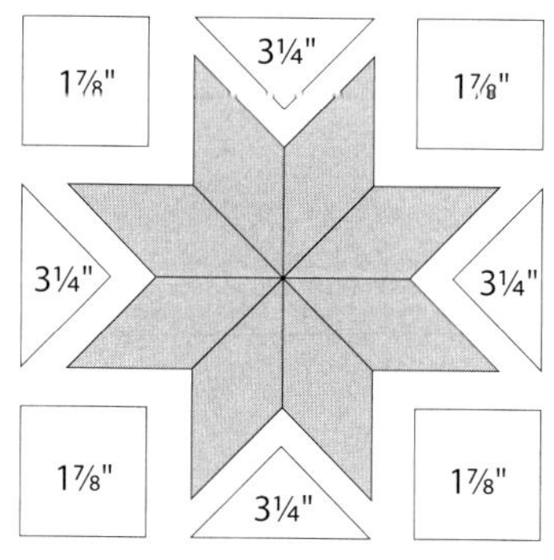

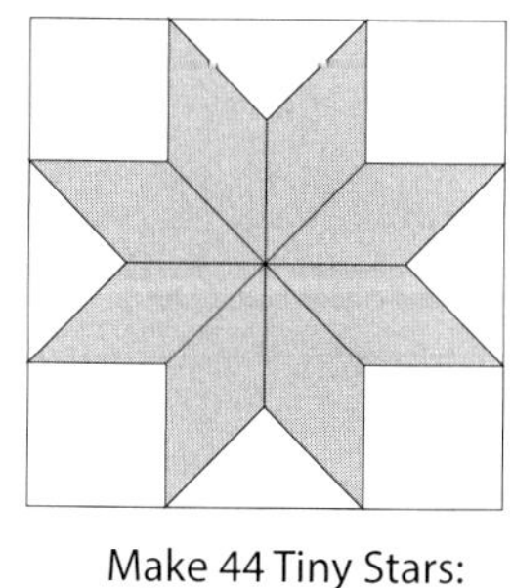
Make 44 Tiny Stars:
5¼" x 5¼" unfinished.

6 Small Stars:

(A) Sew 2–1½" x 21" strips together: dark and light. Stagger the strips about 1". *See diagram.* Press seams open. Make 56 strip sets. Align the 45° line on the ruler with the strip set edge, and cut a 45° angle on the strip set. Align the 1½" line with this cut edge and the 45° line on the ruler on one of the seams to cut the strips. Cut 448 sections. Mark dots ¼" from the points of the diamonds.

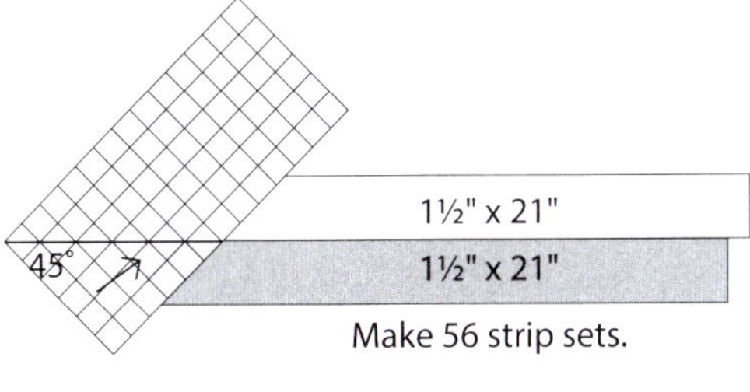

Make 56 strip sets.

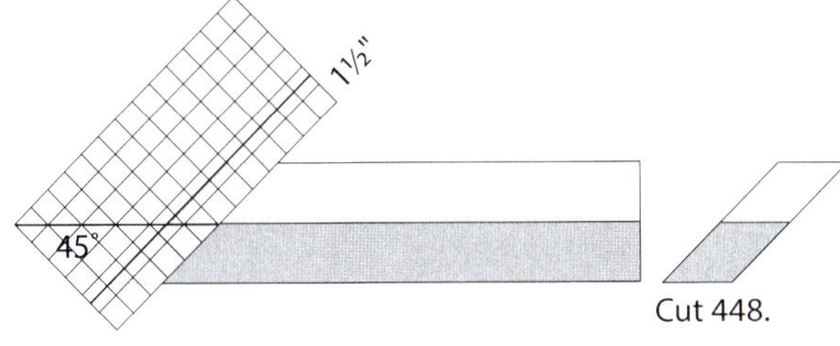

Cut 448.

(B) Combine 2 strips to make a diamond. Make 224 diamonds. Mark dots ¼" from the points of the diamonds.

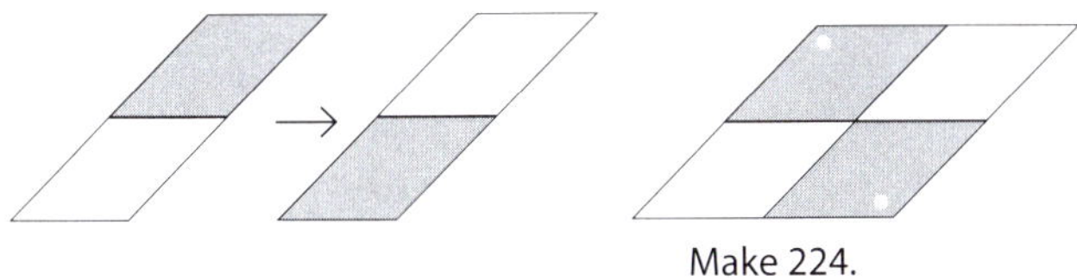
Make 224.

(C) Combine 8 diamonds, 4-3¼" background squares, and 4-5¼" background quarter-square triangles to make Small Star. Trim to 10" x 10". Make 28.

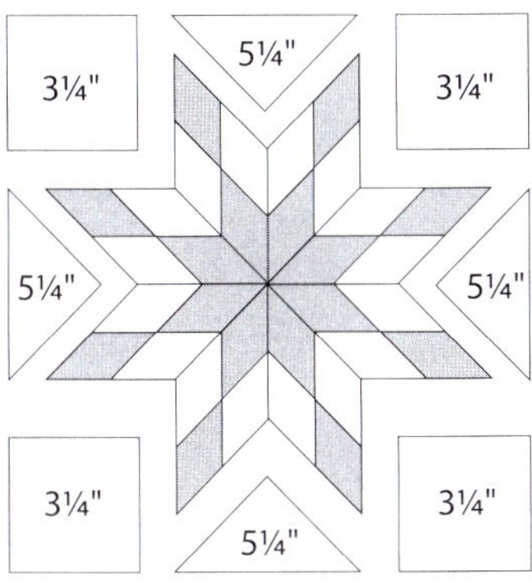

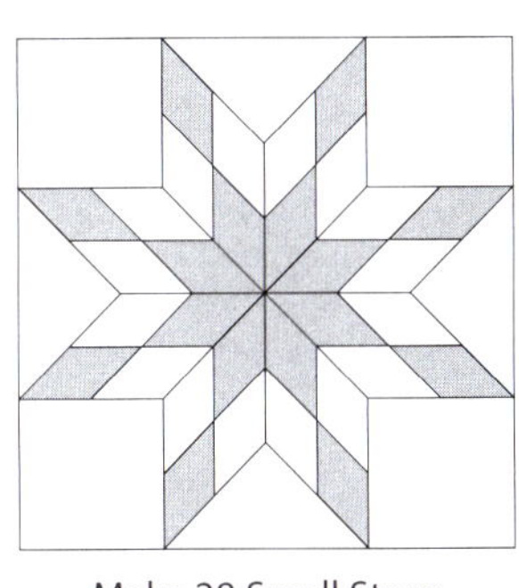
Make 28 Small Stars:
10" x 10" unfinished.

"Y" seam basics

Mark small dots where the ¼" seams meet on the fabrics.

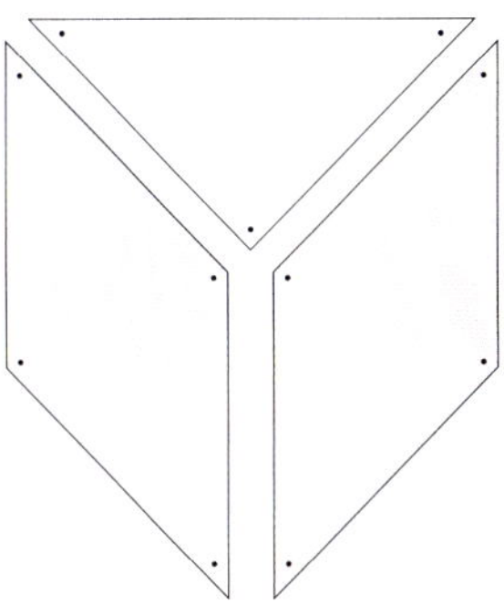

Sewing 2 diamonds together: Pin the seam. Start sewing at the edge. Continue stitching to the next dot, stopping your stitches at the dot backstitch.

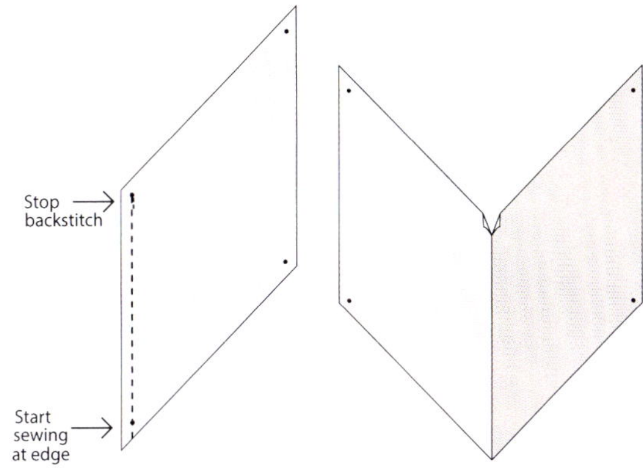

Sewing the "Y" seam: Lock your stitch at the dot, then sew to the next dot. Stop at the dot, and backstitch to lock the seam.

To join the next side, pivot the fabric, push the seam allowance between the diamonds away, and lock your stitch at the dot. Sew to the next dot. Stop at the dot, and backstitch.

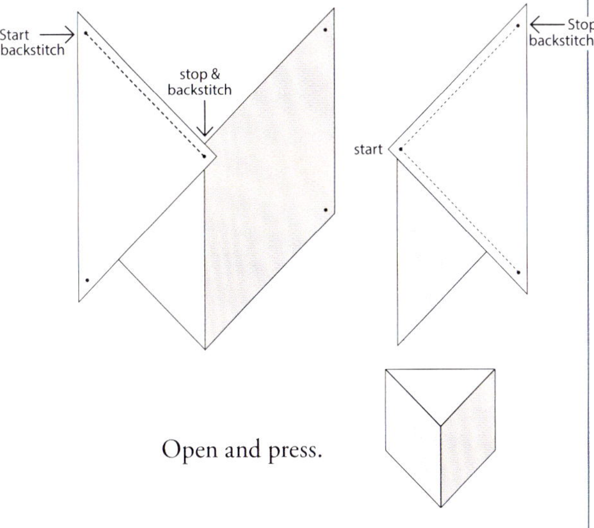

Open and press.

7 **Large Star:**

(A) Sew 10-1½" x 21" strips together as shown. Stagger the strips about 1". Press seams open. Make 10 strip sets. Align the 45° line on the ruler with the strip set edge, and cut a 45° angle on the strip set. Align the 1½" line with this cut edge and the 45° line on the ruler on one of the seams to cut the strips. Cut 8 strips from each of the 10 sections for a total of 80 sections.

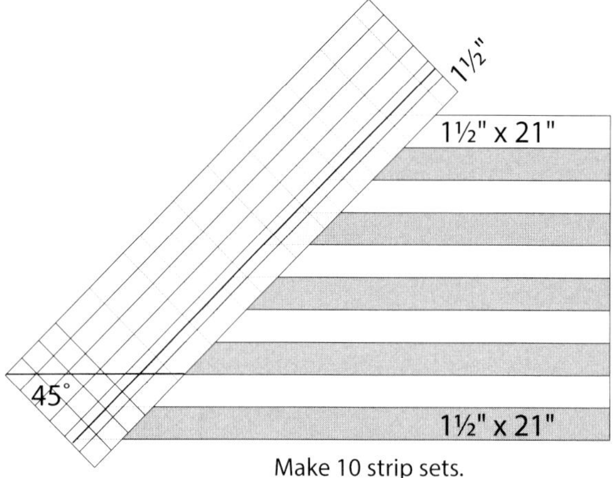

Make 10 strip sets.

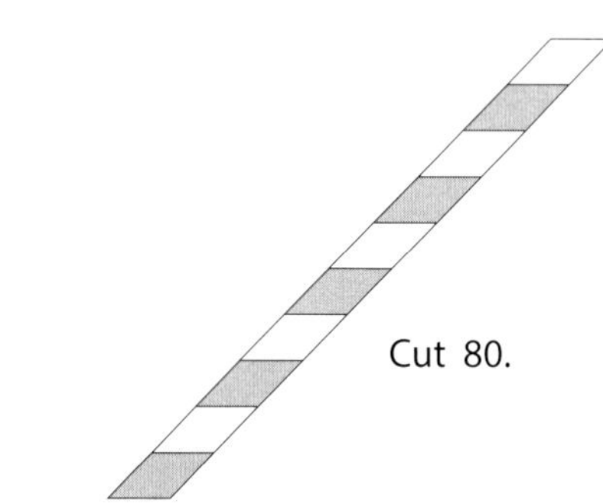

Cut 80.

(B) Combine 10 strips as shown to make a diamond. Make 8. Mark dots ¼" from the points of the large diamonds.

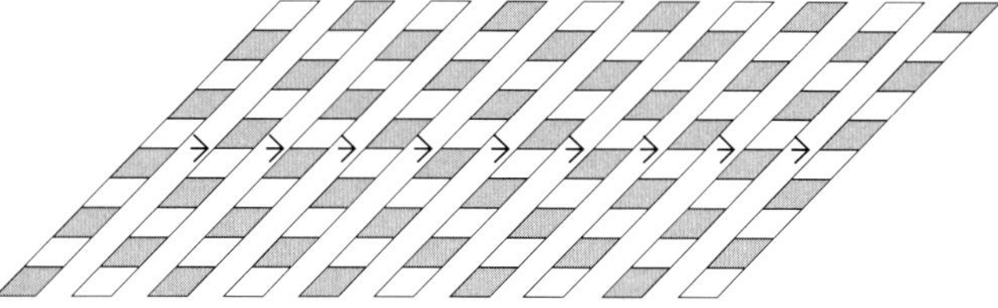

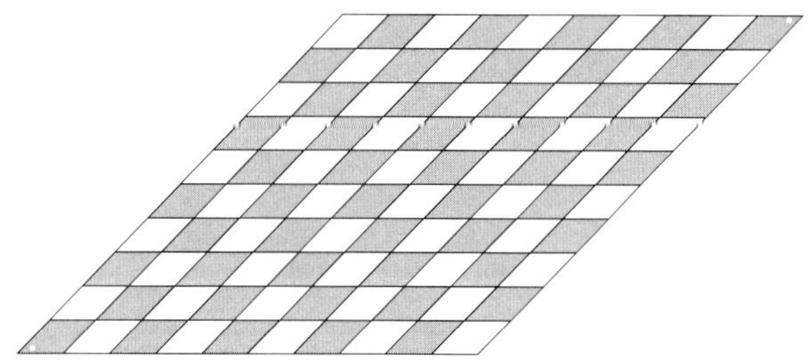

Make 8 Large Diamonds.

(C) Combine 8 Large Diamonds, 4 Medium Stars, and 4 Half Stars to make the Large Star. Trim to 48" x 48".

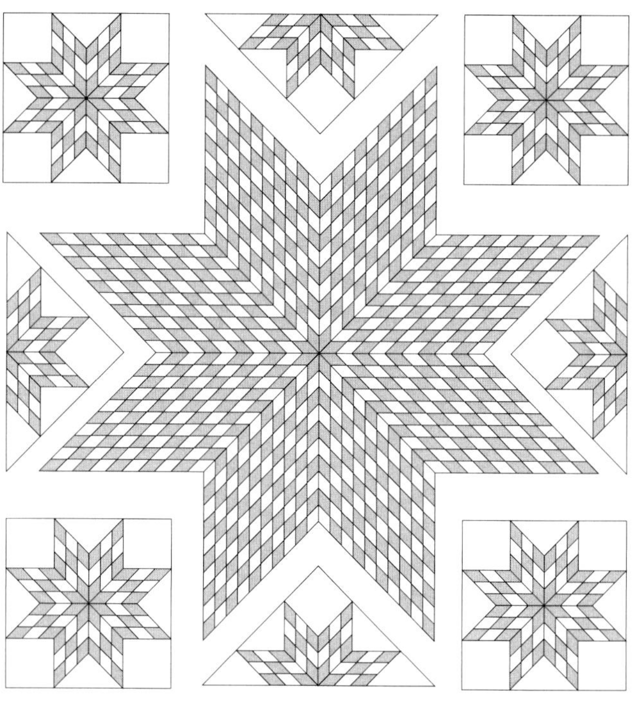

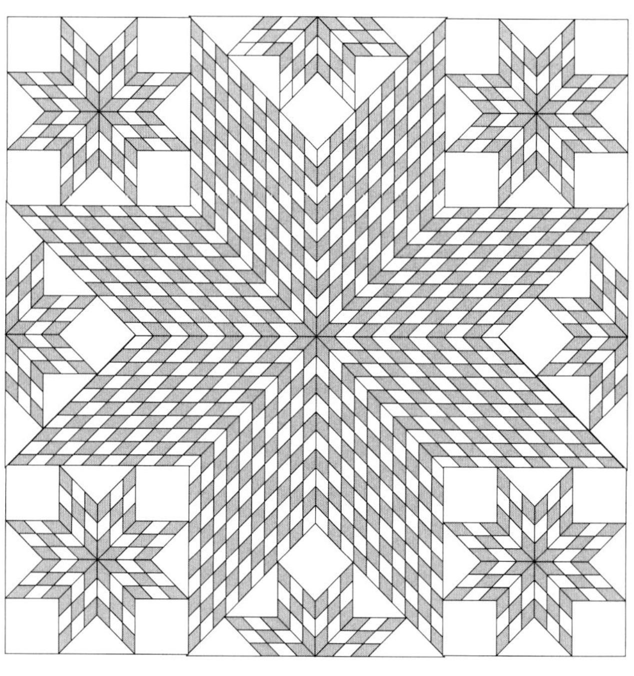

Trim to measure
48"x48" unfinished.

8 Arrange and sew 10 Tiny Stars in one row. Make 2 rows. Sew to the sides of the Large Star.
Arrange and sew 12 Tiny Stars in one row. Make 2 rows. Sew to the top and bottom.
Arrange and sew 6 Small Stars in one row. Make 2 rows. Sew to the sides of the Large Star.
Arrange and sew 8 Small Stars in one row. Make 2 rows. Sew to the top and bottom.

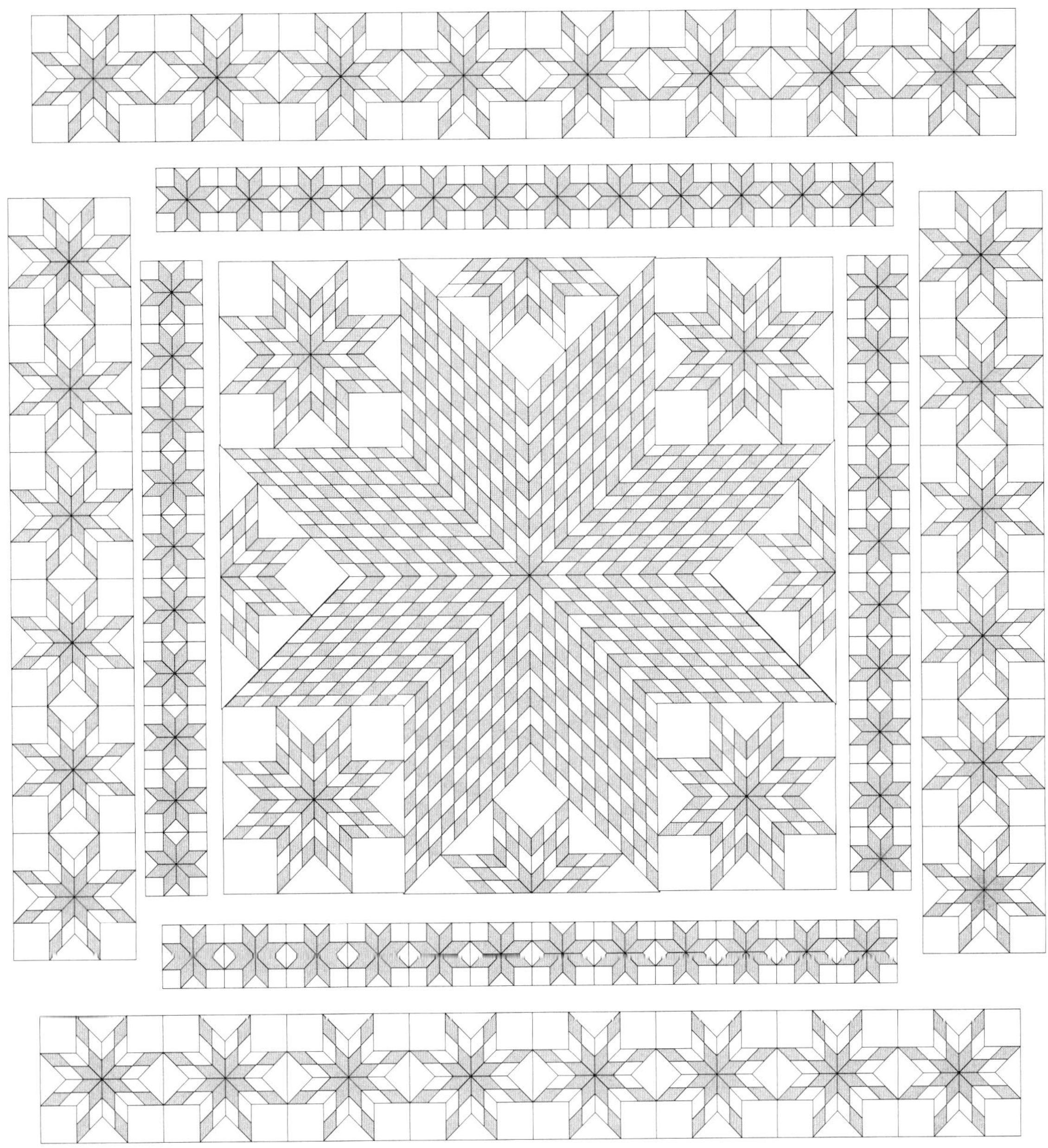

Unfinished quilt top is 76½"x 76½".

9 **Quilting:**

1. Layer quilt in the following order:
   a) Quilt back, right side down, 81" x 81".
   b) Batting 81" x 81". (I prefer Hobbs for best results.)
   c) Quilt top, right side up, 76½" x 76½".
2. Baste layers together.
3. Quilt by hand or machine. The front cover quilt was quilted on a long-arm quilting machine.

10 **Binding:**
Refer to My Sewing Basket on page 48 for binding directions.

MONKEY BUSINESS

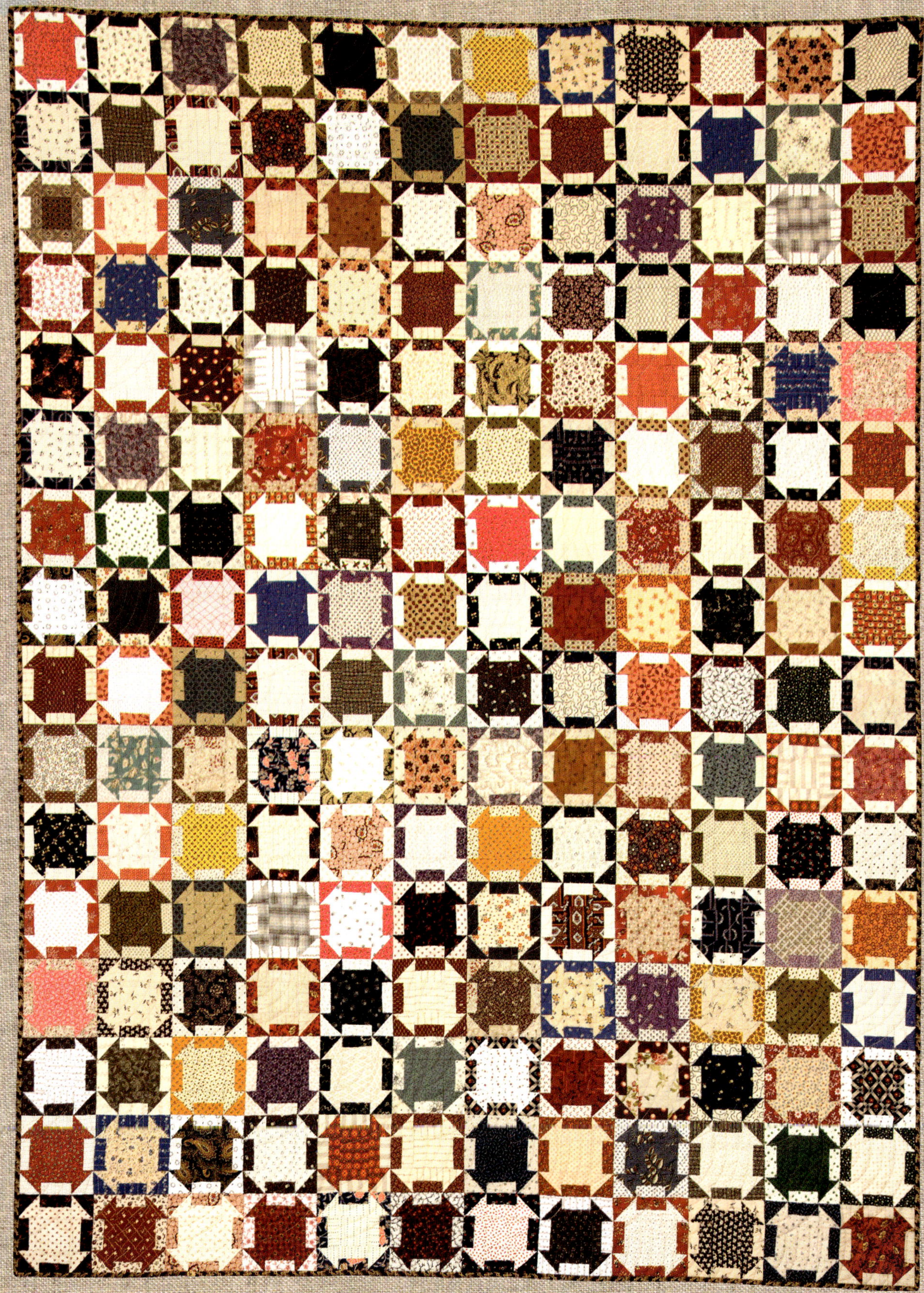

Based on the traditional monkey wrench pattern, this quilt of reversed light and dark fabrics is a barrel of fun for any boy. Taking the pattern all the way to the edge adds geometric impact.

MONKEY BUSINESS

Finished quilt size: 60½" x 80½".

Fabric Requirements

Blocks: 96-light 10½" x 6" rectangles in a variety of colors
96-dark 10½" x 6" rectangles in a variety of colors

Binding: ⅔ yard

Backing: 4½ yards

Fabric Cutting

Blocks:
From EACH of the 96-10½" x 6" light rectangles, cut:
2-1¼" x 10½" strips
4-2⅜" squares, cut in half once on the diagonal to make 8 half-square triangles
1-2½" square

From EACH of the 96-10½" x 6" dark rectangles, cut:
2-1¼" x 10½" strips
4-2⅜" squares, cut in half once on the diagonal to make 8 half-square triangles
1-2½" square

Binding:
7-2½" x width of fabric strips

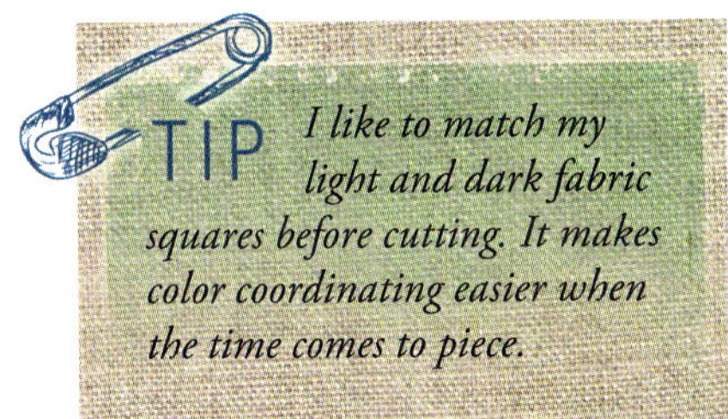

Use a ¼" seam allowance. Press in the direction of the arrows.

1 To make 1 A and 1 B block, use 1 light and 1 dark print for each set:

(A) Join 1 light and 1 dark 2⅜" half-square triangle. Repeat to make 8 half-square triangle blocks, and push seam allowance toward the dark fabric.

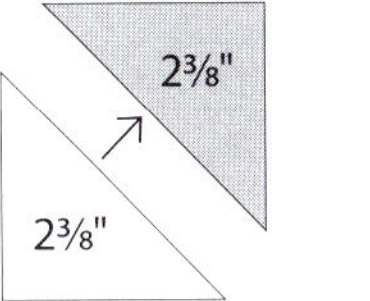

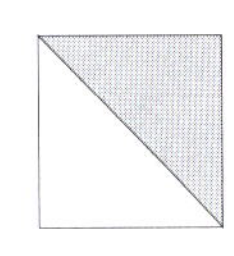

Make 8 Half-Square Triangles: 2" x 2" unfinished.

(B) Join 1 light and 1 dark 1¼" x 10½" strip. Make 2 strip sets. Cut the strip sets into 8-2½" wide strip units; there is a ½" extra length for trimming the beginning and end of strip.

Make 2 strip sets.

Cut 8.

(C) Arrange and sew 4 half-square triangle blocks, 4 strip units, and 1-2½" dark square in 3 rows as shown. Join the rows to make Block A.

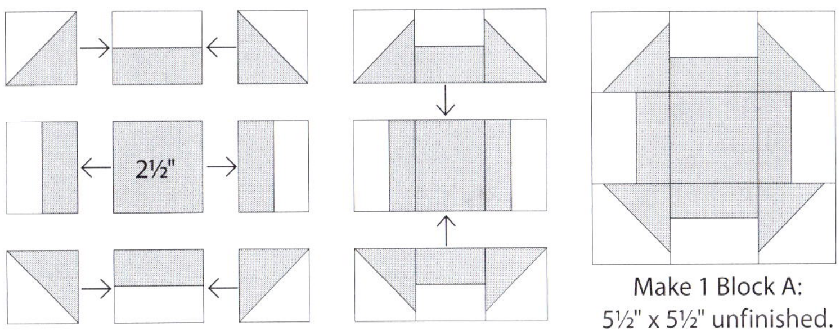

Make 1 Block A: 5½" x 5½" unfinished.

(D) Arrange and sew 4 half-square triangle blocks, 4 strip units, and 1-2½" light square in 3 rows as shown. Join the rows to make Block B.

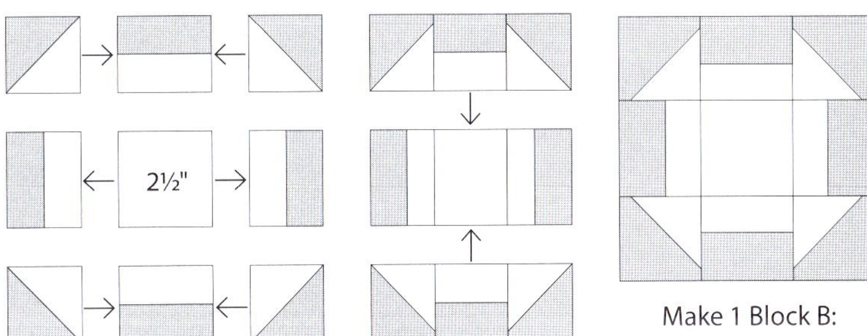

Make 1 Block B: 5½" x 5½" unfinished.

(E) Repeat to make a total of 96 sets of 1 A and 1 B block.

2 Assembly:

(A) Arrange and sew 6 block As and 6 block Bs in 1 row as shown. Repeat to make 16 rows.

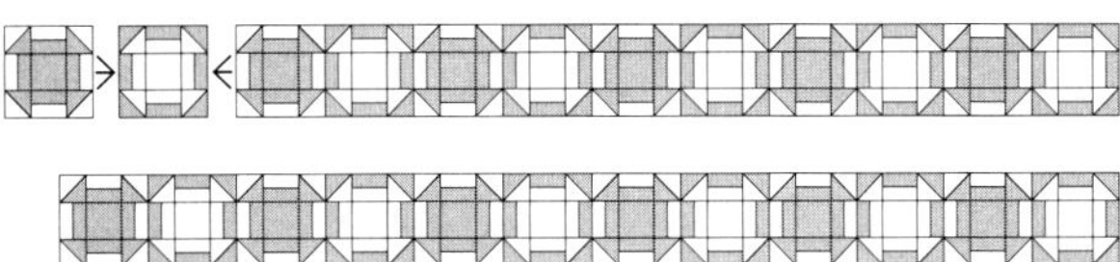

Make 16 Rows:
60½" x 5½" unfinished.

(B) Join the 16 rows, noting that the even rows are rotated 180°.

3 Quilting:

1. Layer quilt in the following order:
   a) Quilt back, right side down, 64½" x 84½".
   b) Batting 64½" x 84½" (I prefer Hobbs for best results.)
   c) Quilt top, right side up, 60½" x 80½".
2. Baste layers together.
3. Quilt by hand or machine. I chose a Baptist Fan overall quilting design for this quilt.

4 Binding:

Refer to My Sewing Basket on page 48 for binding directions.

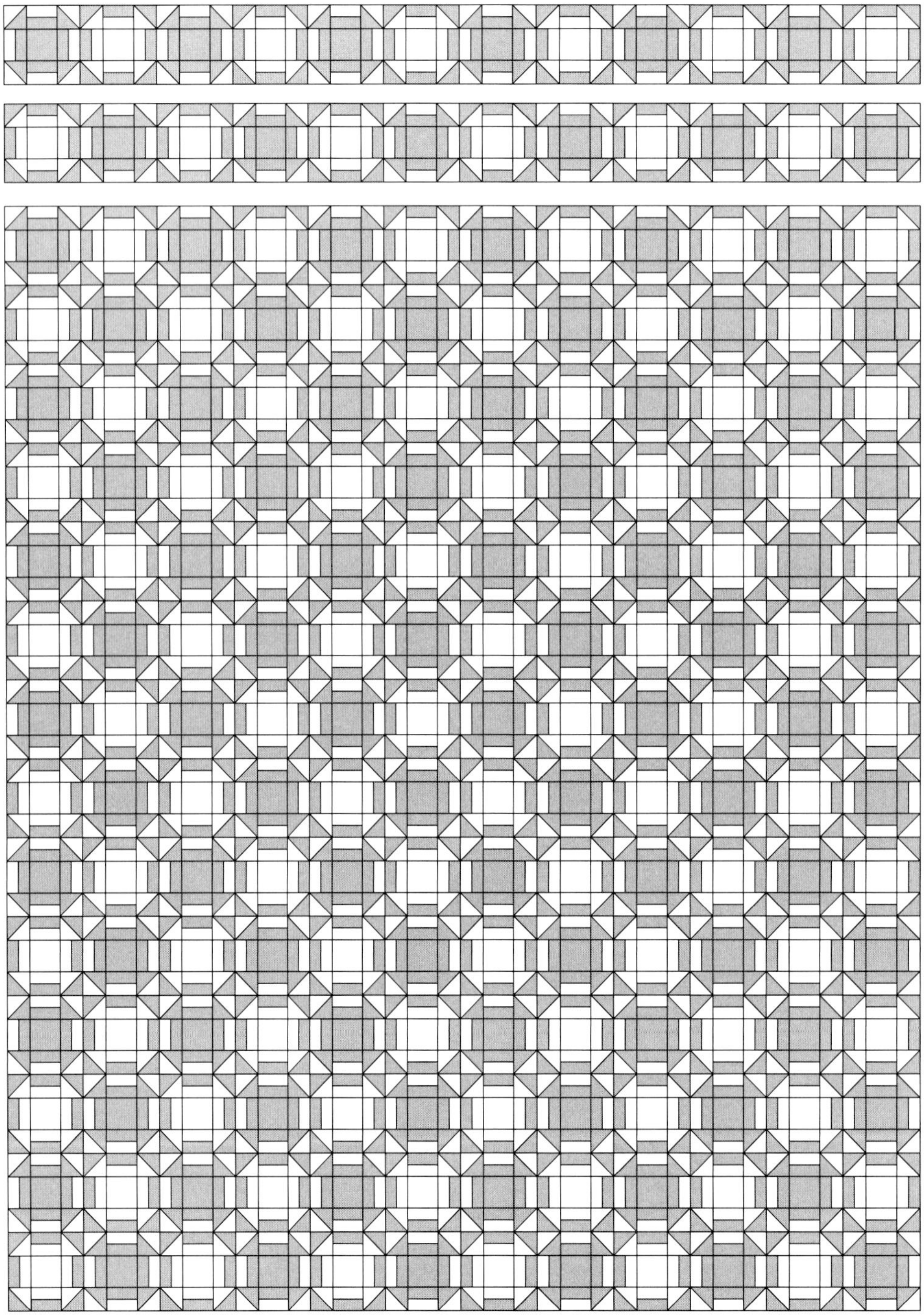

Unfinished quilt top is 60½" x 80½".

LOOKING GLASS

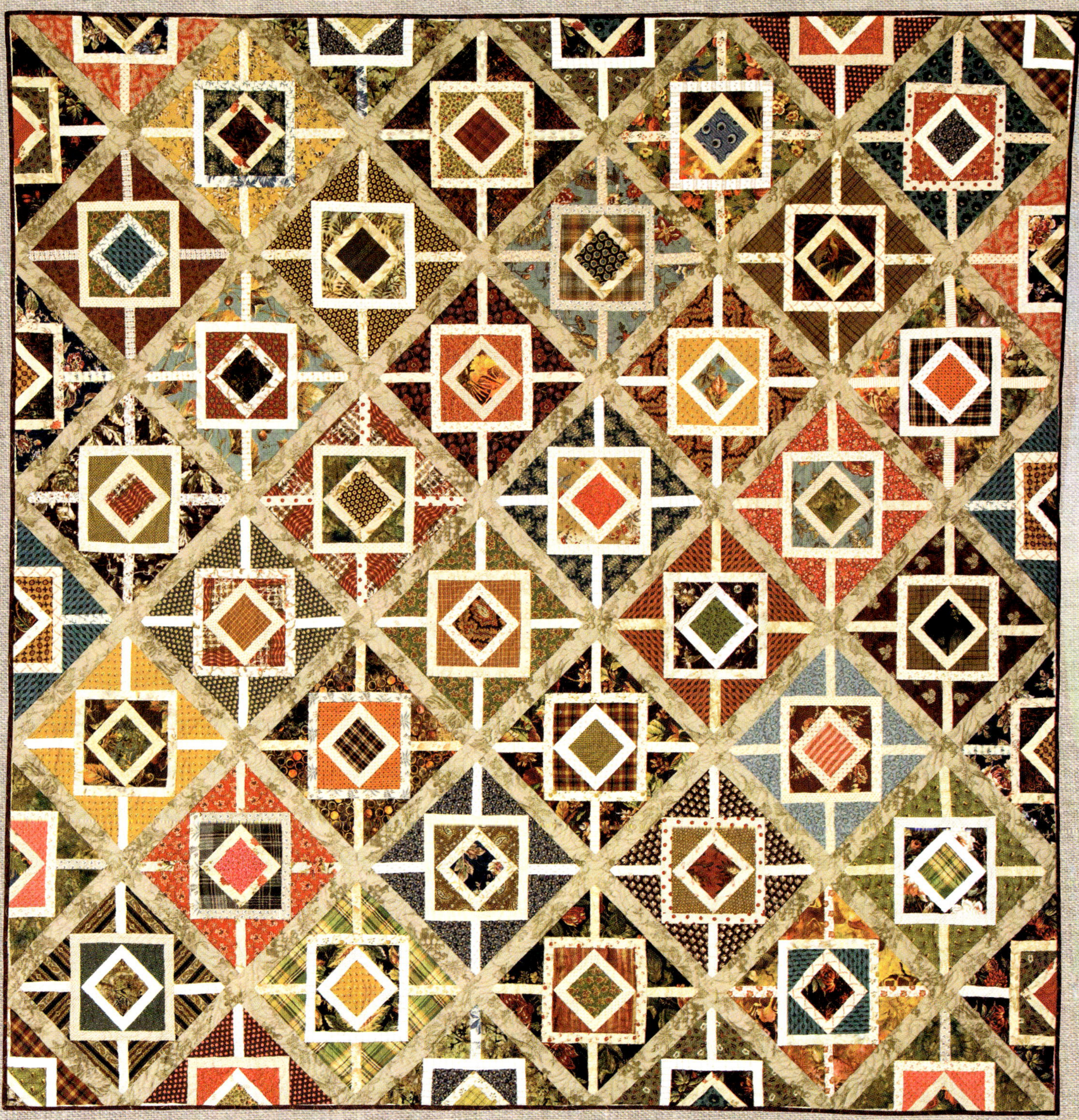

Stacks of scraps are secretly wishing they could be part of this showcase quilt. Shuffle each of 50 different fabrics to arrange 50 individual blocks, squared and set on-point between light sashing strips. Like peeking through a hole in a picket fence, the pattern invites you to love it up-close.

LOOKING GLASS

Finished quilt size: 83" x 83".

Fabric Requirements

Blocks:

Multi-color prints: 50 fat eighths (9" x 21")

Light prints: 25 fat eighths (9" x 21")

Sashing: 2½ yards

Binding: ⅔ yard

Backing: 5 yards

Fabric Cutting

Blocks:

Multi-color prints:

From EACH of the 50-9" x 21" prints, cut: (see diagram)

2-6¼" squares, cut twice on the diagonal to make 8 quarter-square triangles (QST)

2-4" squares, cut once on the diagonal to make 4 half-square triangles (HST)

1-3½" square

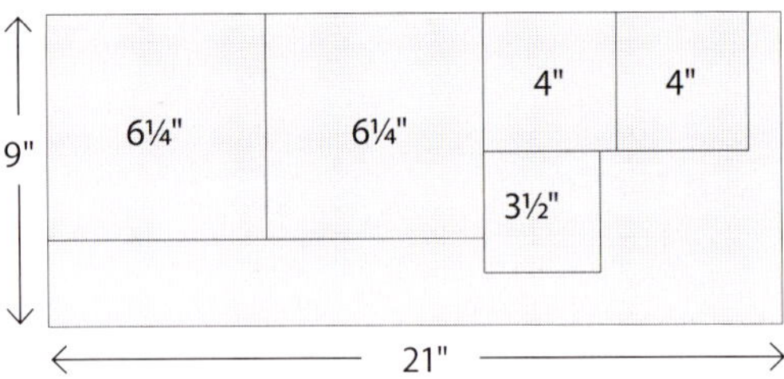

Light prints (used for the interior block sashing):

From EACH of the 25-9" x 21" prints, cut:

6-1¼" x 21" strips for a total of 150 strips

From the 150 strips, cut:

50 sets of: 2-1¼" x 8¼", 2-1¼" x 6⅞", 2-1¼" x 5", 2-1¼" x 4½" and 2-1¼" x 3½" strips

Sashing:

34-2½" x width of fabric strips

From 14 strips, cut 39-2½" x 11½" strips and 2-2½" x 15½" sashing strips

Sew 20 strips end to end. From this long strip, cut:

2-2½" x 50½" sashing strips

2-2½" x 76½" sashing strips

2-2½" x 102½" sashing strips

2-2½" x 128½" sashing strips

Binding:

9-2½" x width of fabric strips

Use a ¼" seam allowance. Press in the direction of the arrows.

These are scrappy blocks.

1 To make one block, select:

Center: 1-3½" square

Half-square triangles (HST): 4 matching 4" triangles

Quarter-square triangles (QST): 8 matching 6¼" triangles

Sashing A: 1 matching set of 2-1¼" x 3½" and 2-1¼" x 5" strips

Sashing B: 1 matching set of 2-1¼" x 6⅞" and 2-1¼" x 8¼" strips

Sashing C: 1 matching set of 4-1¼" x 4½" rectangles

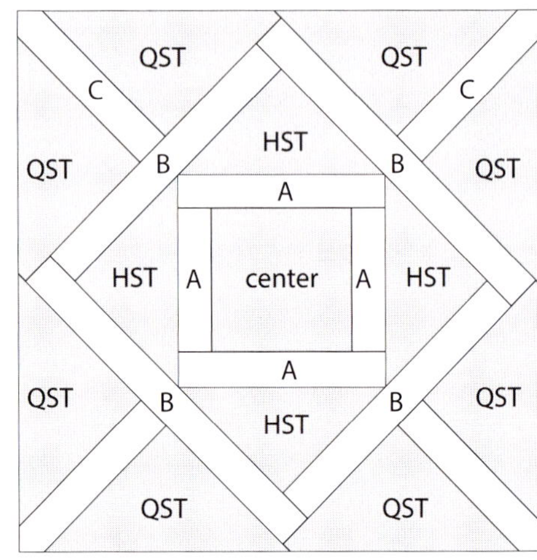

Block is 11½" x 11½" unfinished.

(A) Sew a 1¼" x 3½" sashing A rectangle to 2 sides of the 3½" center square. Sew 2-1¼" x 5" Sashing A rectangles to the remaining 2 sides. Make 1. Press seams toward the sashing.

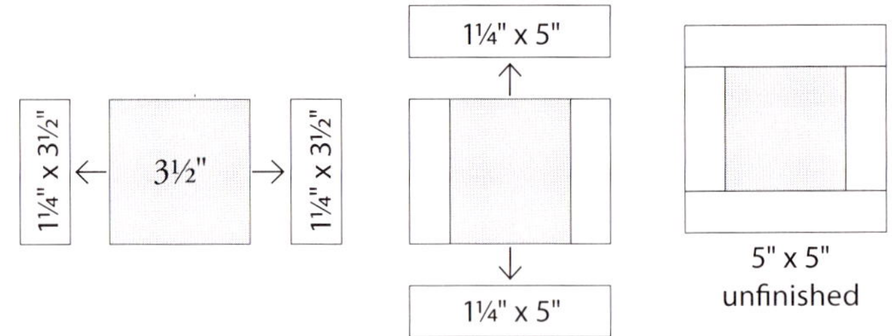

(B) Sew a 4" half-square triangle to 2 sides of the previous unit. Sew a 4" half-square triangle to the remaining 2 sides. Press seams toward the triangles.

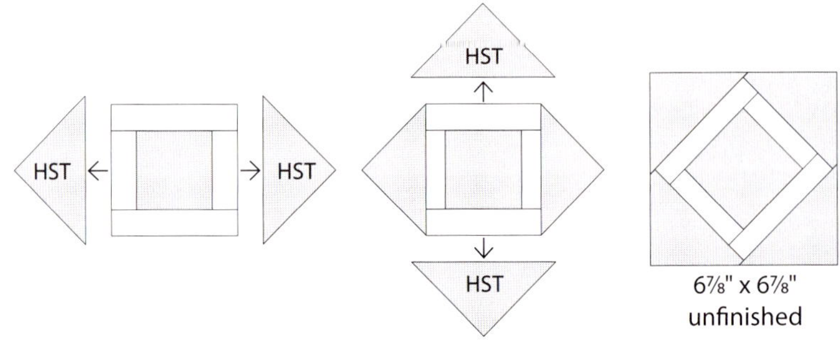

Step 1 continued.

(C) Sew a 1¼" x 6⅞" sashing B rectangle to 2 sides of the previous unit. Sew a 1¼" x 8¼" sashing B rectangle to the remaining sides. Press seams toward the sashing.

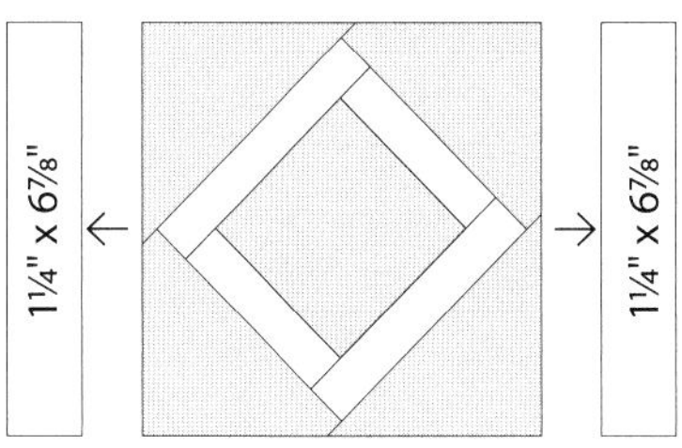

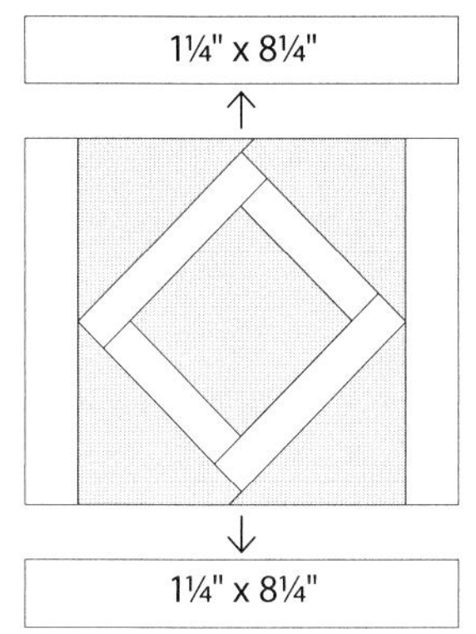

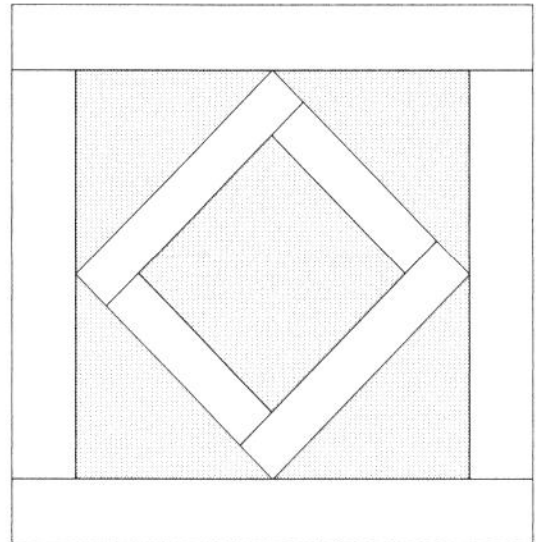

8¼" x 8¼" unfinished

(D) Add 6¼" quarter-square triangles to the side of a sashing C rectangle as shown. Make 4. Press seams toward the sashing.

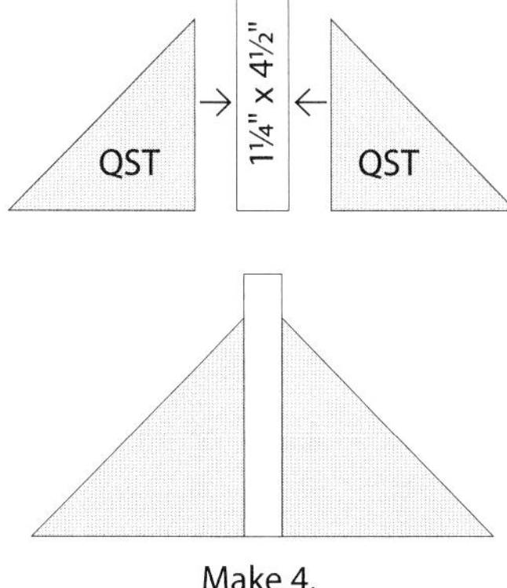

Make 4.

(E) Sew the units from step "D" to the sides of step "C". Press seams toward the sashing.

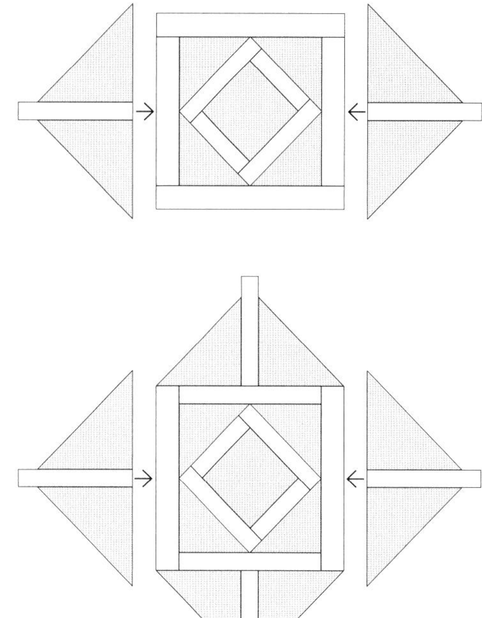

(F) Trim the block to 11½" square with seams.

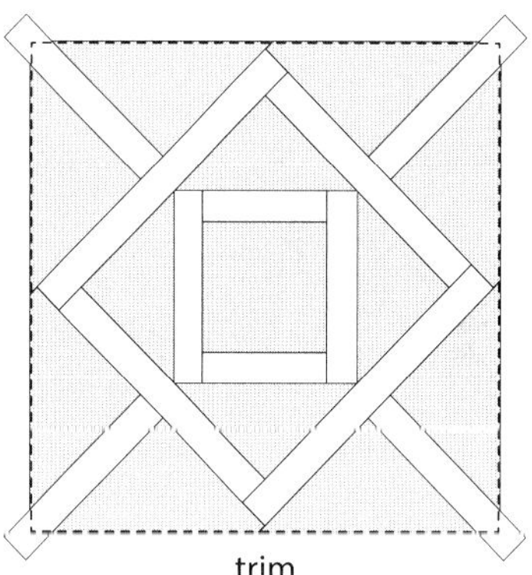

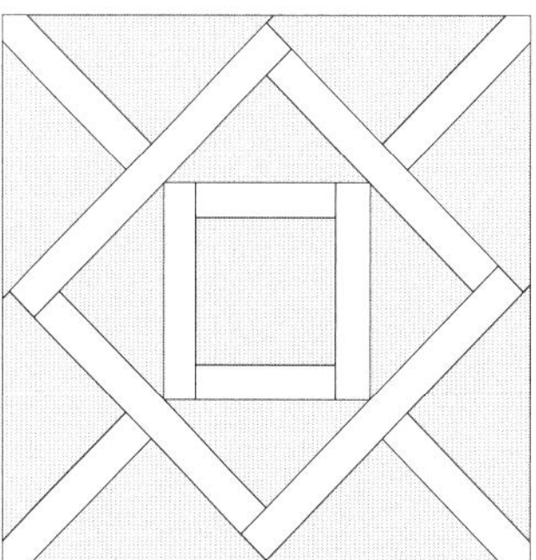

11½" x 11½" unfinished

Repeat step 1 to make a total of 50 blocks.

2 Assembly: Sew the blocks and 2½" x 11½" sashing strips in rows following the diagram. The 2 outside rows use 2½" x 15½" sashing strips. Press the seams toward the sashing. Sew the rows and sashing together. Use pins to keep blocks in line across the sashing.

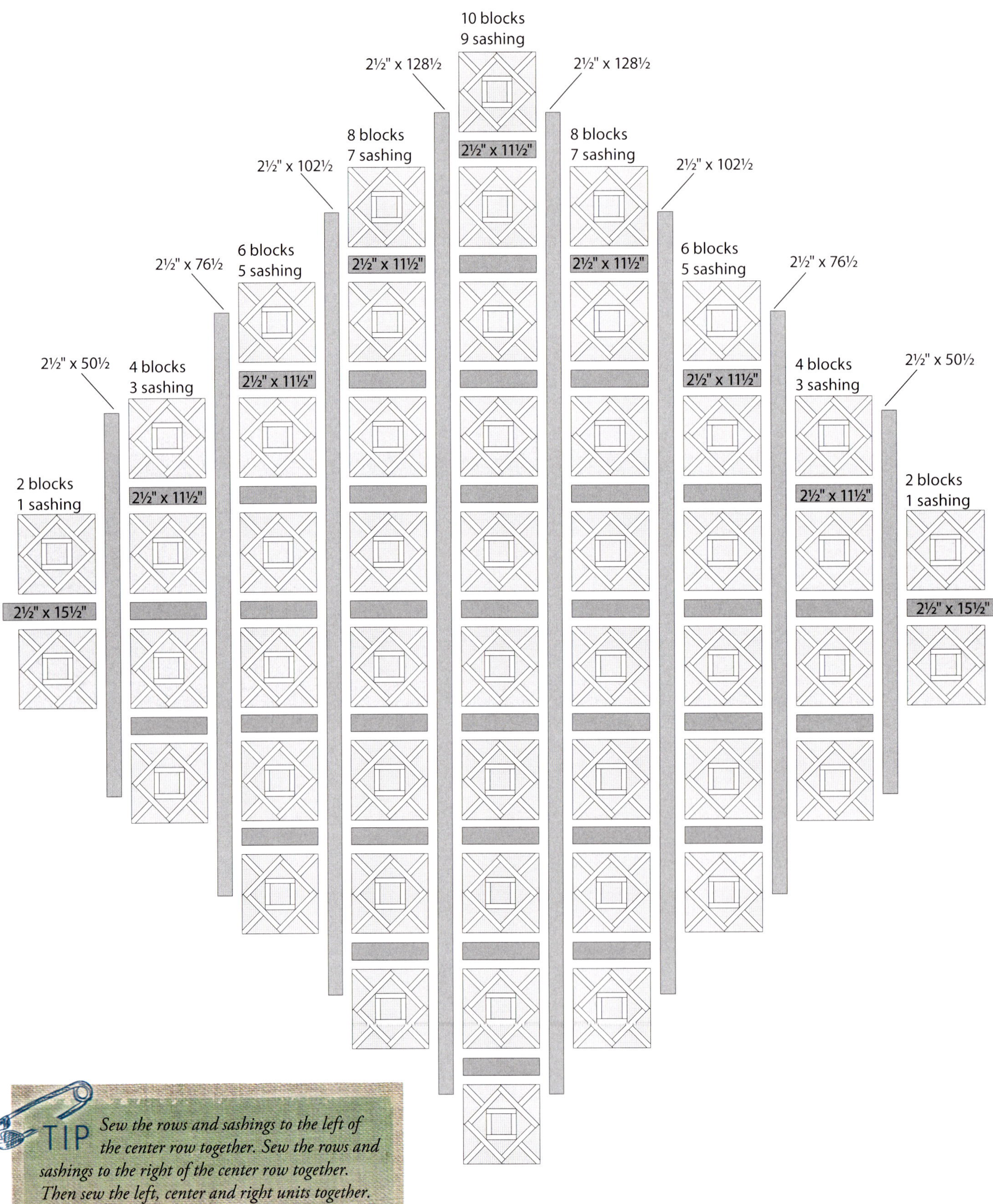

TIP *Sew the rows and sashings to the left of the center row together. Sew the rows and sashings to the right of the center row together. Then sew the left, center and right units together.*

3 Press the quilt top flat. Square the quilt sides using a rotary cutter and ruler. Leave a ¼" seam allowance beyond the points.

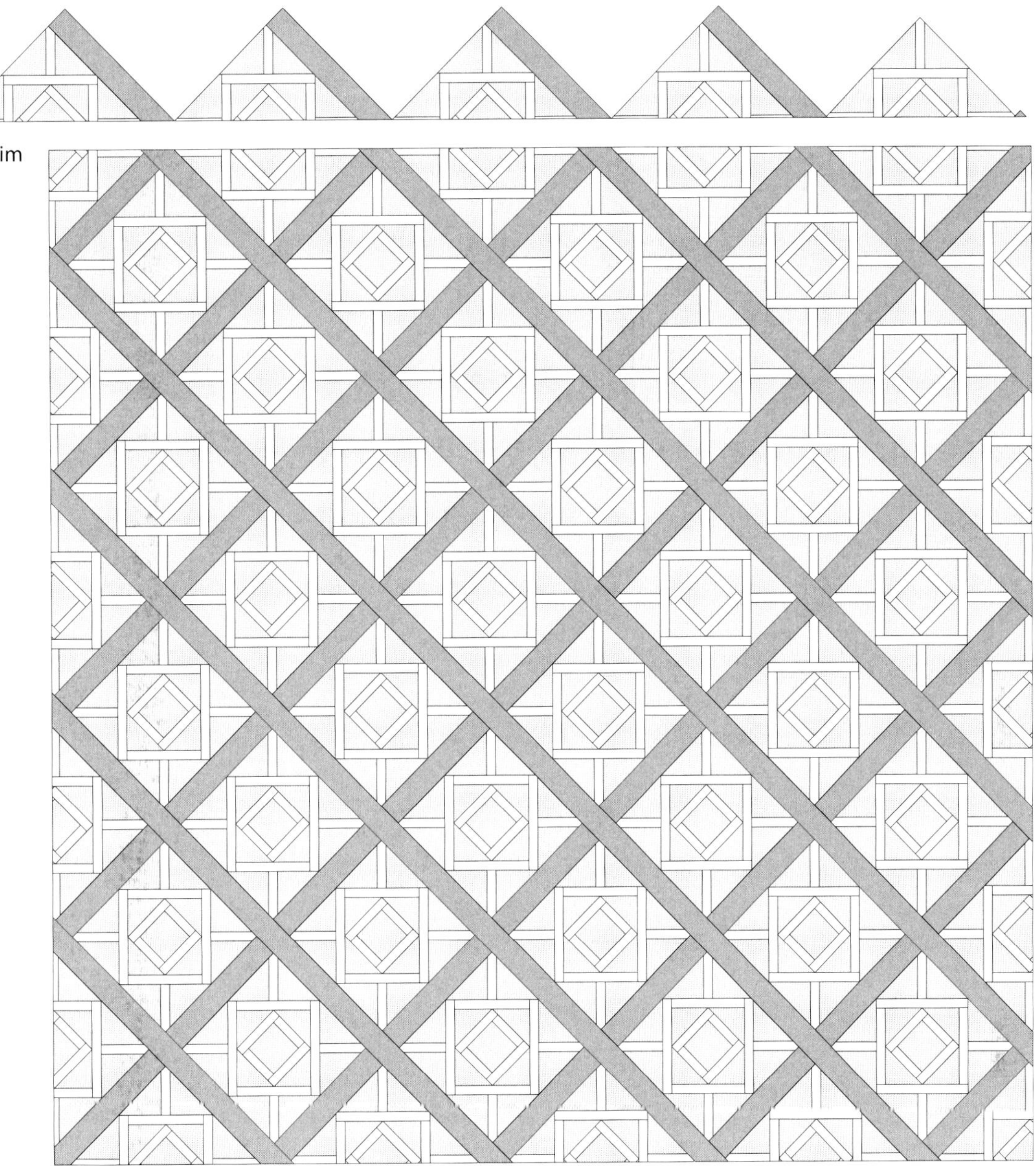

Unfinished quilt top is 83" x 83".

4 **Quilting:**

1. Layer quilt in the following order:
   a) Quilt back, right side down, 87" x 87".
   b) Batting 87" x 87". (I prefer Hobbs for best results.)
   c) Quilt top, right side up, 83" x 83".
2. Baste layers together.
3. Quilt by hand or machine. This quilt was quilted with an overall design on a long-arm quilting machine.

5 **Binding:**

Refer to My Sewing Basket on page 48 for binding directions.

LOVE *at* FIRST SIGHT

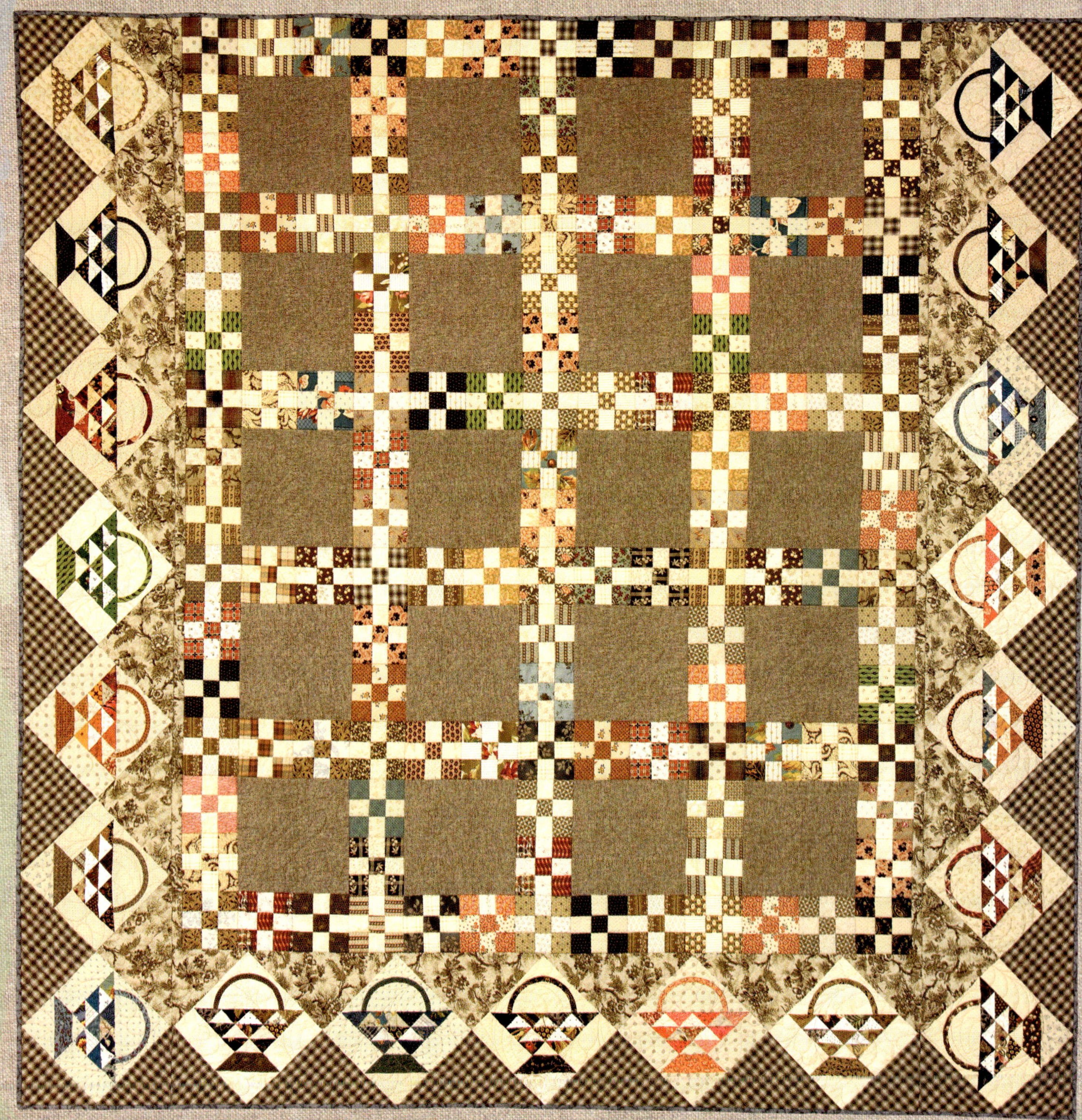

Popular nine patch and basket patterns give your scraps a place to shine. A soft taupe background is especially effective in making the scrappy colors pop. Inspired by a quilt from the Grand Rapids Public Museum, this variation is made for a bed. The baskets fall in just the right place to make a stand-up and stand-out border, which runs along only three sides of the quilt, allowing space at the top for the pillows.

LOVE AT FIRST SIGHT

Fabric Requirements

Baskets: 10 dark fat eighths (9" x 21")
10 light fat sixths (12" x 21")
Nine Patches:
26 dark fat eighths (9" x 21")
13 light fat eighths (9" x 21")
Light Setting Squares: 1⅓ yards
Light Inner Border: ¼ yard
Dark Setting Triangles: 1½ yards
Binding: 3/4 yard
Backing: 5 yards

Fabric Cutting

Baskets (dark prints):
From EACH of the 10 dark 9" x 21" prints, cut: (see diagram)
1-5½" x 9" rectangle to use with triangle paper
1-4⅜" square, cut once on the diagonal to make
2 half-square triangles
2 handles using the template
4-2⅜" squares, cut in half once on the diagonal to
make 8 half-square triangles

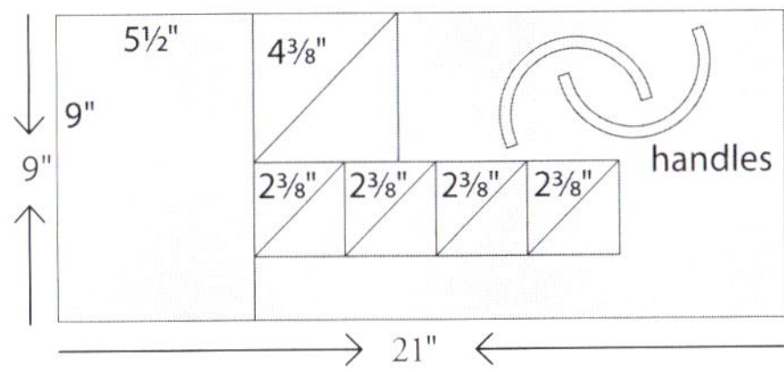

Baskets: (light prints)
From EACH of the 10 light 12" x 21" prints, cut:
1-5½" x 9" rectangle
1-6⅞" square, cut once on the diagonal to make
2 half-square triangles
1-4⅜" square, cut once on the diagonal to make
2 half-square triangles
4-2½" x 5" rectangles
2-2" squares

Nine Patches:
From EACH of the 26 **dark** 9" x 21" prints, cut:
2-2" x 21" strips
1-1¾" x 21" strip
From the strip, cut 2-1¾" x 10½" strips
From EACH of the 13 **light** 9" x 21" prints, cut:
1-1¾" x 21" strip
1-2" x 21" strip
From the strip, cut 2-2" x 10½" strips

Light Setting Squares:
5-9" x width of fabric strips
From the strips, cut 20-9" squares

Light Inner Border:
4-1¼" x width of fabric strips
Sew the strips end to end. From this long strip,
cut 2-1¼" x 68½" borders

Dark Setting Triangles:
3-12½" x width of fabric strips
From the strips, cut 8-12½" squares cut twice on the
diagonal to make 32 quarter-square triangles
1-6⅞" x width of fabric strip
From the strip, cut 6-6⅞" squares cut once on the
diagonal to make 12 half-square triangles

Binding: 8-2½" x width of fabric strips

Finished quilt size: 79¾" x 79¾".

Use a ¼" seam allowance. Press in the direction of the arrows.

1 Half-Square Triangle units:

(See page 69 for an alternative to using triangle paper.)

Cut one LBQ 1½" finished size Triangle Exchange paper into two 6-square sections. Cut 10 sections total from 5 sheets of paper.

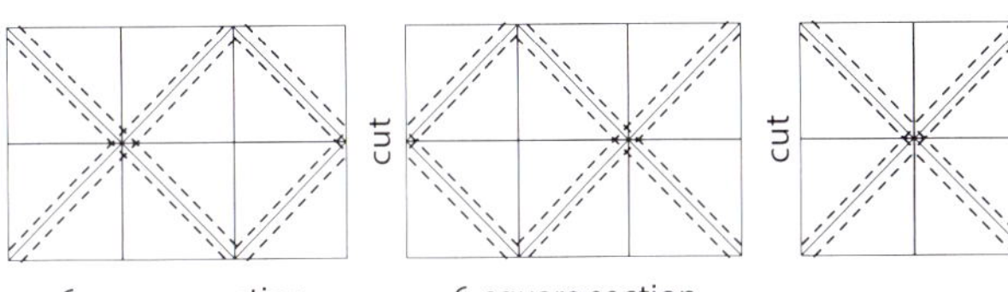

(A) Select one print and one background 5½" x 9" strip. Layer the dark print and light print, right sides together with the background print on the top. Press.

Following the LBQ Triangle Exchange paper directions, place the paper on top of the fabrics and pin. Sew the half-square triangle units using the dashed lines as guides. Remember to use a 50-wt thread and a smaller stitch length.

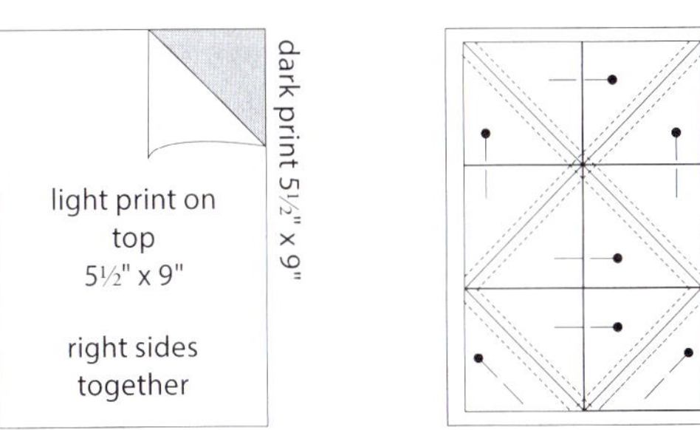

(B) Cut the triangles apart, using the solid lines as guides. *Do not remove the paper.*

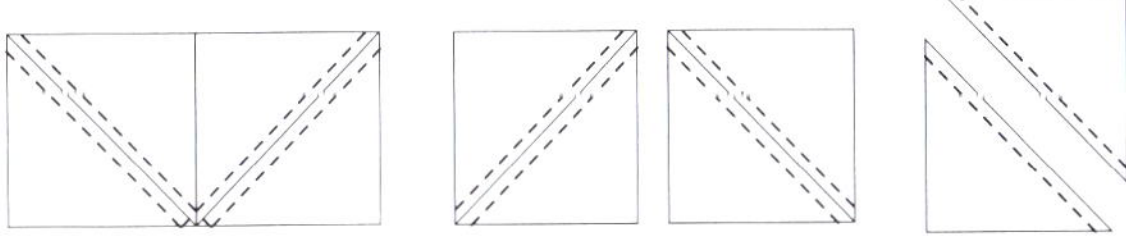

(C) Flip the triangle over so that the print is on the top. Press the half-square triangle unit open. Trim the "dog ears" and remove the paper. One *trimmed* LBQ 1½" Triangle Exchange paper makes 12 half-square triangle units.

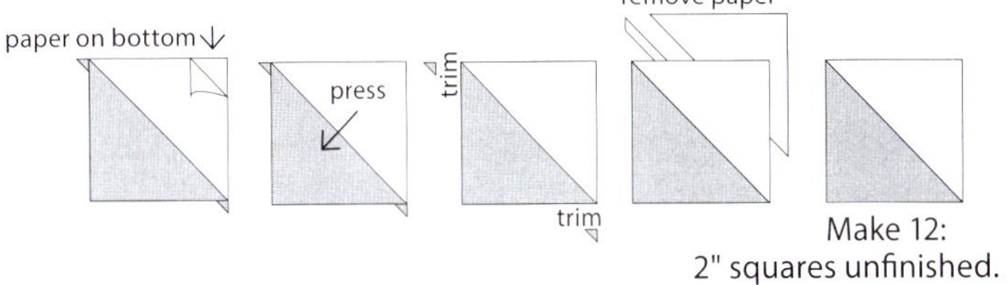

Make 12:
2" squares unfinished.

Repeat to make 10 matching sets of 12 half-square triangle units.

2 **Baskets:** Make 2 matching baskets.

(A) Select: 10 basket half square triangle units
8-2⅜" dark basket triangles
2-4⅜" dark basket triangles
2 dark handles from the template
2-4⅜" light triangles
2-6⅞" light triangles
2-2" light squares
4-2½" x 5" light rectangles

(B) Arrange 3 basket half-square triangle units and 3-2⅜" basket half-square triangles in rows as shown; sew together. Press the rows in opposite directions. Join the rows. Add 1-2½" x 5" light rectangle. Make 2.

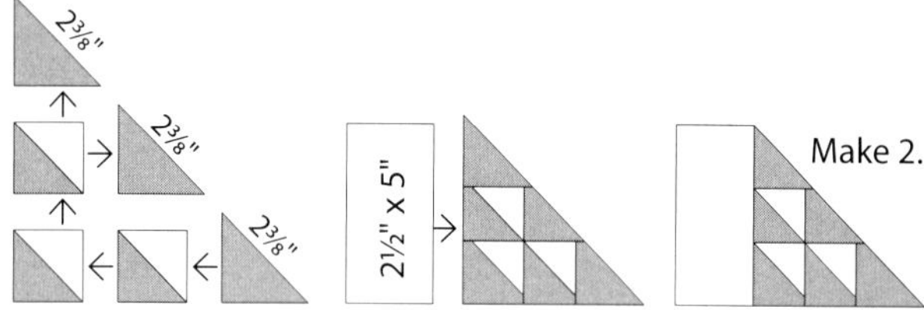

(C) Arrange 2 basket half-square triangle units and 1-2⅜" basket half-square triangle in a row as shown, sew together. Add 1-2½" x 5" light rectangle. Make 2.

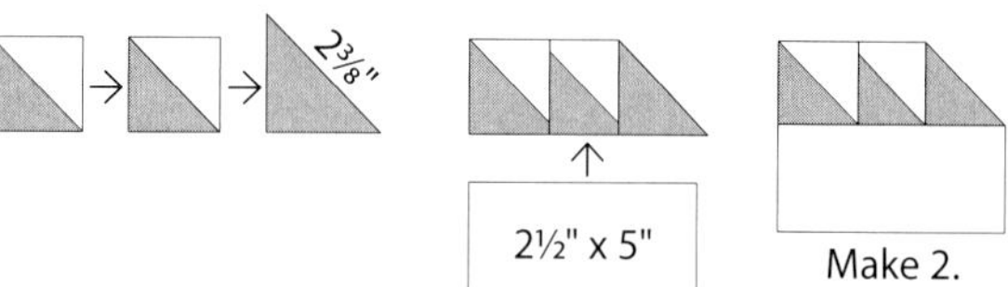

(D) Sew 1-4⅜" basket and 1-4⅜" light triangle together. Sew 1-2" light triangle on the diagonal to the unit. Trim ¼" from the sewn line. Press to form a triangle. Add to the unit from step C.

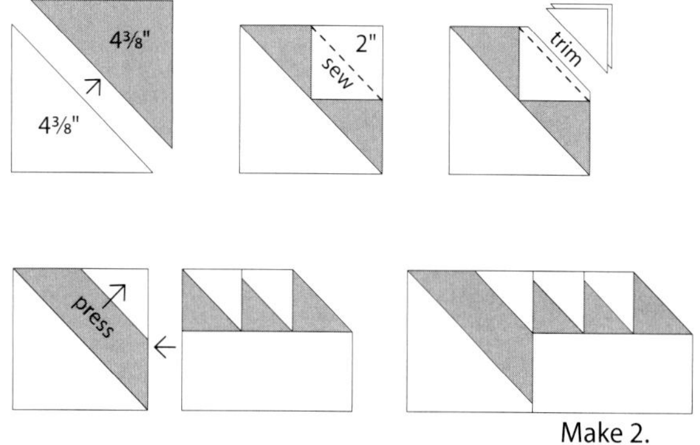

(E) Assemble the bottom of the basket as shown.

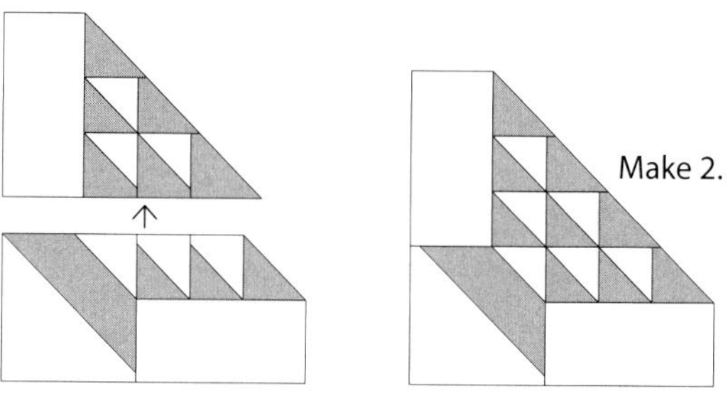

(F) Using your favorite appliqué technique, add the handle to the 6⅞" light triangle. I used machine applique to secure my handles in place; see My Sewing Basket on page 48 for appliqué details. Finish assembling the basket as shown, and repeat the steps to make 19 total. You have cut enough fabric for 20; you might want to use the last one for a label on the back of your quilt like I did.

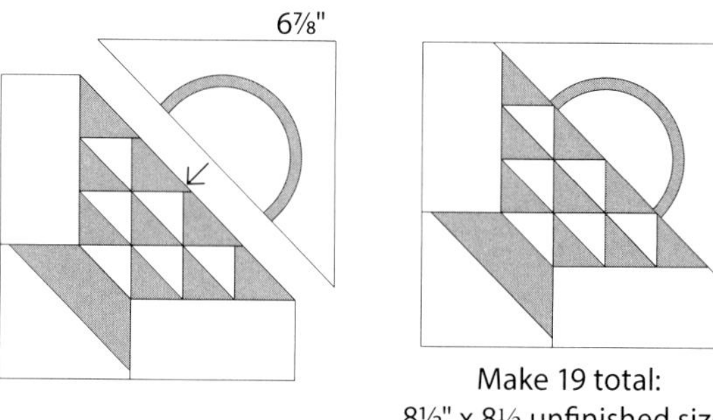

Make 19 total:
8½" x 8½ unfinished size.

3 **Nine Patches:** Use the same dark print and same light print in the nine patch.

(A) Sew 2-2" x 21" matching dark strips and 1-1¾" x 21" light strip together as shown. Cut into 10 units.

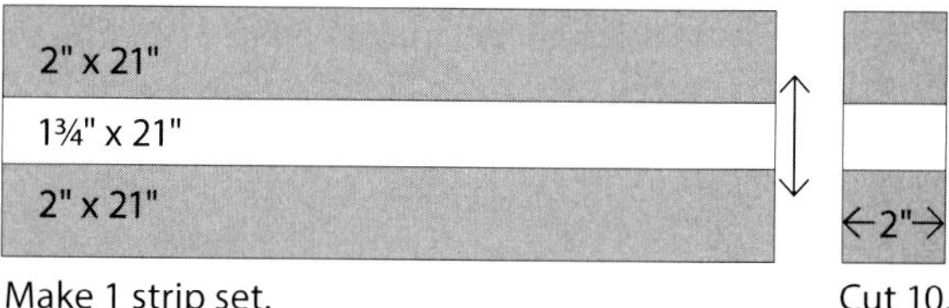

(B) Sew 2-2" x 10½" matching light strips and 1-1¾" x 10½" dark strip together as shown. Cut into 5 units.

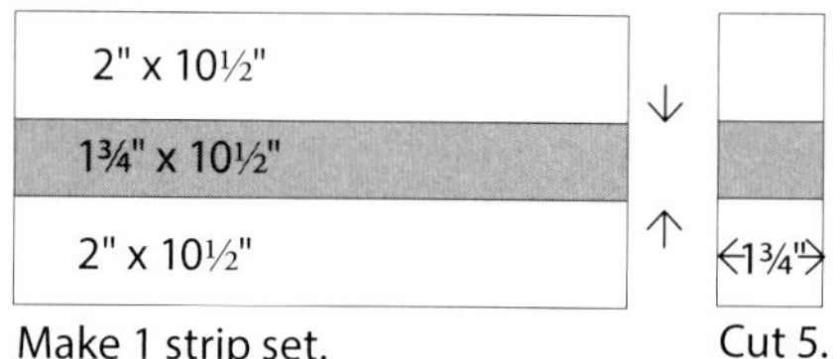

(C) Join units as shown to make a nine patch.

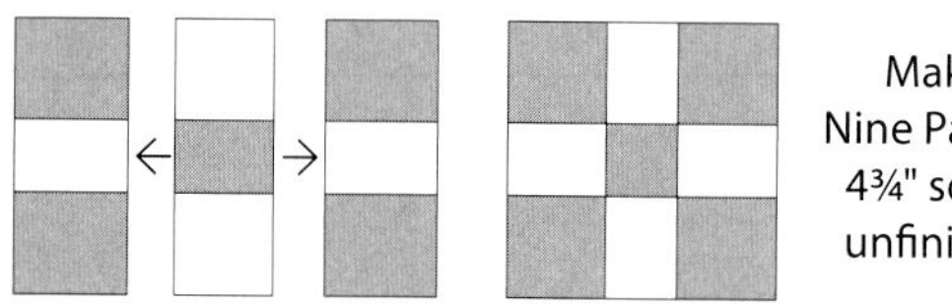

Make 5 Nine Patches: 4¾" square unfinished.

(D) Repeat steps 3(A)-(C) to make a total of 128 nine patches.

4 **Assemble Quilt Center:** Arrange 13-nine patches as shown to make row A; sew together. Make 6 total. Arrange 10-nine patches and 4-9" light squares as shown to make row B; sew together. Make 5 total. Join rows A and B. Sew 1-1¼" x 68½" light strip to each side of the quilt center.

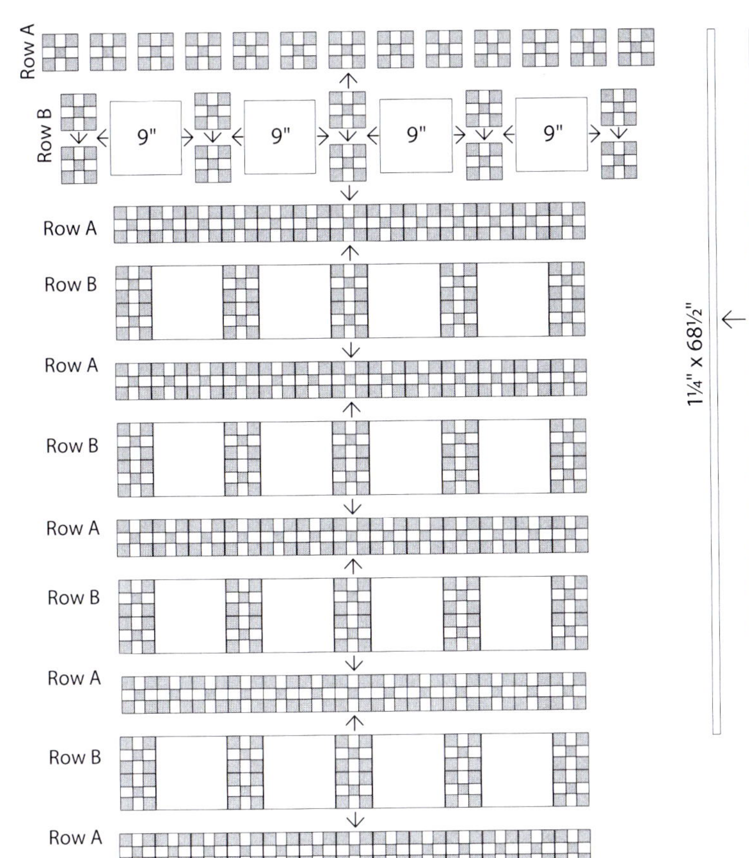

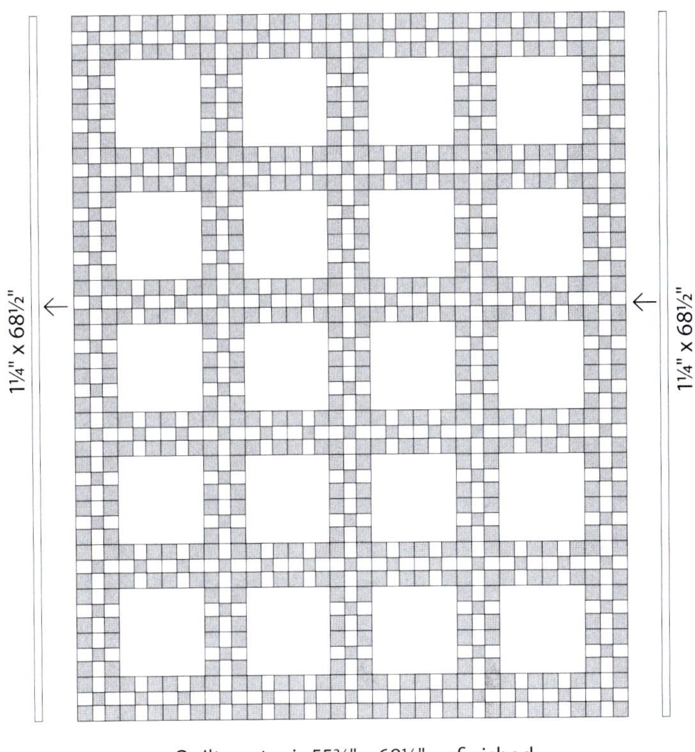

Quilt center is 55¾" x 68½" unfinished.

Quilt center is 57¼" x 68½" unfinished, including the inner borders.

5 Join 5 basket blocks, 8 quarter-square triangles, and 4 corner half-square triangles to make one basket border.
Join 7 basket blocks, 12 quarter-square triangles, and 4 corner half-square triangles to make two large basket borders.

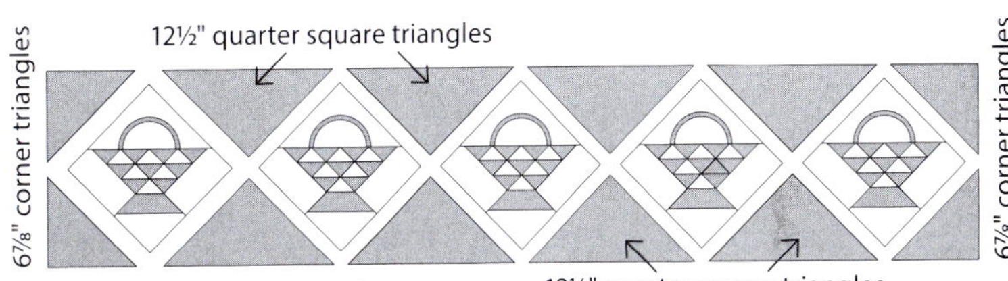

Make 1 Basket Border.

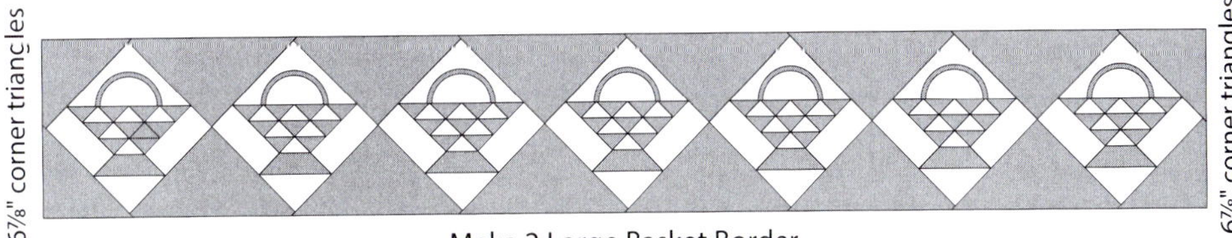

Make 2 Large Basket Border.

Alternative to using the triangle paper:

1. Cut 1 light and 1 dark 2⅜" square. Cut the squares once on the diagonal.
2. Layer one dark and one light triangle right sides together. Sew together along diagonal using a ¼" seam allowance.
3. Press your triangles open and trim the bunny ears. Makes 2 half-square triangle units.

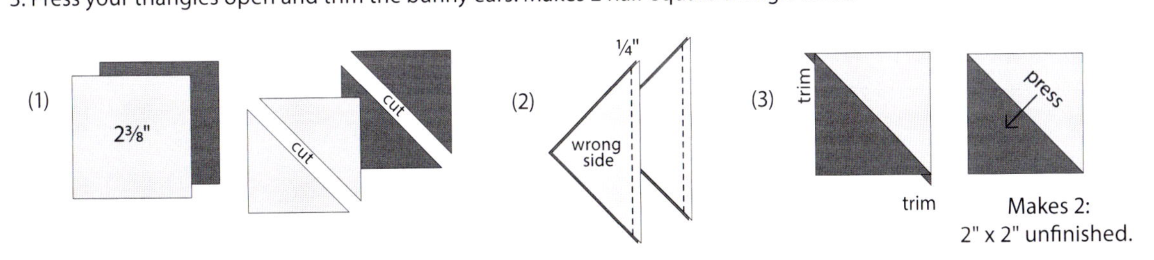

6 Sew the basket border to the quilt bottom, and then sew the large basket borders to the quilt sides. Press seam allowance away from the basket borders.

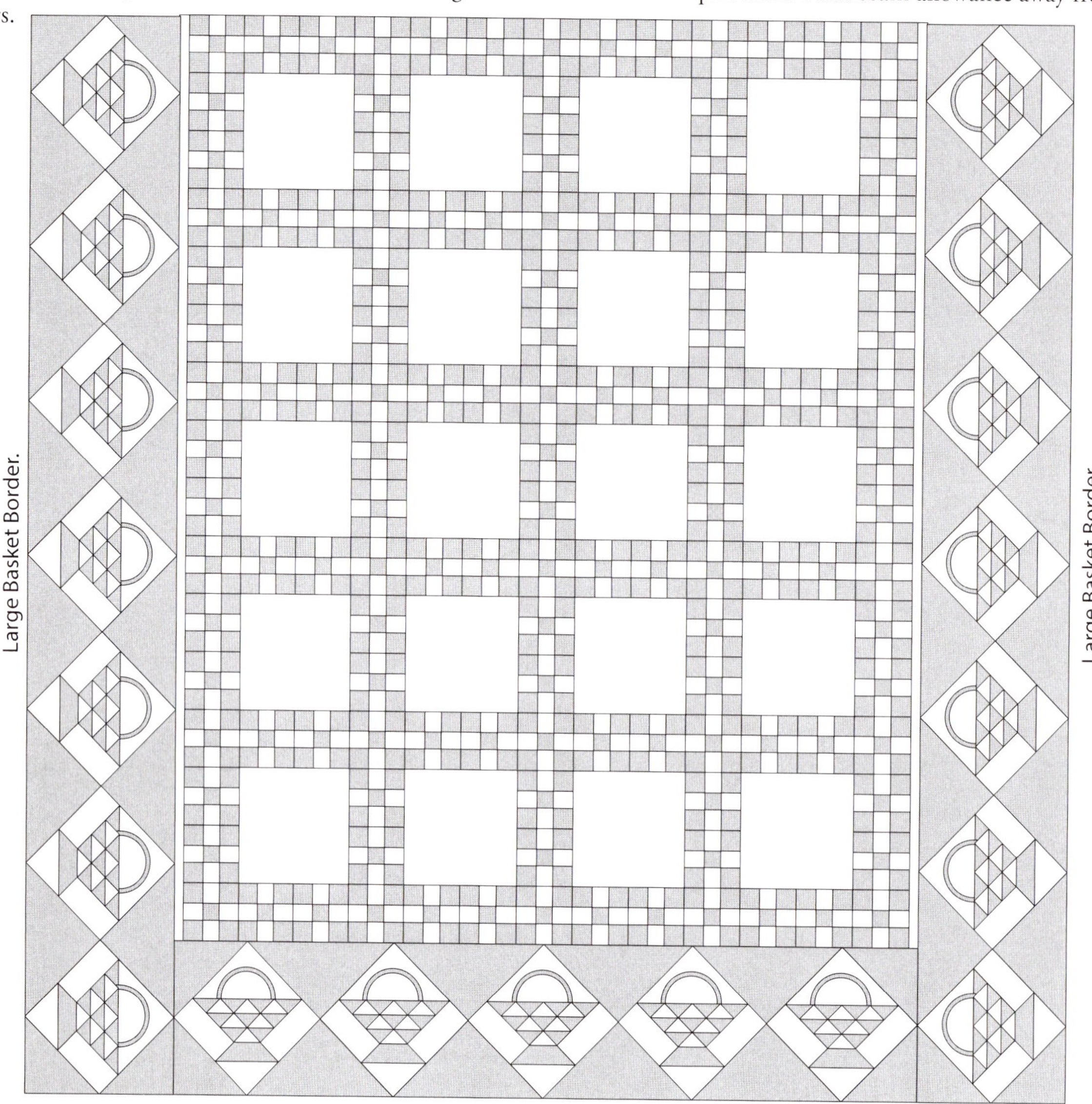

Basket Border.

> **TIP** *I used the same color fabric for my inner border strips on the left and right side of the quilt as I used for the border setting triangles. To add detail to the quilt, you might want to choose a different color for the inner border.*

Basket Handle template, actual size. Seam allowances only included where indicated.

seam allowance

seam allowance

7 **Quilting:**

1. Layer quilt in the following order
   a) Quilt back, right side down, 84" x 84".
   b) Batting 84" x 84". (I prefer Hobbs for best results.)
   c) Quilt top, right side up, 79¾" x 79¾".
2. Baste layers together.
3. Quilt by hand or machine. This quilt was quilted on a long-arm quilting machine.

8 **Binding:**

Refer to My Sewing Basket on page 48 for binding directions.

BASKET *of* SCRAPS

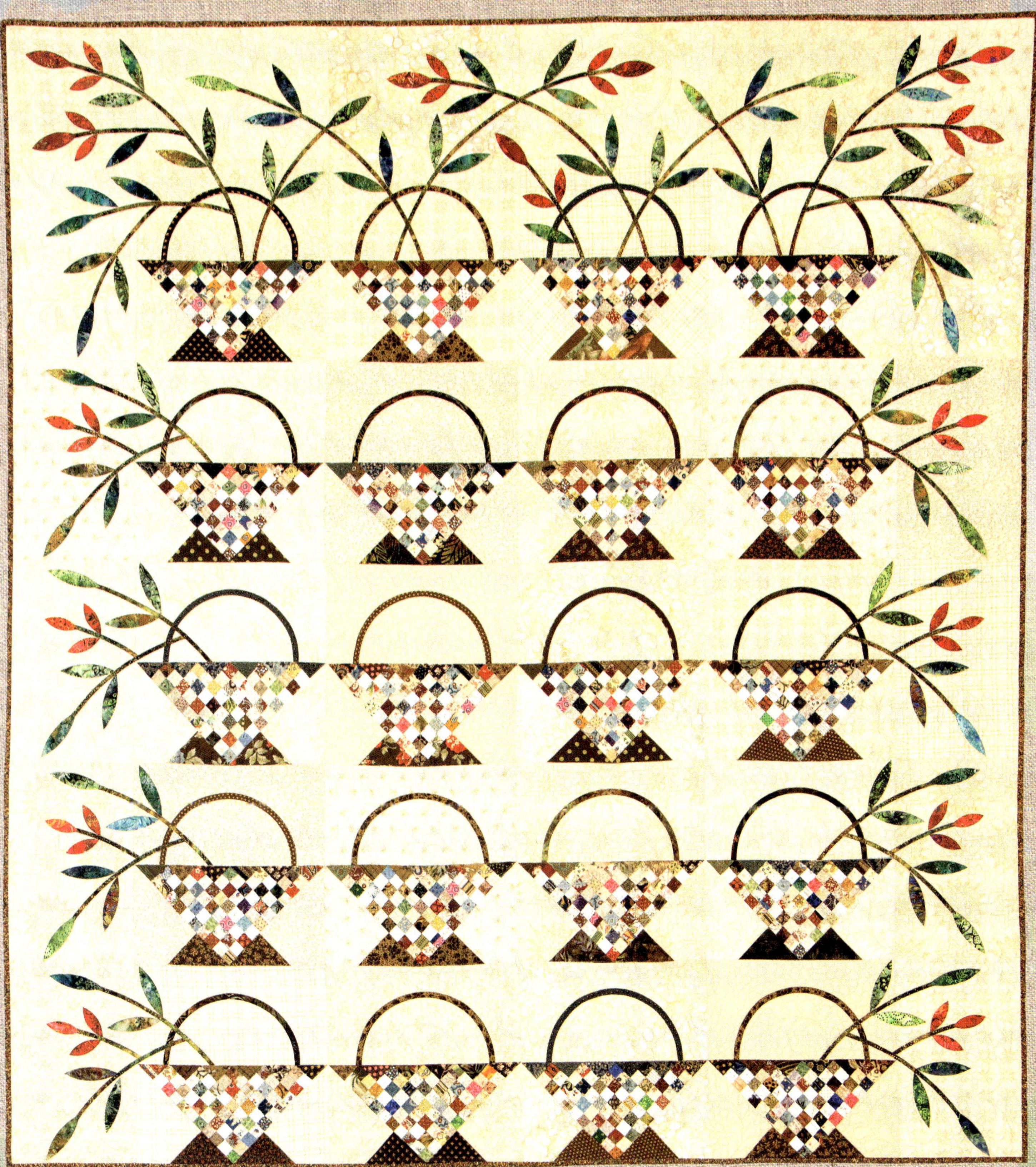

Fill these welcome baskets to the brim with all your favorite fabrics. Appliquéd flowery branches and leaves—as if cut fresh from the garden—spill into a free-form border. The empty space between the baskets is open to your stitching imagination. This quilt is perfect for practicing some of your favorite quilting design stitches like feathers and pebbles.

BASKET OF SCRAPS

Finished quilt size: 67½" x 72¼".

Fabric Requirements

Baskets and Appliqué:
20 multi-color fat eighths
10 brown fat eighths

Background:
16-14" x width of fabric lights

Binding:
⅔ yard brown fabric

Backing:
4¼ yards fabric

Fabric Cutting

Baskets (multi-color):
From EACH of the 20 dark fat eighths, cut
2-1¼" x 21" strips (total 40 strips)
From remaining multi-color fat eighths, cut
30-3⅜" squares, cut in half twice on the diagonal to make 4 quarter-square triangles (QST). You need 120 triangles.

Handles and Basket Feet (brown):
From EACH of the 10 brown fat eighths, cut:
2-4¾" squares
2-¾" x 12" bias strips

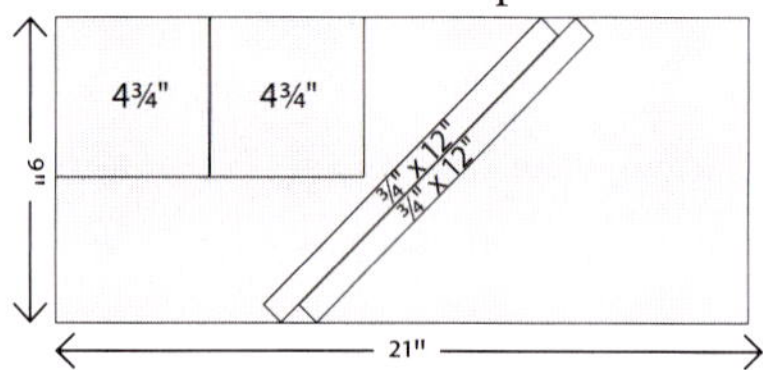

Background:
From each of 10 light fabrics, cut for baskets:
2-6⅞" x 13¼" rectangles
2-7" x 7" squares
4-1¼" x 21" strips
From remaining light fabrics, cut for border:
14-8½" x 13¼" rectangles
2-8½" x 8½" squares

Appliqué:

Template	Description	Cut	Color
A	Leaf	7	Red
B	Leaf	38	Red
E	Leaf	95	Green
G	Stem	37	Brown
½ G	Stem	8	Brown

Binding:
8-2½" x width of fabric strips

Use a ¼" seam allowance. Press seams in the direction of the arrows.

1 **Handles:**

(A) Follow the instructions on the **Clover Fusible Bias Tape Maker** package to prepare the ⅜" x 12" basket handles using ¾" x 12" bias strips.

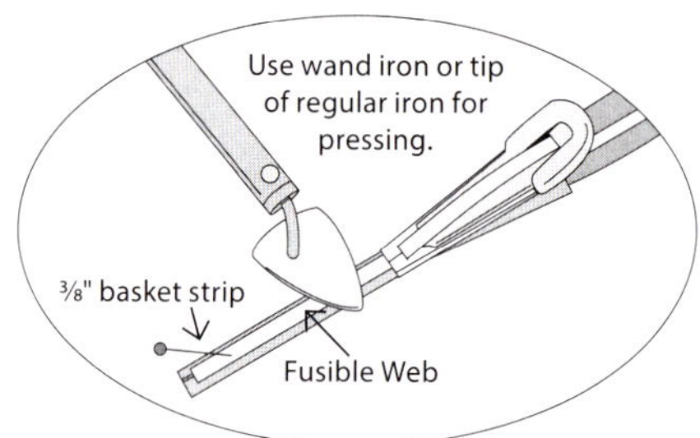

(B) Remove the paper tape from the handle to reveal the adhesive. Finger press a 13¼" x 6⅞" background rectangle in half to find the center, then place the rectangle on your ironing board. Center your arch template on rectangle, aligning the guidelines.

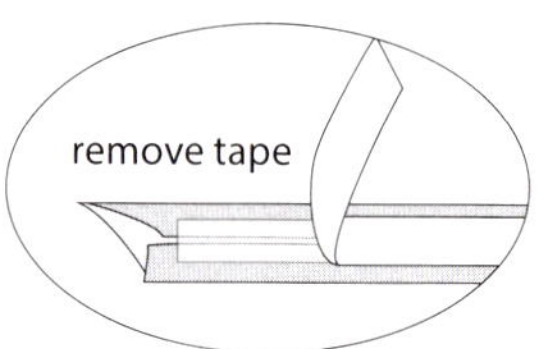

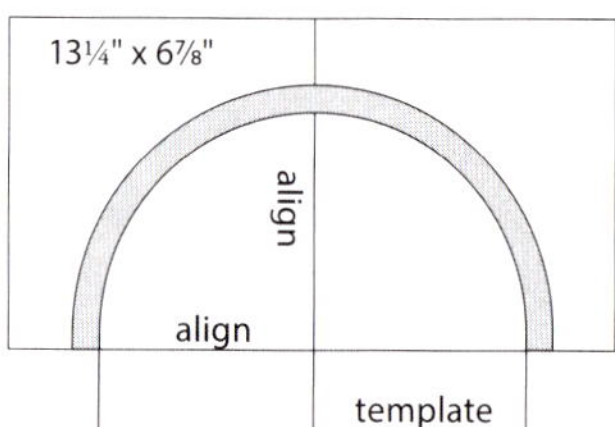

(C) *Make sure that the exposed adhesive on the handle faces your fabric as you iron.* Since you only have two hands and you need three for this step, secure the starting edge of your handle to the rectangle with a pin, and use your iron to hold the template. Place your iron at the base of the template, and glide the point in a circular motion, beginning on one side over the template arch and basket handle. The cardboard template will ensure that all your basket handles are uniform. NOTE: When ironing to secure the handle, DO NOT overheat the adhesive. Wait a few seconds to allow the handle to cool before you move it.

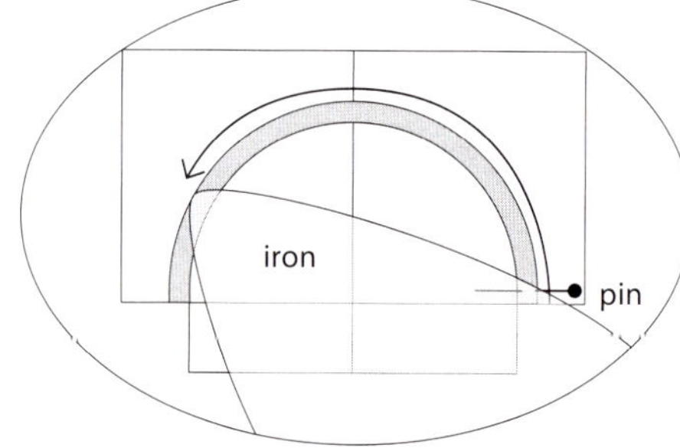

(D) Appliqué the handle by hand or machine. See directions from My Sewing Basket on page 48. Repeat to make 20 handles.

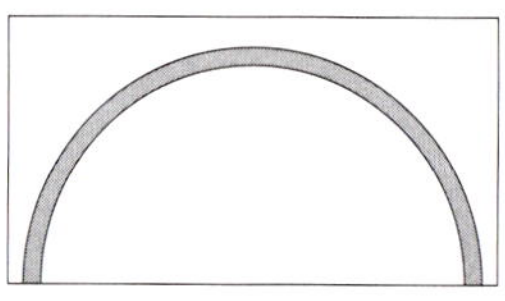

Make 20 handles:
13¼" x 6⅞" unfinished.

2 Baskets:

(A) Join a 1¼" x 21" dark and 1¼" x 21" background strip as shown. Make 40 strip sets. Cut 600-1¼" units. Join two units to make a four patch. Make 300 four patches.

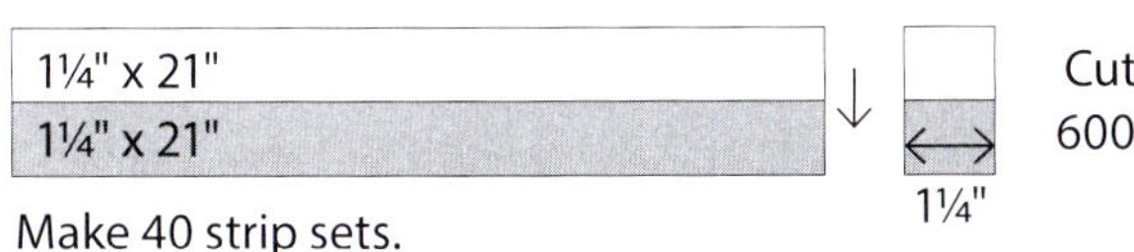

Make 40 strip sets.

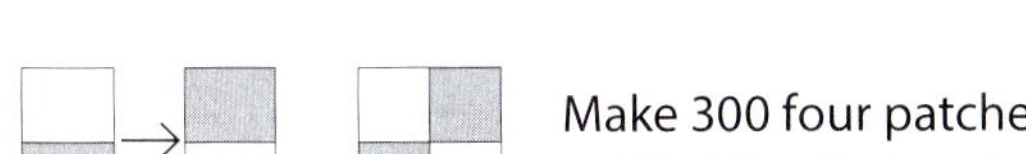

Make 300 four patches:
2" x 2" unfinished.

(B) Arrange and sew 15 four patches and 6-3⅜" quarter square triangles (QST) in 6 rows as shown. Press the odd rows in one direction and the even rows in the opposite direction. Join the rows. Repeat to make 20 baskets.

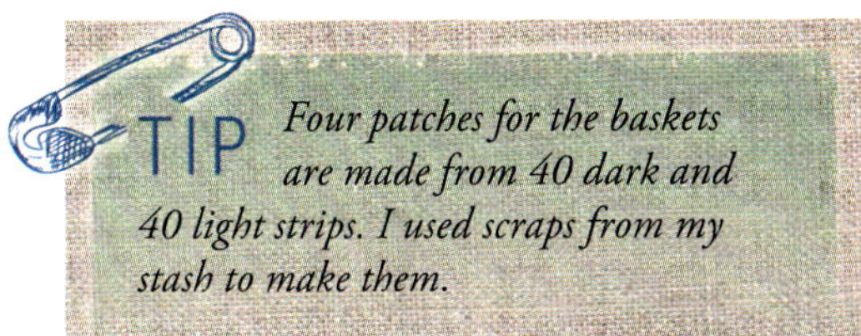

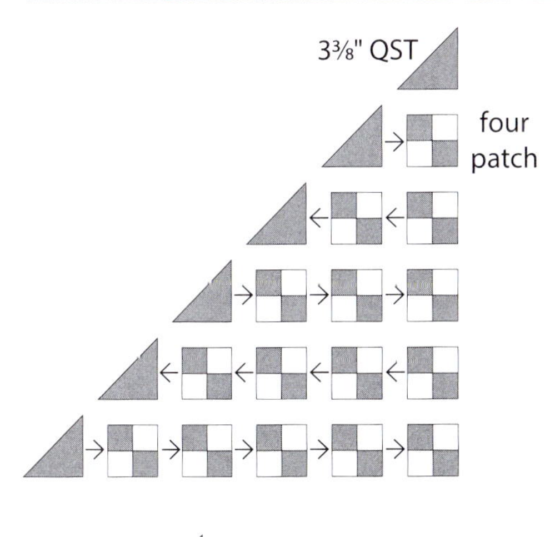

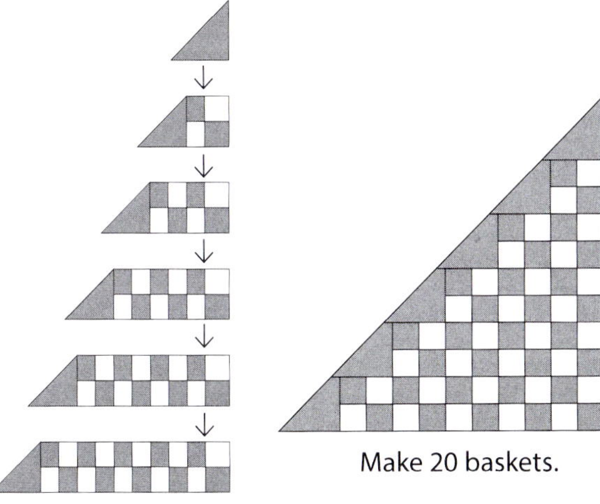

Make 20 baskets.

(C) Draw a diagonal line from corner to corner on the wrong side of 20-4¾" squares. Layer one marked square, right sides together, on the corner of a 7" background square as shown. Sew on the diagonal line. Trim ¼" from the sewn line. Press to the corner to form a triangle. Cut in half on the diagonal as shown. Repeat to make 20 basket feet.

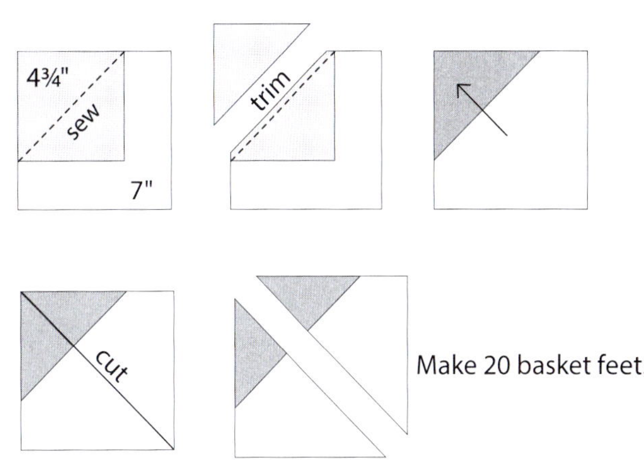

Make 20 basket feet.

(D) Join the basket, feet and handle as shown to make one basket. Repeat to make 20 baskets.

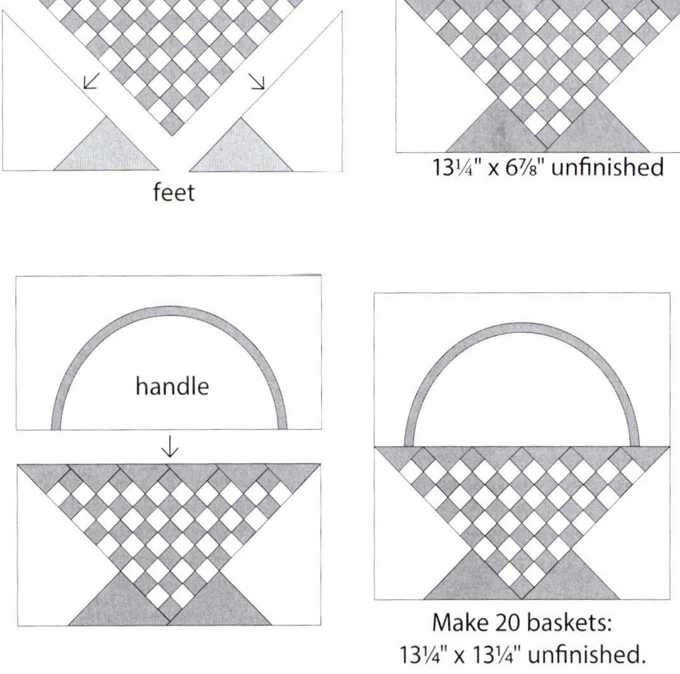

Make 20 baskets:
13¼" x 13¼" unfinished.

3 Assemble Quilt Top: Sew 20 baskets, 14-8½" x 13¼" background rectangles and 2-8½" x 8½" corner squares into 6 rows as shown below. Sew the rows together.

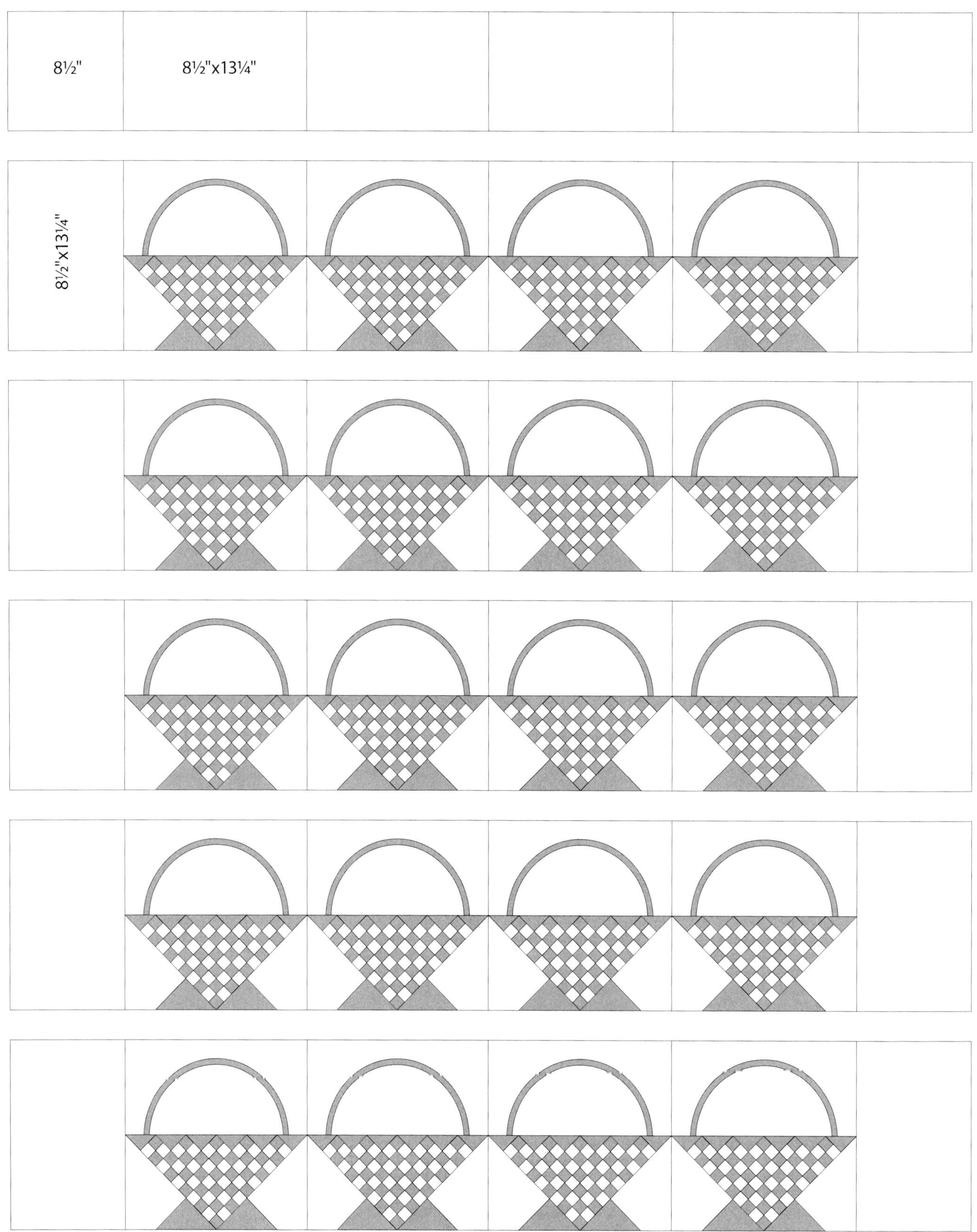

4 **Appliqué**: Choose your favorite appliqué method from My Sewing Basket on page 48 and appliqué shapes (A, B, E, G and ½ G) from page 50 to complete the quilt top.

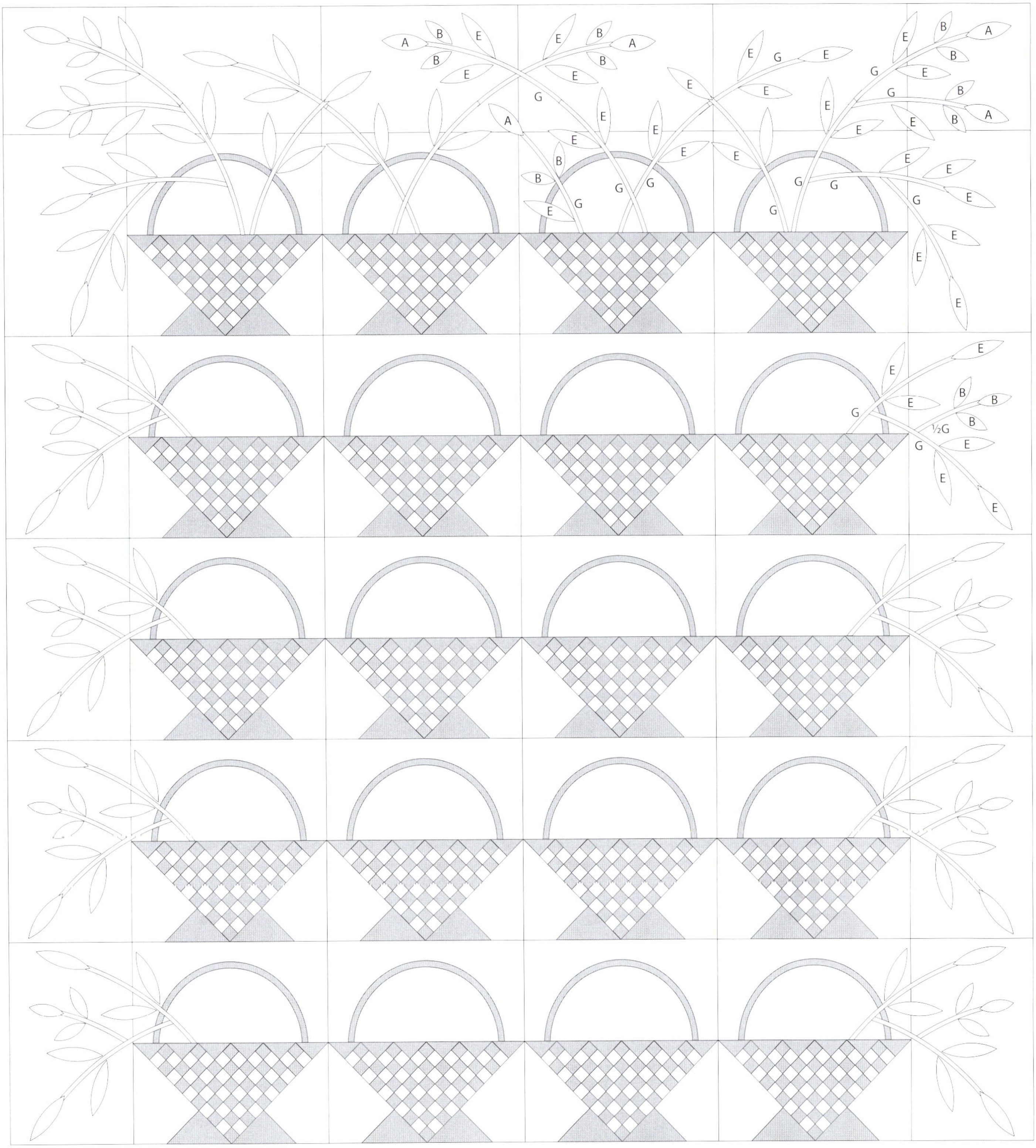

Unfinished quilt top is 67½" x 72¼".

5 **Quilting:**

1. Layer quilt in the following order:
   a) Quilt back, right side down, 71½" x 76¼".
   b) Batting 71½" x 76¼" (I prefer Hobbs for best results.)
   c) Quilt top, right side up, 67½" x 72¼".
2. Baste layers together.
3. Quilt by hand or machine. This quilt was custom-quilted with feathers and pebbles on a long-arm machine.

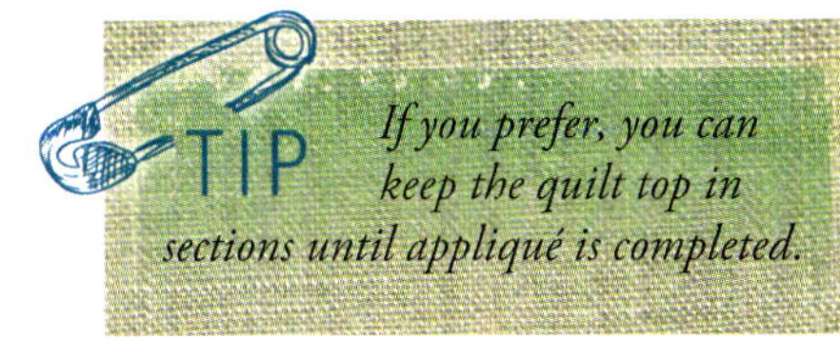

6 Binding:

Refer to My Sewing Basket on page 48 for binding instructions.

ARCH TEMPLATE

Trace the arch template on poster board or lightweight cardboard.

Align to the bottom of rectangle

center

Align to the bottom of rectangle

SLOW *and* STEADY

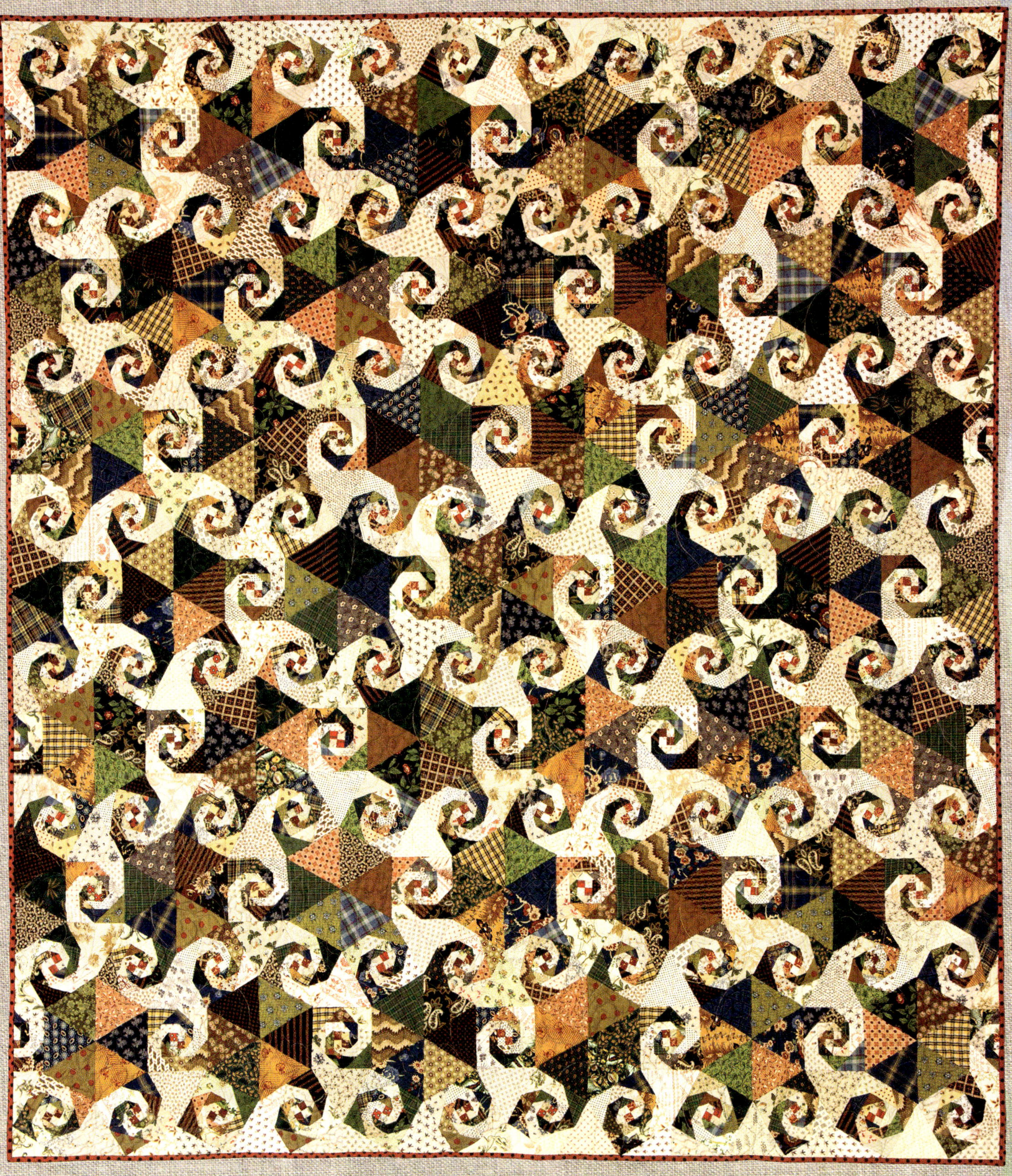

Here is the project for those extra special scraps you've been saving! This quilt looks difficult, but like anything else in life, take one stitch at a time, and you will cross the finish line. Sixty-degree triangles in light and dark fabrics put this Snail Trail pattern on the fast track to smiles.

SLOW AND STEADY

Finished quilt size: 72" x 76".

Fabric Requirements

Blocks:
45-6" x width of fabric strips from dark fabrics
45-6" x width of fabric strips from light fabrics
15-1" x 21" strips from red fabrics
15-1" x 21" strips from light fabrics

Binding: ⅔ yard red fabric for binding

Backing: 4½ yards fabric for backing

Fabric Cutting

Blocks:
15-1" x 21" red strips, cut 284 1" x 1" squares
15-1" x 21" light strips, cut 284 1" x 1" squares
From each of 45-6" dark strips, cut:
4-2⅞" x 2⅞" squares, cut on the diagonal to make 8 half-square triangles
4-2¼" x 2¼" squares, cut on the diagonal to make 8 half-square triangles
4-1⅞" x 1⅞" squares, cut on the diagonal to make 8 half-square triangles
4-1⅝" x 1⅝" squares, cut on the diagonal to make 8 half-square triangles
From remaining fabrics, cut 252 triangles as shown in step 2 using template on page 81.

From each of 45-6" light strips cut:
4-2⅞" x 2⅞" squares, cut on the diagonal to make 8 half-square triangles
4-2¼" x 2¼" squares, cut on the diagonal to make 8 half-square triangles
4-1⅞" x 1⅞" squares, cut on the diagonal to make 8 half-square triangles
4-1⅝" x 1⅝" squares, cut on the diagonal to make 8 half-square triangles
From remaining fabrics, cut 128 triangles as shown in step 2 using template on page 81.

Binding: 8-2½" x width of fabric strips

Use a ¼" seam allowance. Press in the direction of the arrows.

1 **Blocks:**
(A) Join 4-1" assorted squares. Make 142.

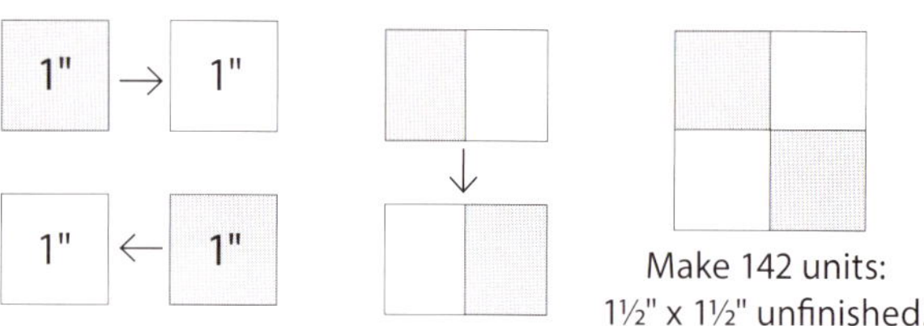

Make 142 units:
1½" x 1½" unfinished.

(B) Add 4-1⅝" assorted half-square triangles. Make 142.

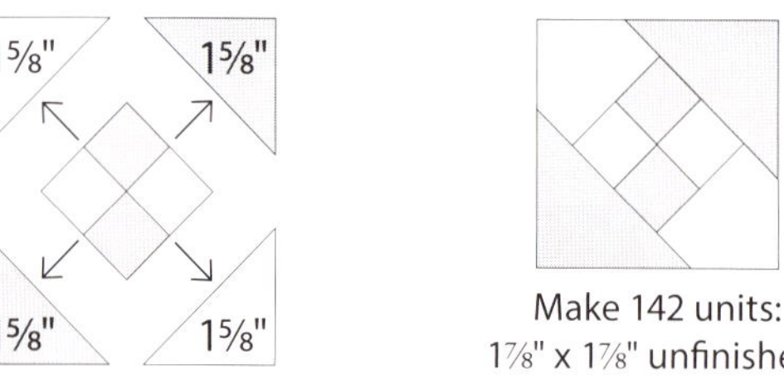

Make 142 units:
1⅞" x 1⅞" unfinished.

(C) Add 4-1⅞" assorted half-square triangles. Make 142.

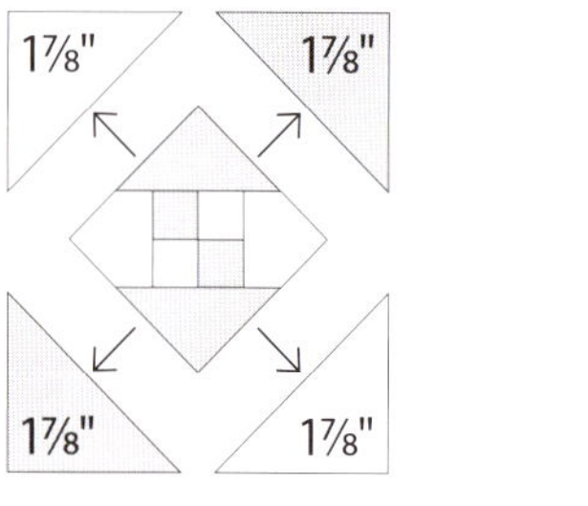

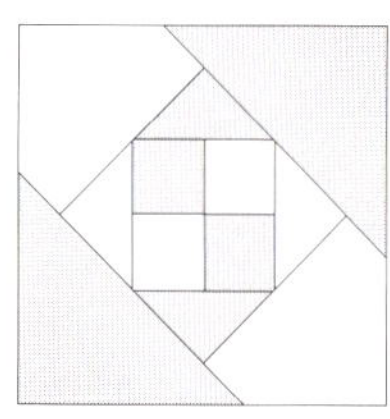
Make 142 units:
2½" x 2½" unfinished.

(D) Add 4-2¼" assorted half-square triangles. Make 142.

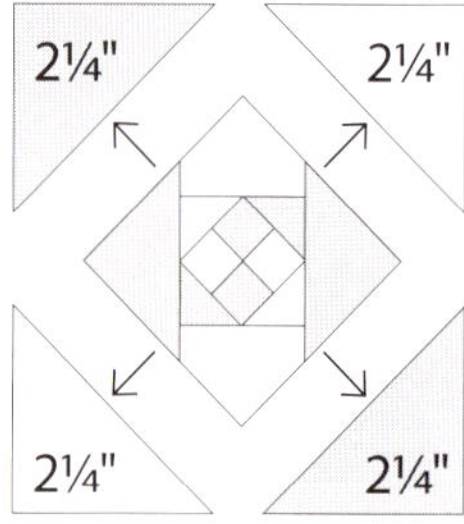

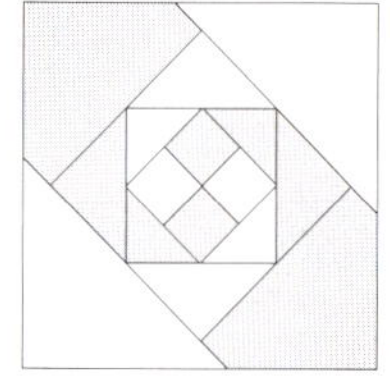
Make 142 units:
3⅜"x 3⅜" unfinished.

(E) Add 4-2⅞" assorted half-square triangles. Make 142.

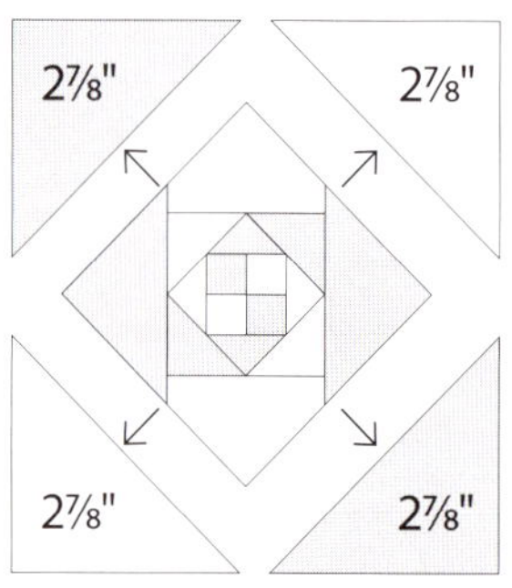

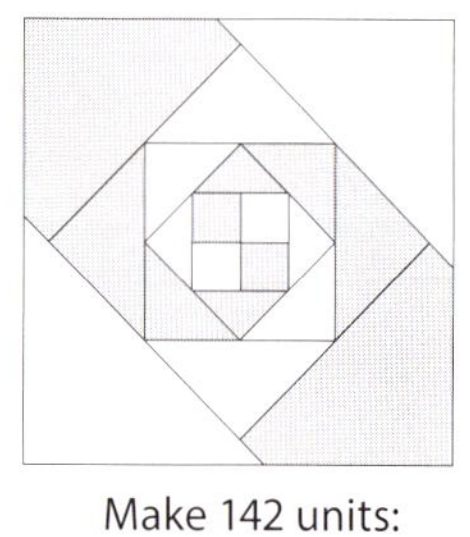
Make 142 units:
4½" x 4½" unfinished.

2 Triangles:

(A) Use Template A from page 81 to cut triangles from the remaining light strips. Trim your strip to 4". Rotate the template as shown. Cut a total of 128 triangles from 45 strips (approximately 3 per strip for a nice variety).

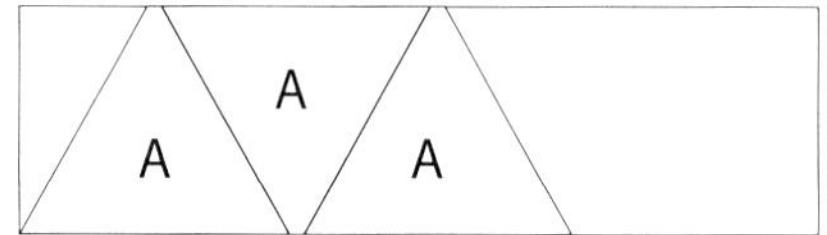

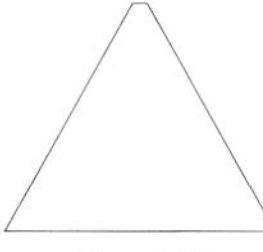

Cut 128.

(B) Use Template A from page 81 to cut triangles from the remaining dark strips. Trim your strip to 4". Rotate the template as shown. Cut a total of 252 triangles from 45 strips (approximately 6 per strip for a nice variety).

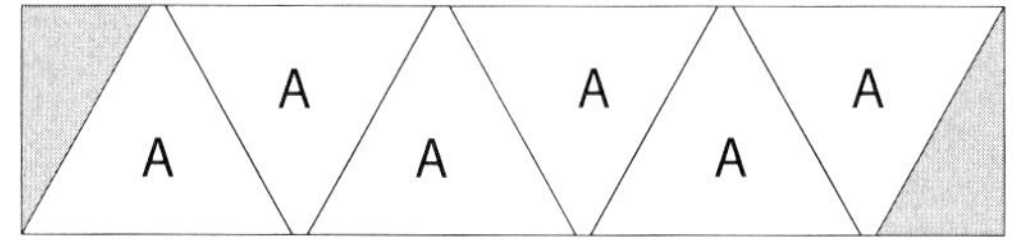

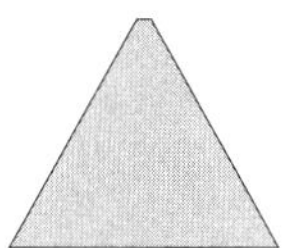

Cut 252.

(C) Arrange and sew 3 dark triangles in 1 row. Make 84. Set aside 6 to be used later for quilt sides.

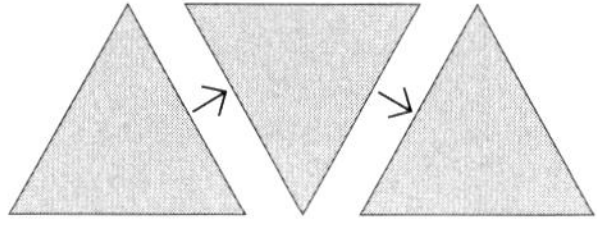

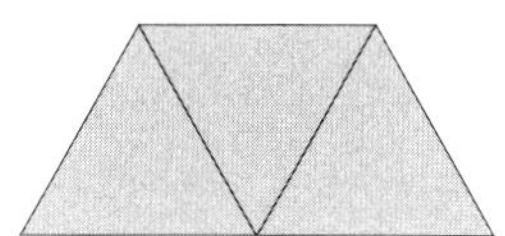

Make 84.

(D) Join 78 units together. Make 39.

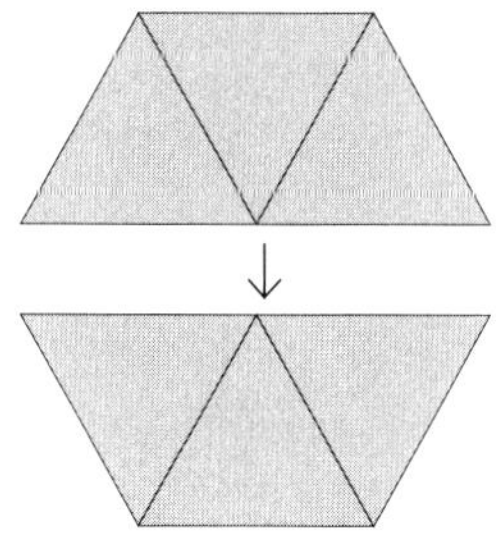

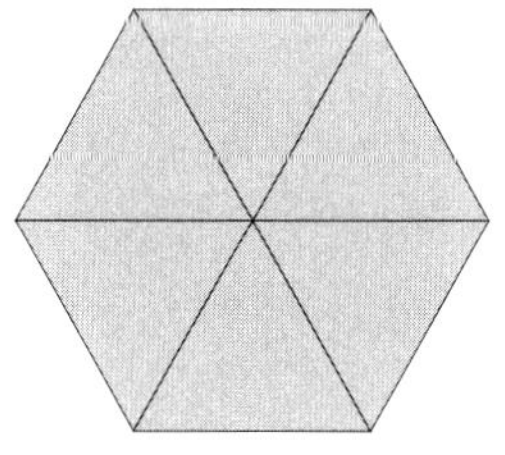

Make 39.

(E) Join 104 blocks with light triangles. Make sure to start and stop sewing ¼" from the end of the seam as shown by the dots in the diagram below.

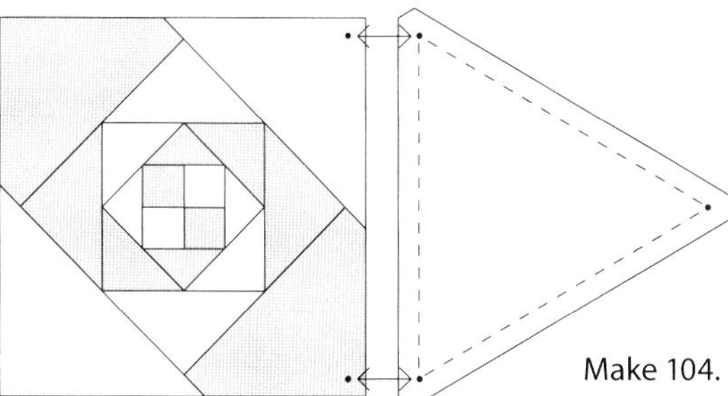

Make 104.

3 Row Assembly:

(A) Prepare 3 rows A and 4 rows B as shown below. When sewing blocks and triangles together, remember to stop and backstitch ¼" away from the start and end of seam.

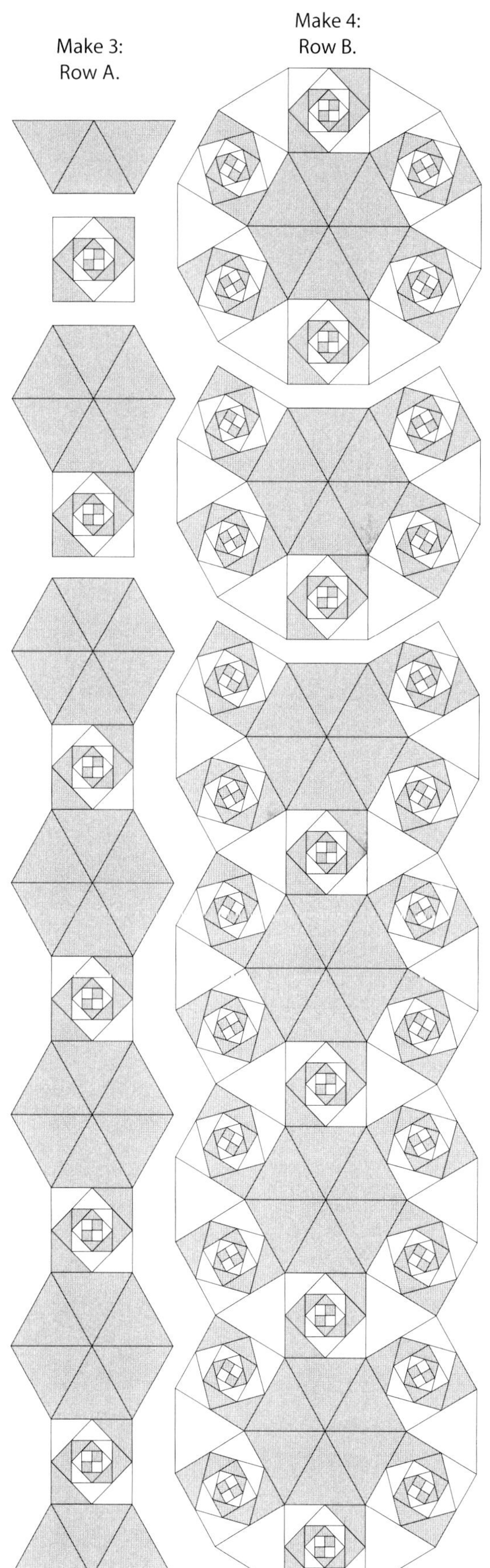

4 Quilt Assembly:

1. Lay out quilt, alternating rows A and B as shown below:
2. Starting from one side, sew rows together, keeping in mind that you will need to stop and backstitch ¼" away from the start and end of seam. You will be sewing one 4" seam at a time. Once your first seam is completed, match your next seam, pin and proceed to sew the next seam.
3. Repeat until all rows are sewn together.
4. Sew 20 light triangles into sets of 2.
5. Add light triangle sets A to the right and left sides of the quilt as shown below.
6. Add 4 single light triangles A to the corners of the quilt.
7. Trim quilt top using ruler and rotary cutter as shown by the dotted line below, keeping as far to the edges as possible.

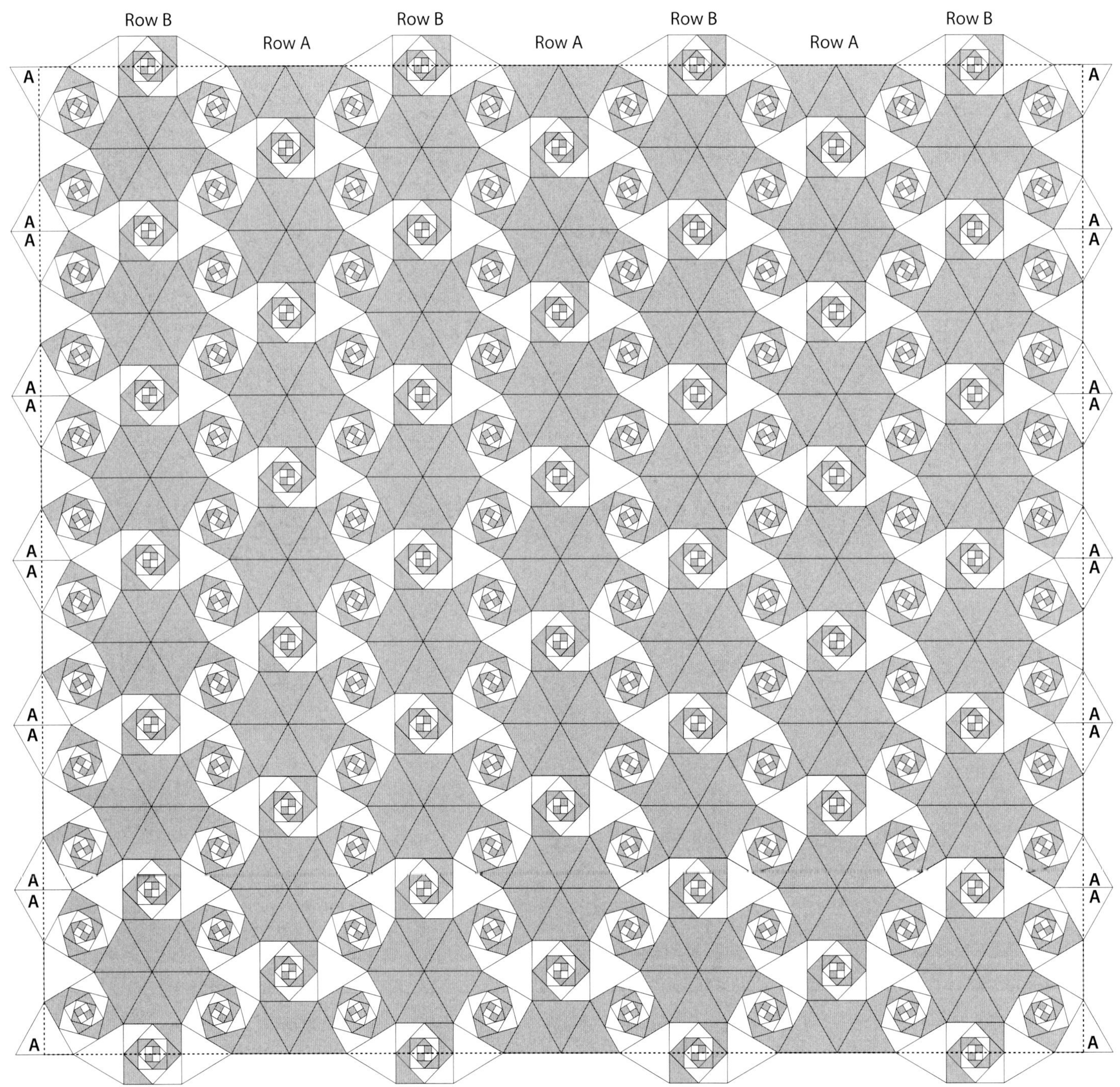

Unfinished quilt size is 72" x 76".

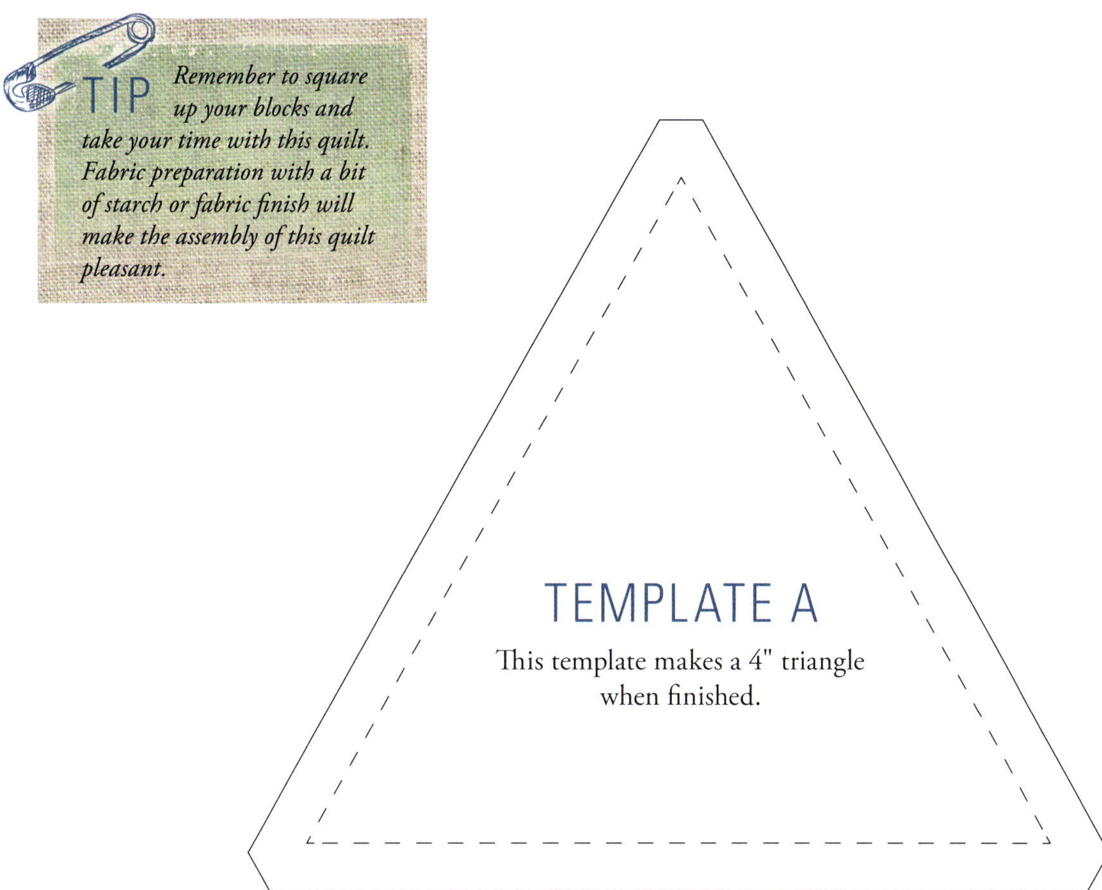

5 **Quilting:**

1. Layer quilt in the following order:
   a) Quilt back, right side down, 76" x 80".
   b) Batting 76" x 80" (I prefer Hobbs for best results.)
   c) Quilt top, right side up, 72" x 76".
2. Baste layers together.
3. Quilt by hand or machine. This quilt was overall quilted on a long-arm quilting machine.

6 **Binding:**

Refer to My Sewing Basket on page 48 for binding instructions.

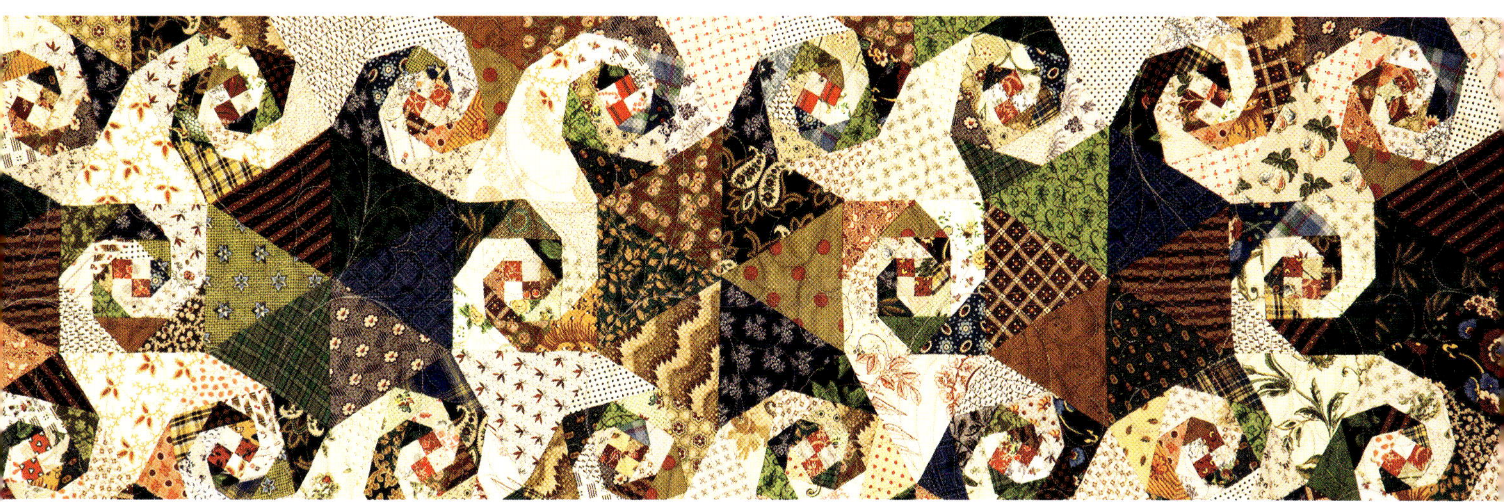

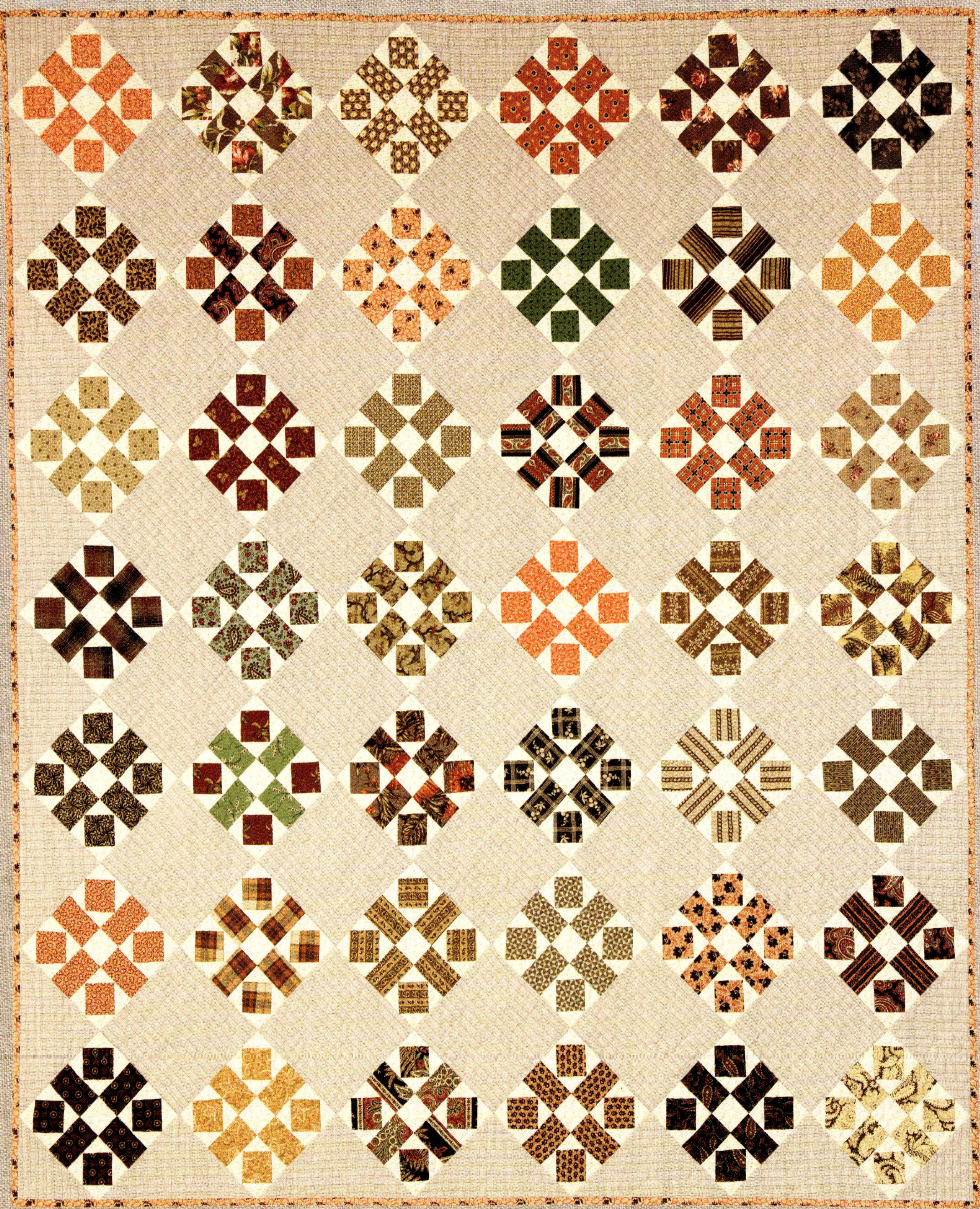

A simple pattern takes on new dimension when set in an elegant linen-like backdrop. Here, a Japanese woven taupe gives each block a quiet applause. Use the alternating empty squares to practice your quilting or embellishment techniques.

SCRAPS ON PARADE

Finished quilt size: 55⅝" x 64⅞".

Fabric Requirements

Blocks: 42-10" squares in a variety of colors

Light: 1⅓ yards

Background: 2 yards

Backing: 3½ yards

Binding: ⅔ yard

Fabric Cutting

Blocks:
From EACH of the 42-10" squares, cut:
4-2¼" squares
4-3" x 2" rectangles

Light:
18-2⅛" x width of fabric strips
From the strips, cut 336-2⅛" squares, cut in half once on the diagonal to make 672 half-square triangles
2 to 3-2" x width of fabric strips
From the strips, cut 42-2" squares

Background:
2-10½" x width of fabric strips
From the strips, cut 6-10½" squares, cut in half twice on the diagonal to make 24 quarter-square triangles (QST). You need 22.
5-7" x width of fabric strips
From the strips, cut 30-7" squares
2-5½" squares, cut once on the diagonal to make 4 half-square triangles (HST)

Binding:
7-2½" x width of fabric strips

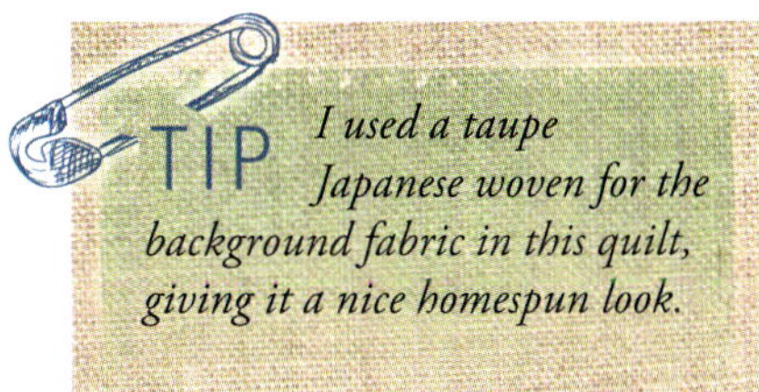

Use a ¼" seam allowance. Press in the direction of the arrows.

1 **Blocks:**

(A) Sew a 2⅛" half square triangle to each side of a 2¼" dark square. Repeat to make 168 units.

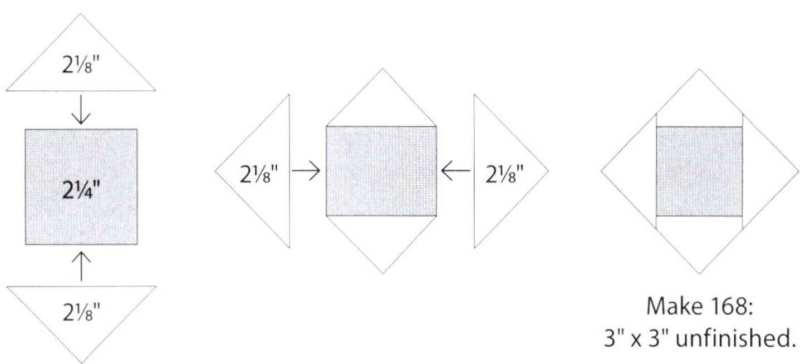

Make 168:
3" x 3" unfinished.

(B) Arrange and sew 4 units, 4-3" x 2" dark rectangles, and 1-2" light square in 3 rows as shown. Join the rows to make 1 block.

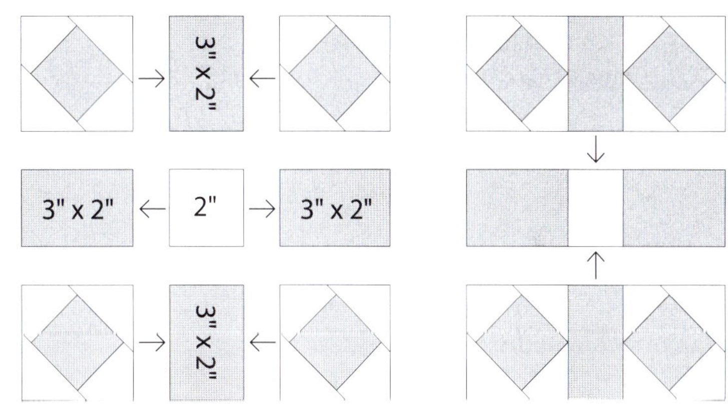

(C) Once block is completed, press and trim to 7" x 7" unfinished size to prepare for quilt assembly. Repeat to make 42 blocks.

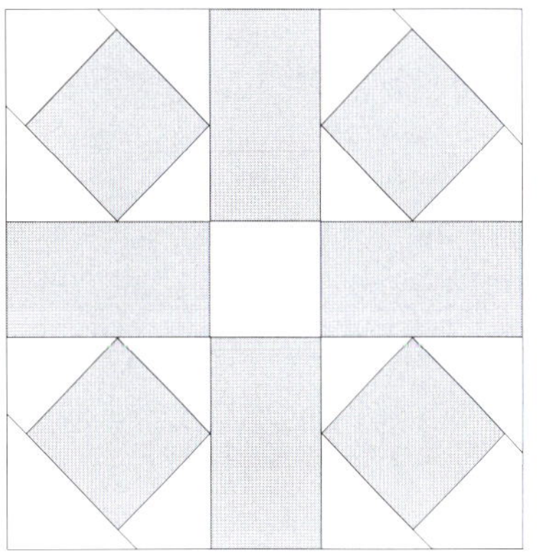

Make 42 blocks:
7" x 7" unfinished.

2 Assemble the 42 blocks, 30-7" background squares, 22 quarter-square triangles (QST), and 4 half-square triangles (HST) in rows as shown. Press seam allowance toward the blocks. Join the rows.

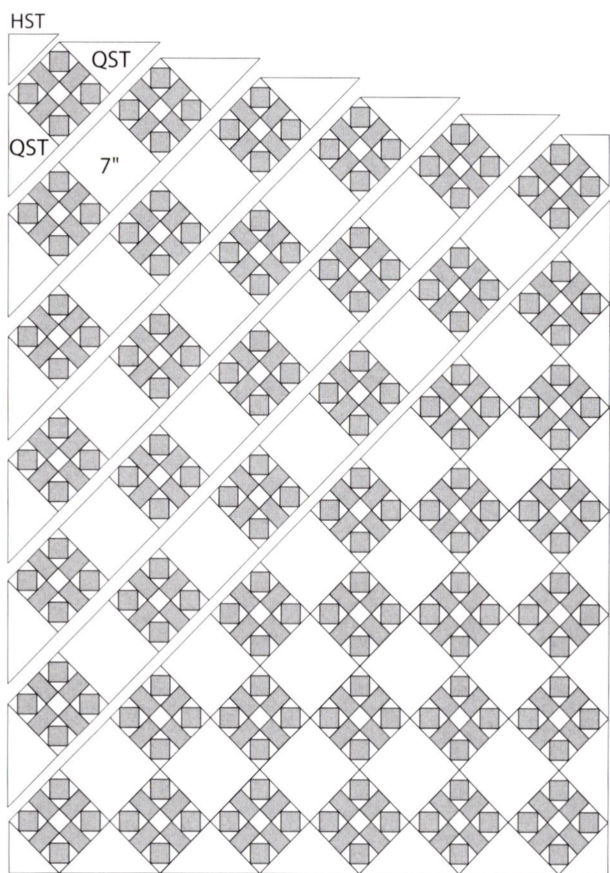

Once quilt top is completed, press to prepare for quilting.

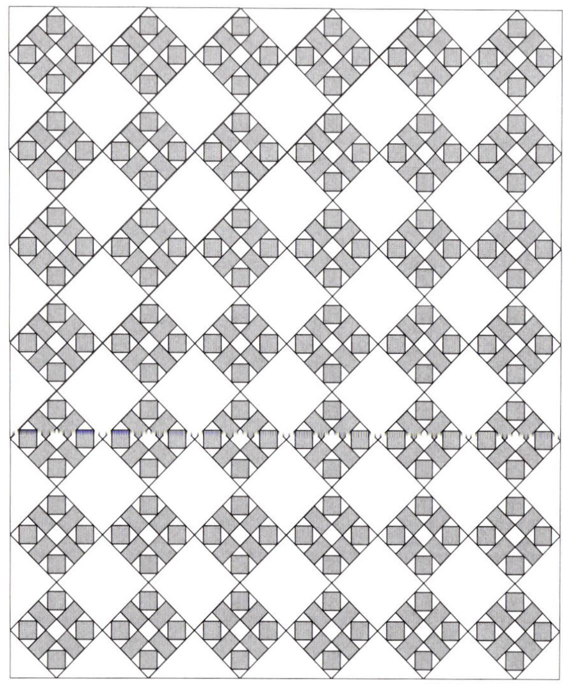

Unfinished quilt top is 55⅝" x 64⅞".

3 **Quilting:**

1. Layer quilt in the following order:
   a) Quilt back, right side down, 60" x 70".
   b) Batting 60" x 70" (I prefer Hobbs for best results.)
   c) Quilt top, right side up, 55⅝" x 64⅞".
2. Baste layers together.
3. Quilt by hand or machine. I chose stitch-in-the-ditch around each block piece and then added a feather wreath to each of the background squares.

4 **Binding:**

Refer to My Sewing Basket on page 48 for binding directions.

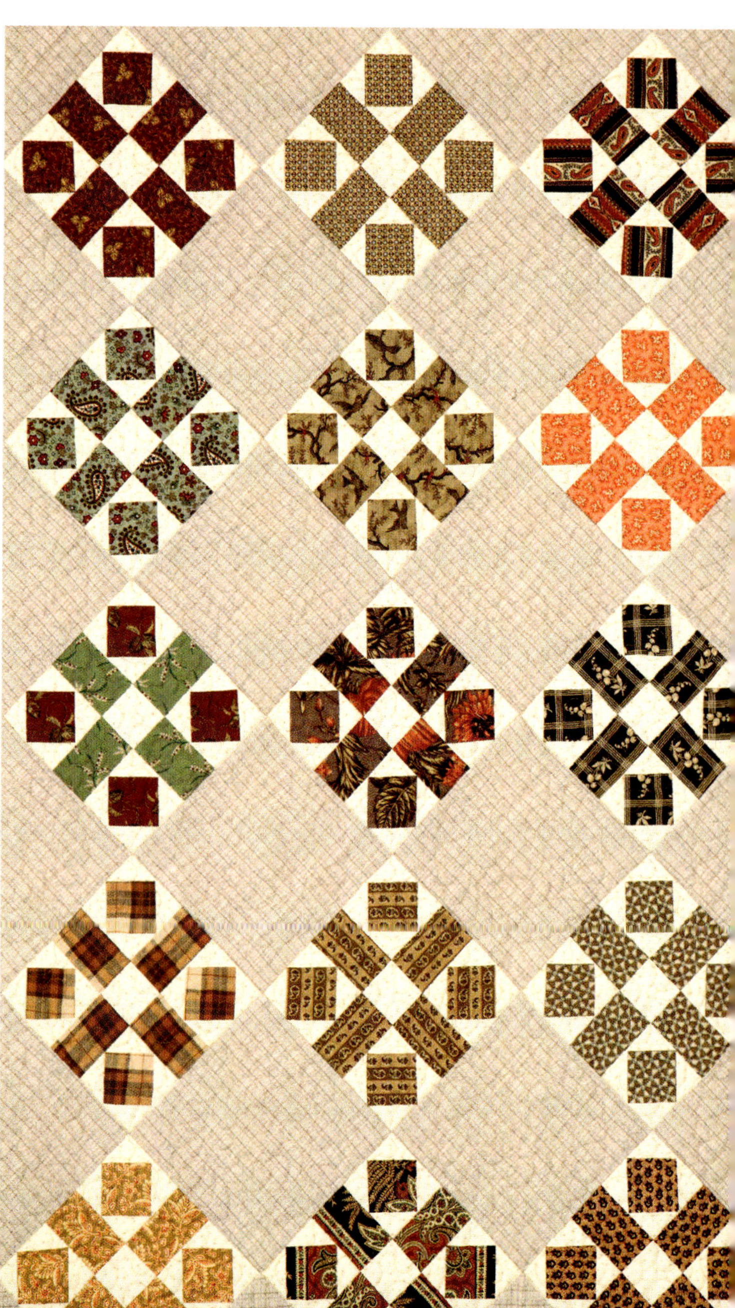

SUNRISE SCRAPS

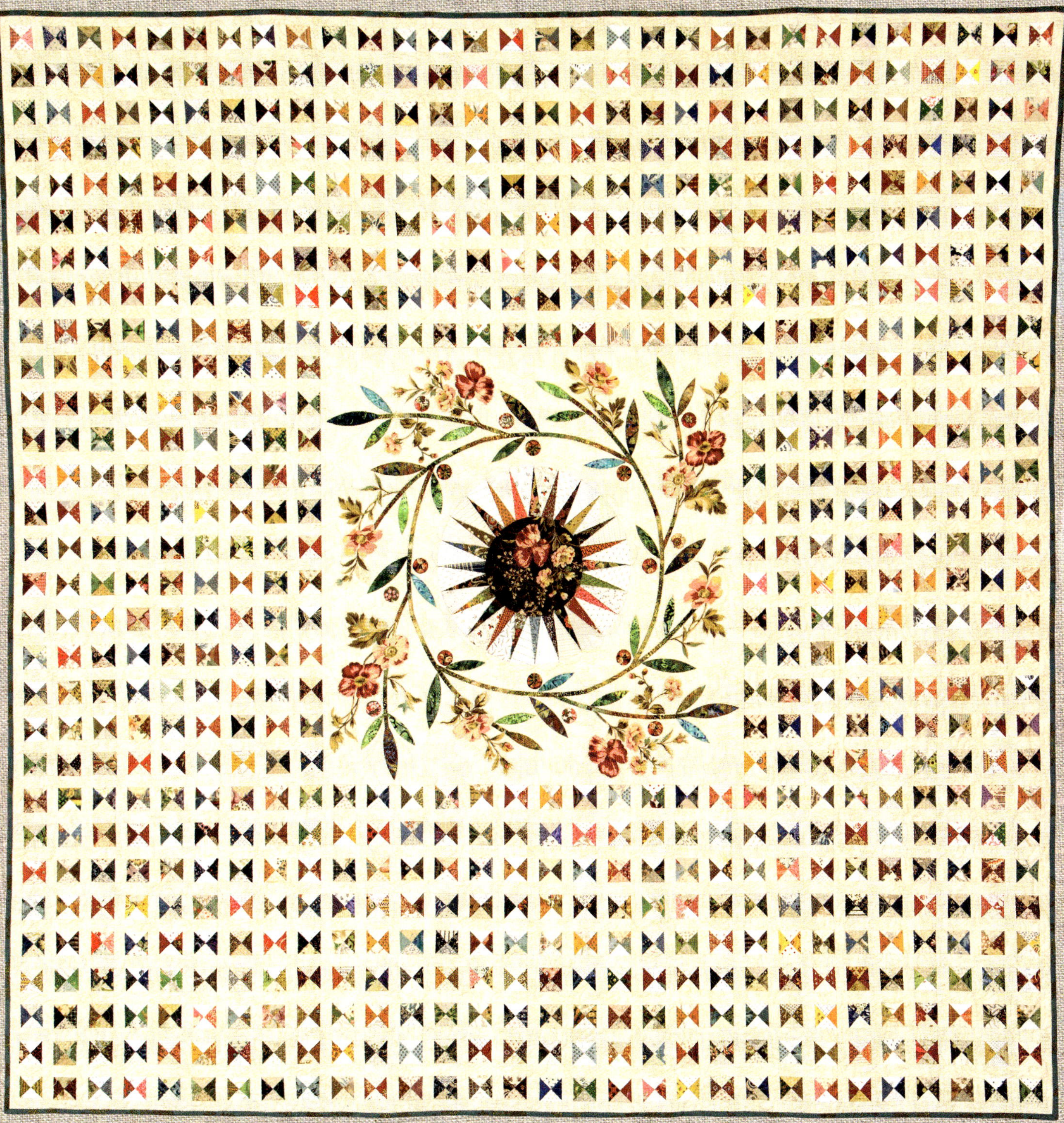

The repetitive process of sewing thousands of little triangles is both meditative and restorative. Tuck some pieces into your bag for an inconspicuous portable project. All the pieces come together in a Broken Dish backdrop with a burst of light and life at the center. Paper piecing, appliqué, and traditional sewing make this quilt an adventure worth taking.

SUNRISE SCRAPS

Finished quilt size: 68¾" x 68¾".

Fabric Requirements

Blocks:
42-10" x 10" squares from dark fabric
42-10" x 10" squares from light fabric

Glow:
24-1½" x 4" rectangles from a variety of dark fabric
24-2¼" x 4" rectangles from a variety of light fabric
1-6¾" x 6¾" square from brown fabric for center

Background:
4¼ yards light fabric for background

Appliqué:
Fat quarter brown fabric
4-9" x 9" squares from a variety of green fabric
½ yard big floral print for broderie appliqué

Backing:
4½ yards fabric

Binding:
⅔ yard blue fabric

Fabric Cutting

Blocks:

From EACH of the 42 dark 10" squares, cut:
9-2¾" square, cut in half twice on the diagonal to make 36 quarter-square triangles (QST). You need 1512 QSTs. (1512 / 4 = 378 squares)

From EACH of the 42 light 10" squares, cut:
9-2¾" square, cut in half twice on the diagonal to make 36 quarter-square triangles (QST). You need 1512 QSTs. (1512 / 4 = 378 squares)

Background:
1-28¼" x 28¼" center square
88-1¼" x width of fabric strips and sub-cut:
- 26 strips 504-1¼" x 2" rectangles
- 15 strips 75-1¼" x 7¼" rectangles
- 43 strips 253-1¼" x 6½" rectangles
- Sew 4 strips into sets of 2 and sub-cut:
  - 1 set to 1¼" x 68¾"
  - 1 set to 1¼" x 68"

Binding:
7-2½" x width of fabric strips

Appliqué: Templates on page 50

Template	Description	Cut	Color
D	Leaf	24	Green
E	Leaf	12	Green
G	Stem	12	Brown
L	Circle	16	Red

Use a ¼" seam allowance. Press in the direction of the arrows.

1 Block A:

(A) Join 2 dark and 2 light quarter-square triangles to make broken dish as shown. Make 756 broken dishes. Set aside 252 broken dishes. Add a 1¼" x 2" background rectangle to remaining 504 units.

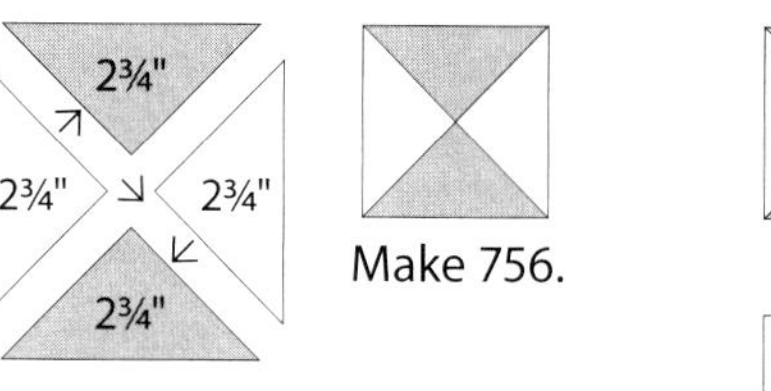

Make 756.

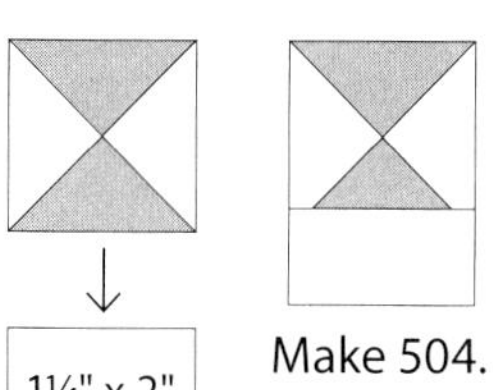

Make 504.

(B) Join 2 units and 1 broken dish in a column as shown. Make 252.

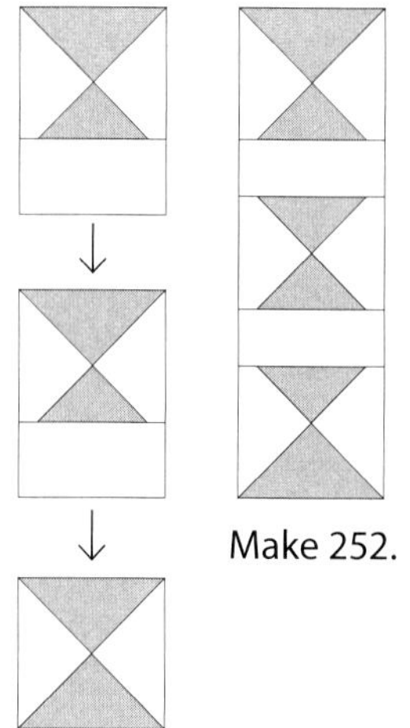
Make 252.

(C) Join 3 columns and 2-1¼" x 6½" background strips as shown. Repeat to make 84 blocks.

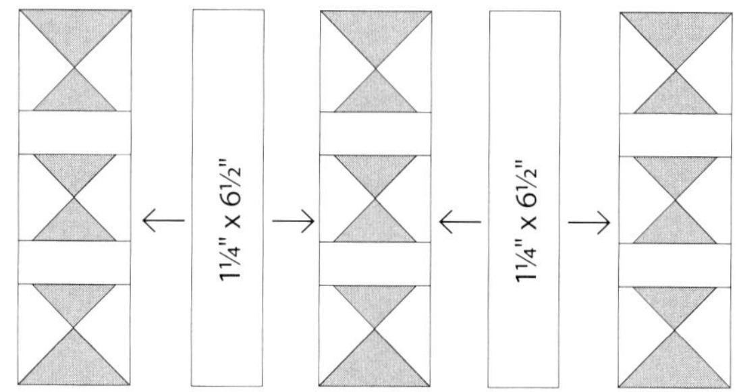

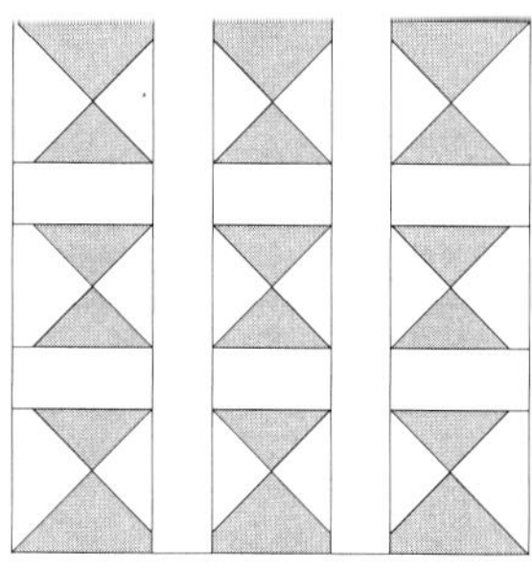
Make 84 Blocks:
6½" x 6½" unfinished.

(D) Prepare blocks for quilt top assembly by adding sashing to them as shown in diagrams below. Push seam allowance toward sashing: 4 - Block A: add 1¼" x 6½ sashing to side of block.
6 - Block B: add 1¼" x 6½ sashing to bottom of block.
74 - Block C: add 1¼" x 6½ sashing to bottom of block and 1¼" x 7¼" sashing to side of block

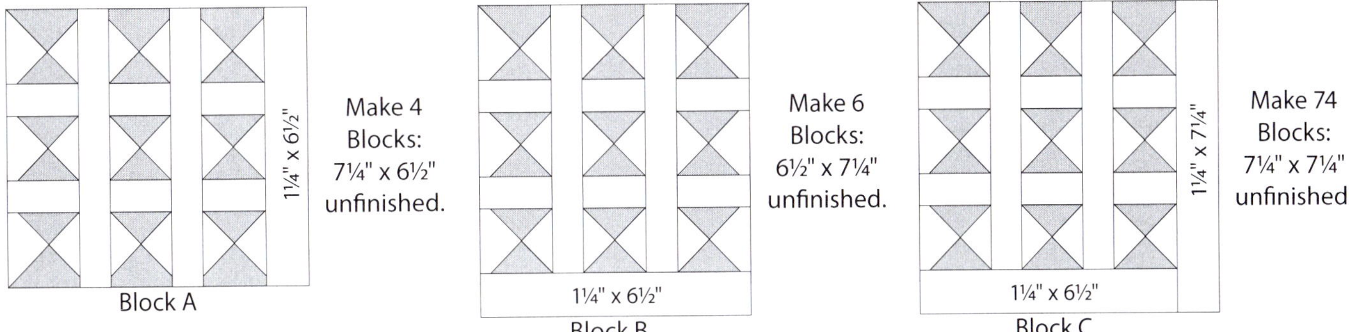

2 Paper Piecing:

Use 24 light rectangles, 24 dark rectangles and 3 copies of the arch on page 90. Compare your copies to the original in the book to check for accuracy. Place fabric on wrong side of paper, and stitch on the line on the opposite side. Use a shorter length stitch to ease paper removal later. After sewing, flip the fabric open, align your next piece on top of the previously sewn piece right sides together, and stitch. Check to ensure your fabric is covering the desired area, and trim away from the seam allowance if needed. Repeat steps, alternating light and dark fabric rectangles until all pieces are sewn in place. Once 3 Arches are completed, sew them together to create the center "glow."

3 Appliqué:

Choose your appliqué method from My Sewing Basket on page 48, and appliqué the glow to the center of the 28¼" background square. Finish glow by appliquéing circle (template on page 91) over the center and a wreath of branches and flowers around it as shown below (see appliqué templates on page 50). Broderie appliqué directions can be found on page 49.

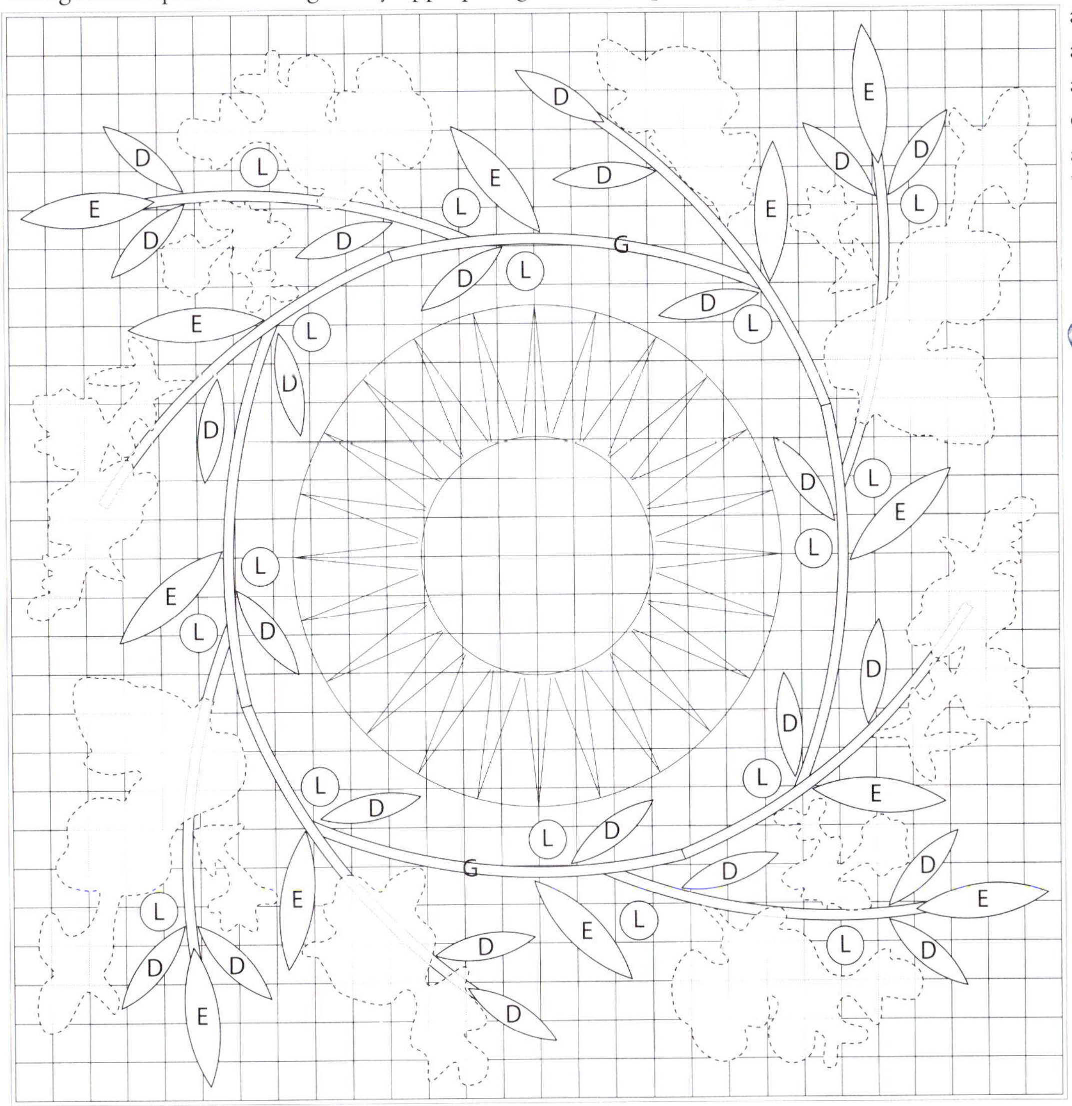

TIP *Place your traditional appliqué shapes first, and then fill the open areas with beautiful flower cutouts from your favorite large print fabric. The flowers can be any color that you would like; I chose red to create a warm "Sunrise" look to the quilt.*

Layout is 20% of actual size, each square represents 1".

4 Assembly:

- Arrange and sew 4 Blocks A and 1-1¼" x 6½" rectangle to create Section A.
- Arrange and sew 6 Block B to create Section B.
- Arrange and sew 4 Block C and 1-1¼" x 7¼" rectangle to create Section C.
- Arrange and sew 6 Block C to create Section D.
- Arrange and sew 4 rows of 10 Block C. Sew 2 rows together to create Section E for top and bottom of quilt.
- Arrange and sew 12 rows of 2 Block C. Sew 6 rows together to create Section F for left and right side of quilt.
- Assemble quilt top in the following order: Sew Sections A, C, B, and D to center square. Sew Sections F to each side of the quilt. Finally, sew Sections E to the top and bottom of the quilt. Remember to press your seam allowance in the direction of the arrows.

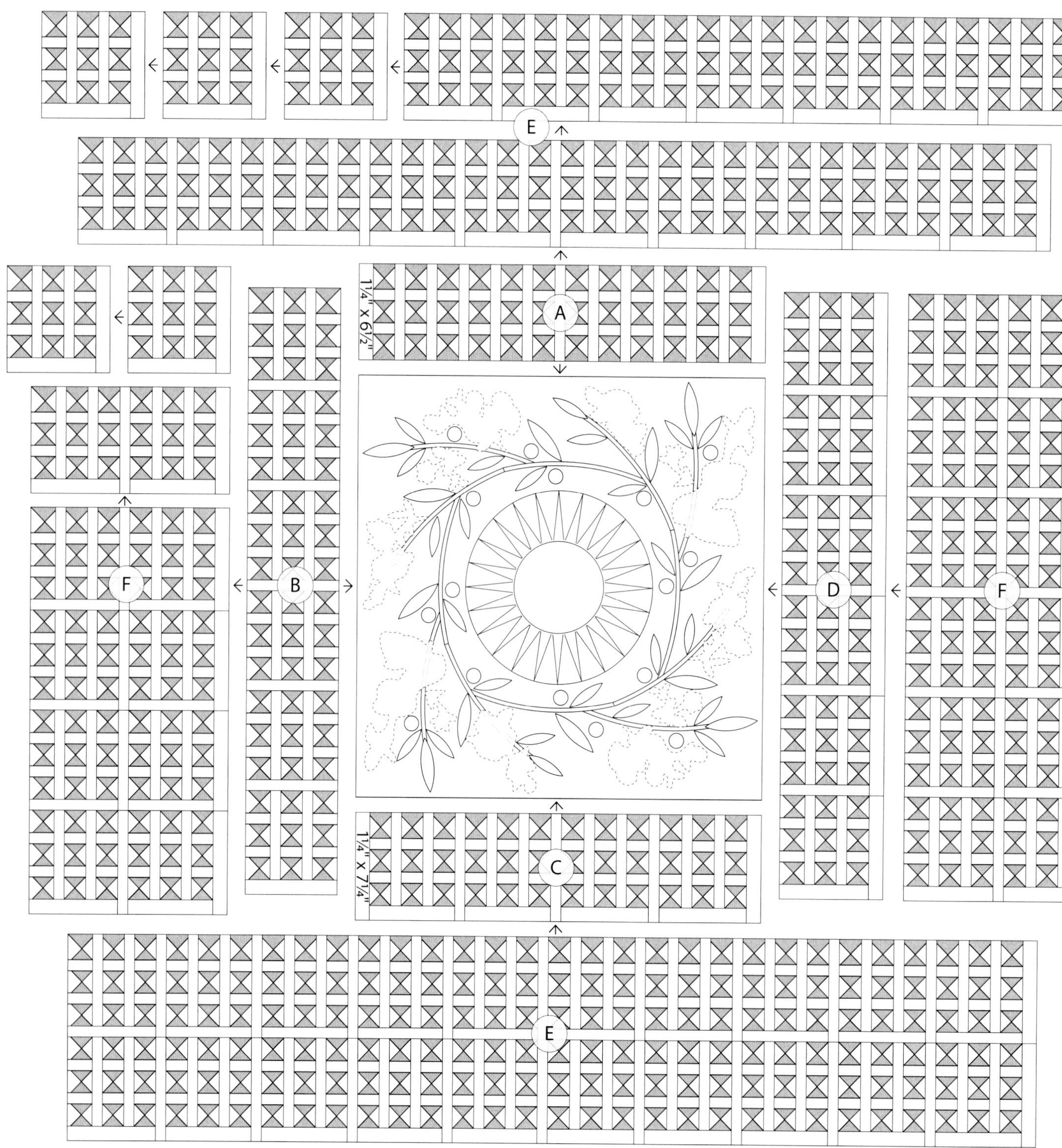

5 Borders:

Add a 1¼" x 68" background strip to the left side of the quilt. Add a 1¼" x 68¾" background strip to the top of the quilt.

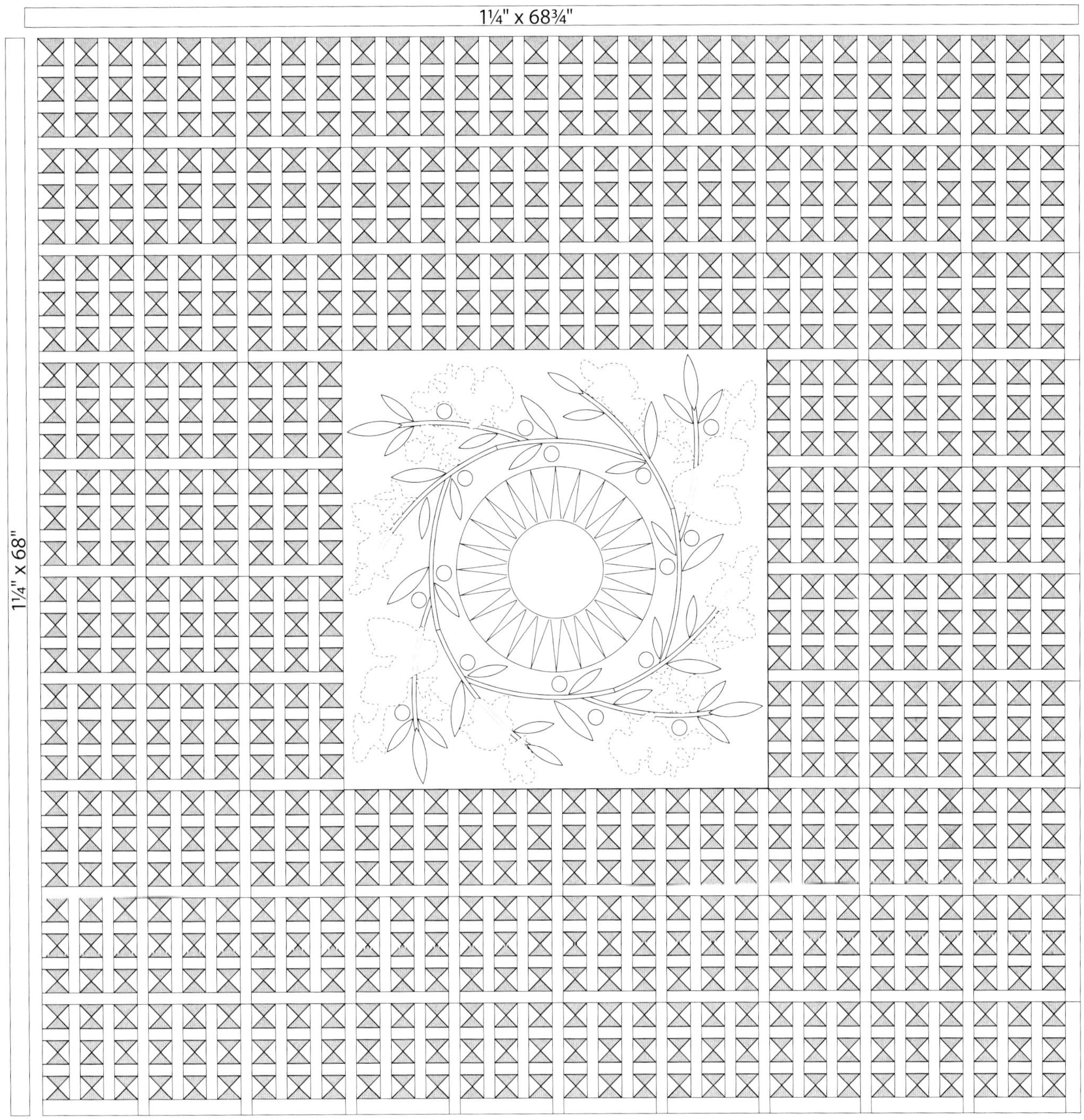

Unfinished quilt size: 68¾"x 68¾".

6 Quilting:

1. Layer quilt in the following order:
   a) Quilt back, right side down, 73" x 73".
   b) Batting 73" x 73" (I prefer Hobbs for best results.)
   c) Quilt top, right side up, 68¾" x 68¾".
2. Baste layers together.
3. Quilt by hand or machine. This quilt was custom-quilted on a long-arm quilting machine with stitch-in-the-ditch around the glow, crackling in the appliqué background, and meandered feather on the remainder of the quilt.

7 Binding:

Refer to My Sewing Basket on page 48 for binding instructions.

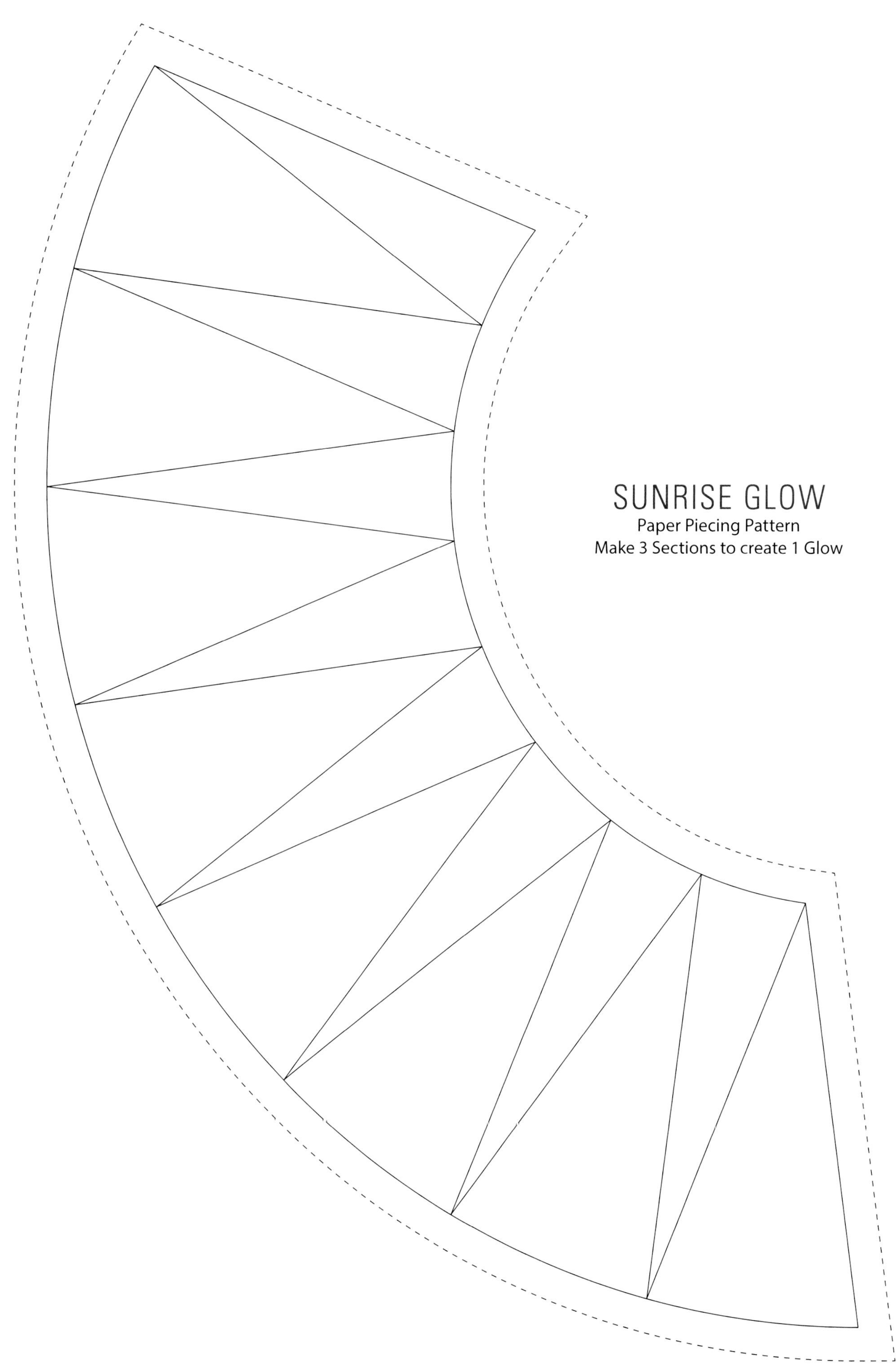
SUNRISE GLOW
Paper Piecing Pattern
Make 3 Sections to create 1 Glow

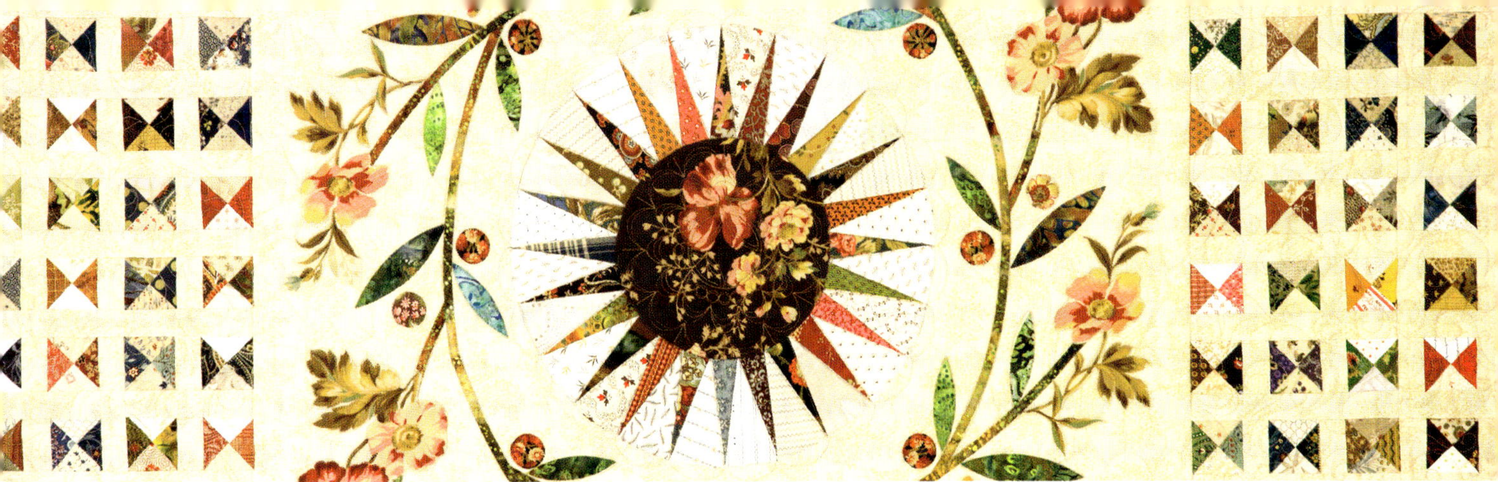

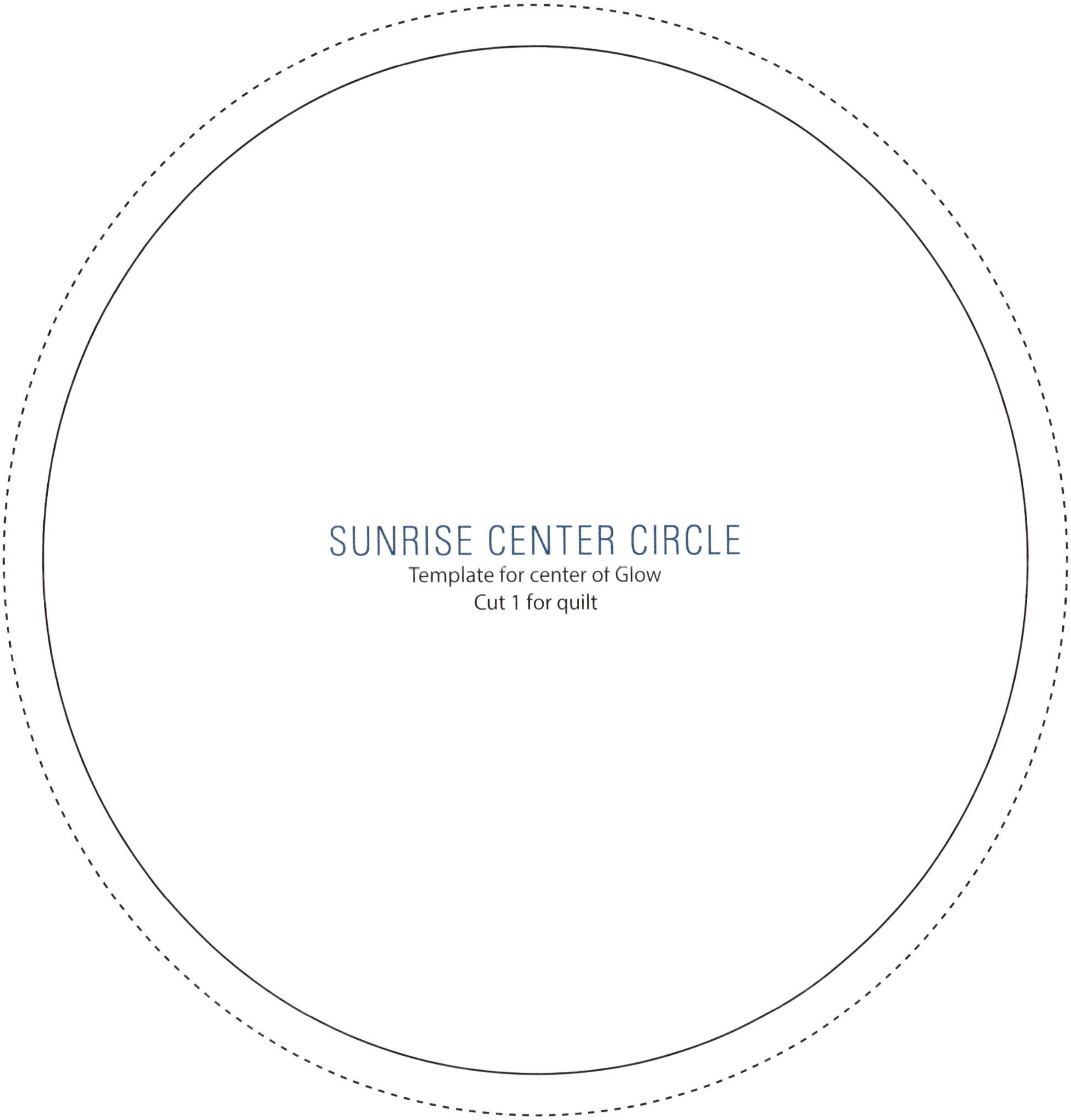

SUNRISE CENTER CIRCLE

Template for center of Glow

Cut 1 for quilt

PRAIRIE STITCHES

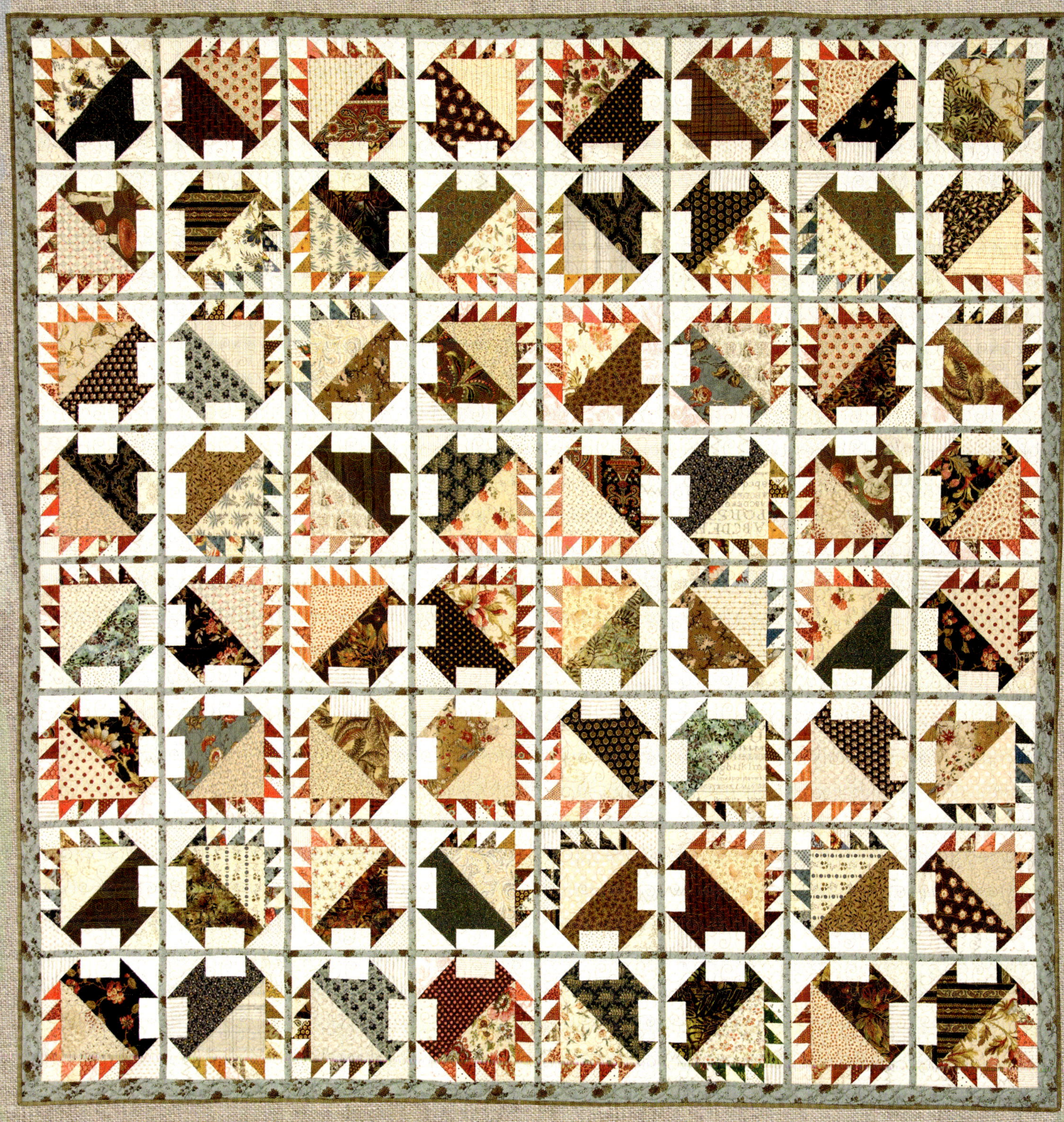

My friend Kim Nimtz of Prairie Stitches Quilt Shoppe encouraged me to design this pattern based on an antique quilt in her collection. A gathering of blocks from many hands, the pattern represents a close quilting community, fortitude, and friendship—all values that live on at Prairie Stitches. The original quilt was designed for each of its makers to personally sign and date.

PRAIRIE STITCHES

Finished quilt size: 80½" x 80½".

Fabric Requirements

Baskets:
Multi-color: 16 assorted fat eighths (9" x 21")
Medium: 16 assorted fat eighths
Brown: 16 assorted fat eighths
Light: 16 assorted fat quarters (18" x 21")
Sashing and Border: 1½ yards (blue)
Binding: ⅔ yard (brown)
Backing: 4⅔ yards (brown)

Fabric Cutting

Multi-color prints:
From EACH of the 16 fat eighths, cut:
1-5½" x 15" rectangle for using 1½" LBQ Triangle Paper
1-2⅜" x 21" strip
From the strip, cut 4-2⅜" squares, cut in half once on the diagonal to make 8 half-square triangles

Light prints:
From EACH of the 16 fat quarters, cut:
1-5½" x 15" rectangle for using 1½" LBQ Triangle Paper
6-3⅞" squares, cut in half once on the diagonal to make 12 half-square triangles
2-2" x 21" strips
From the strips, cut 8-2" x 3½" rectangles and 4-2" squares

Medium prints:
From EACH of the 16 fat eighths, cut:
2-6⅞" squares, cut in half once on the diagonal to make 4 half-square triangles

Brown prints:
From EACH of the 16 fat eighths, cut:
2-6⅞" squares, cut in half once on the diagonal to make 4 half-square triangles
4-2⅜" squares, cut in half once on the diagonal to make 8 half-square triangles

Sashing and Border (blue):
28-1" x width of fabric strips:
From 14 strips, cut 56-1" x 9½" rectangles
Sew 2 strips together. Repeat to make 7.
Trim these 7 long strips to 1" x 76"
8-2½" x width of fabric strips:
Sew 2 strips together. Repeat to make 4
Trim 2 long strips to 76"
Trim 2 long strips to 80½"

Binding (brown):
8-2½" x width of fabric strips

Use a ¼" seam allowance. Press in the direction of the arrows.

You will be making 16 sets of 4 matching baskets for a total of 64 baskets.

1 **Half-Square Triangle Units:**
(See page 95 for an alternative to using triangle paper.)

Cut one LBQ 1½" Triangle Exchange paper into two sections. You will need 16 sections. Set aside the 4 squares for another project.

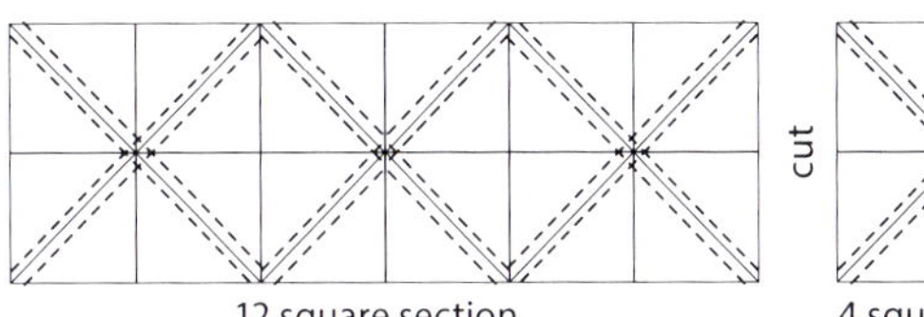

(A) Select one print and one background 5½" x 15" strip. Layer the print and background strip, right sides together, with the background print on the top. Press.

Following the LBQ Triangle Exchange paper directions, place the paper on top of the fabrics and pin. Sew the half-square triangle units using the dashed lines as guides. Remember to use a 50-wt thread and a smaller stitch length.

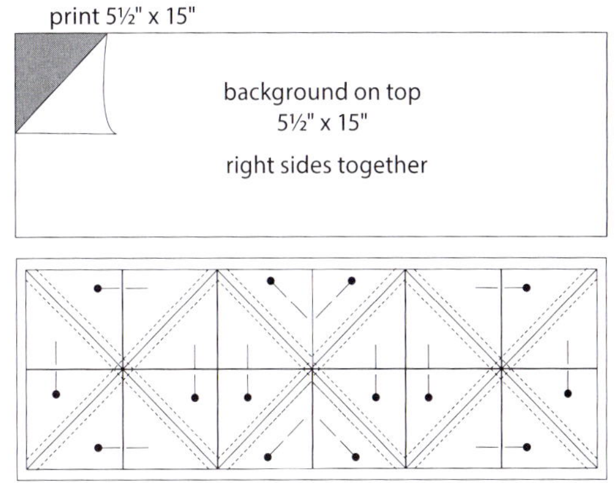

(B) Cut the triangles apart, using the solid lines as guides. *Do not remove the paper.*

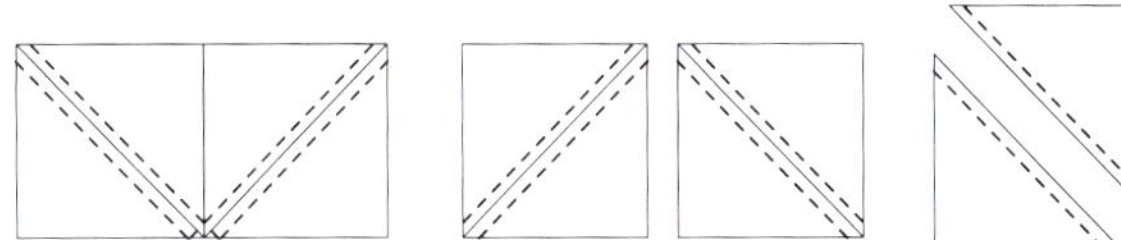

(C) Flip the triangle over so that the print is on the top. Press the half-square triangle unit open. Trim the "dog ears" and remove the paper. One *trimmed* LBQ 1½" Triangle Exchange paper makes 24 half-square triangle units.

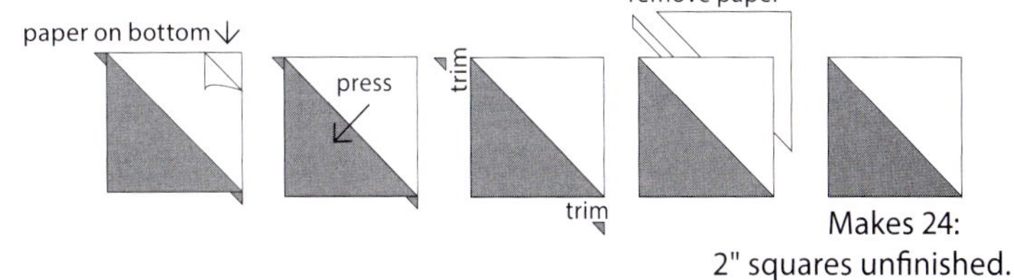

Repeat to make 16 matching sets of 24 half-square triangle units.

2 Baskets:

To make 4 matching baskets, select:
Note: Use the multi-color and light prints that match the half-square triangles units.

Multi-color & light half-square triangle units:	
	24 matching units
Multi-color:	8-2⅜" half-square triangles
Light:	4-2" squares
	8-2" x 3½" rectangles
	12-3⅞" half-square triangles
Medium:	4-6⅞" half-square triangle
Brown:	4-6⅞" half-square triangle
	8-2⅜" half-square triangles

(A) Sew 1-6⅞" Brown and 1-6⅞" Medium triangle together.

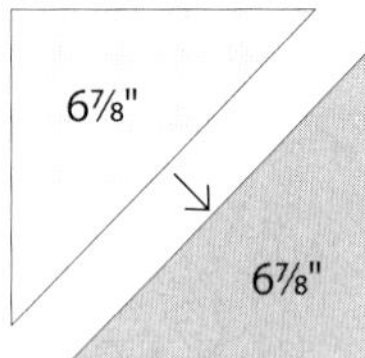

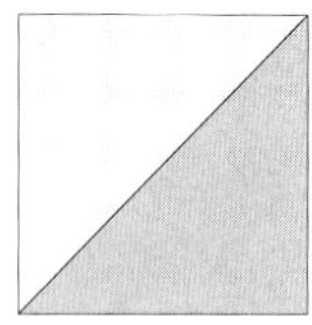

Make 4:
6½" x 6½"
unfinished.

(B) Basket handle: Join 1-2" light square, 3 half-square triangle units and 1-2⅜" multi-color half-square triangle as shown. Make 4.

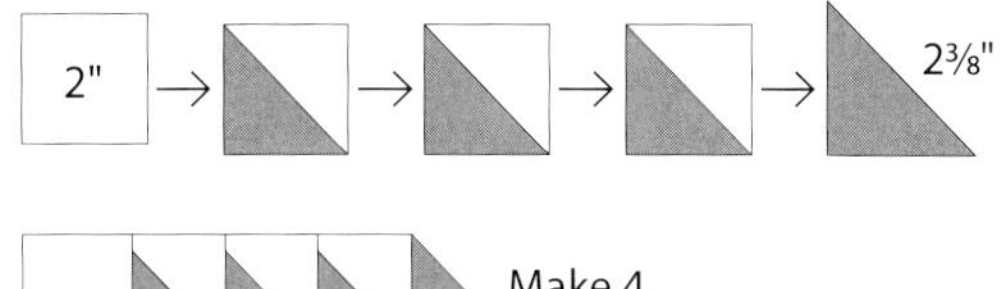

Make 4.

Join 3 half-square triangle units and 1-2⅜" multi-color half-square triangle as shown. Make 4.

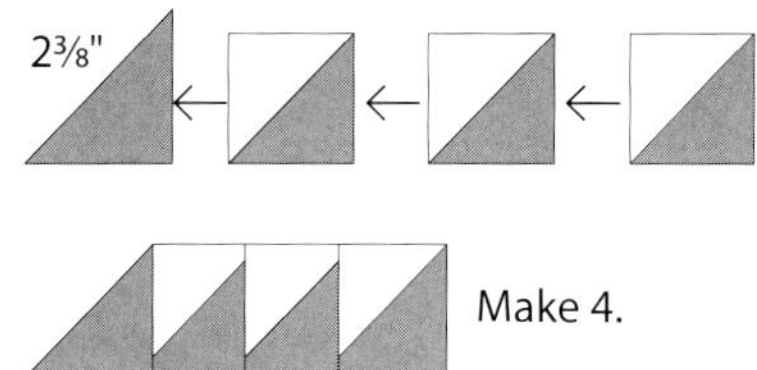

Make 4.

Add the handles to the basket. Make 4.

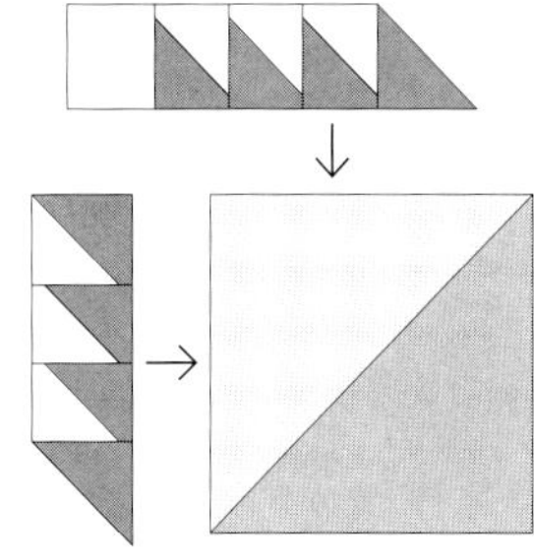

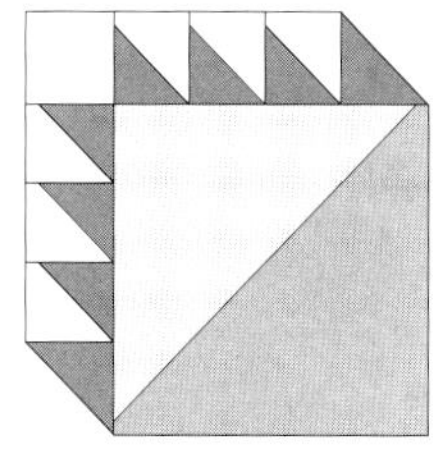

Make 4:
6½" x 6½" unfinished.

(C) Basket feet: Join 1-2" x 3½" Light rectangle and 2-2⅜" Brown half-square triangles as shown. Make 8.

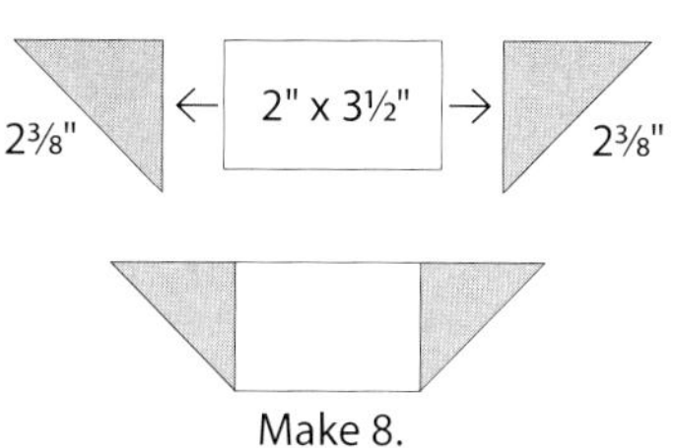

Make 8.

(D) Assemble the baskets as shown. Make 4 baskets. Repeat to make a total of 64 baskets.

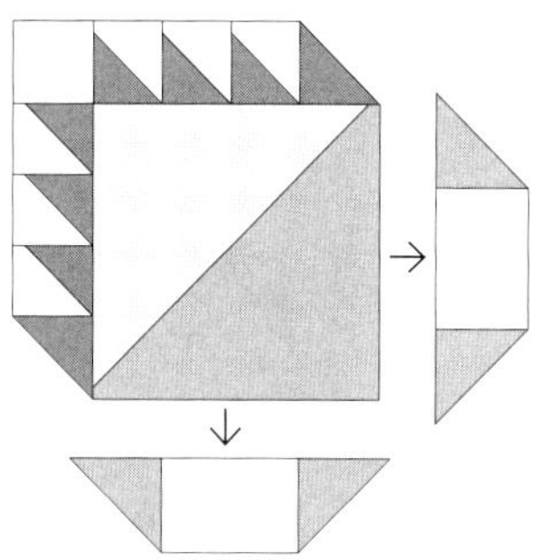

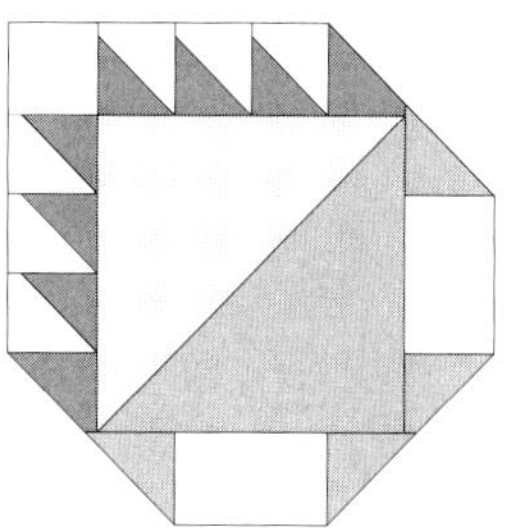

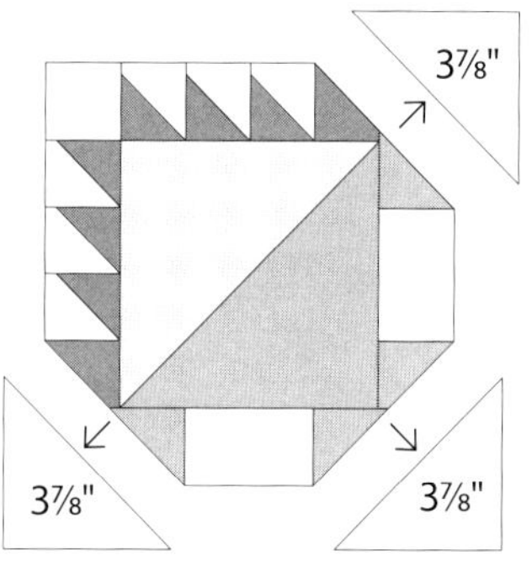

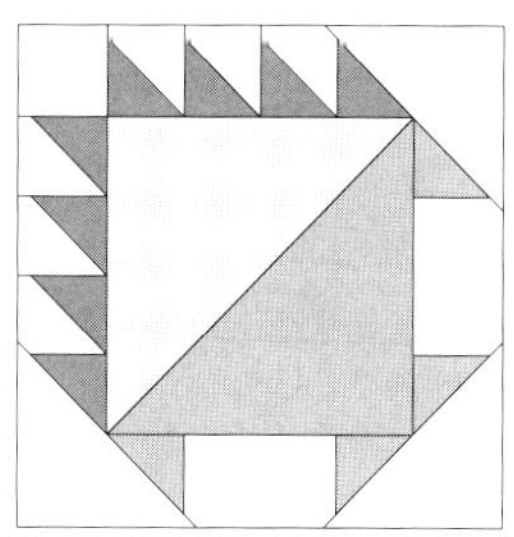

Make 64 total:
9½" x 9½" unfinished.

3 **Assemble Quilt Center:** Arrange 8 baskets and 7-1" x 9½" sashing strips as shown to make row A; sew together. Make 8 total. Join rows A and 7-1" x 76" strips together as shown.

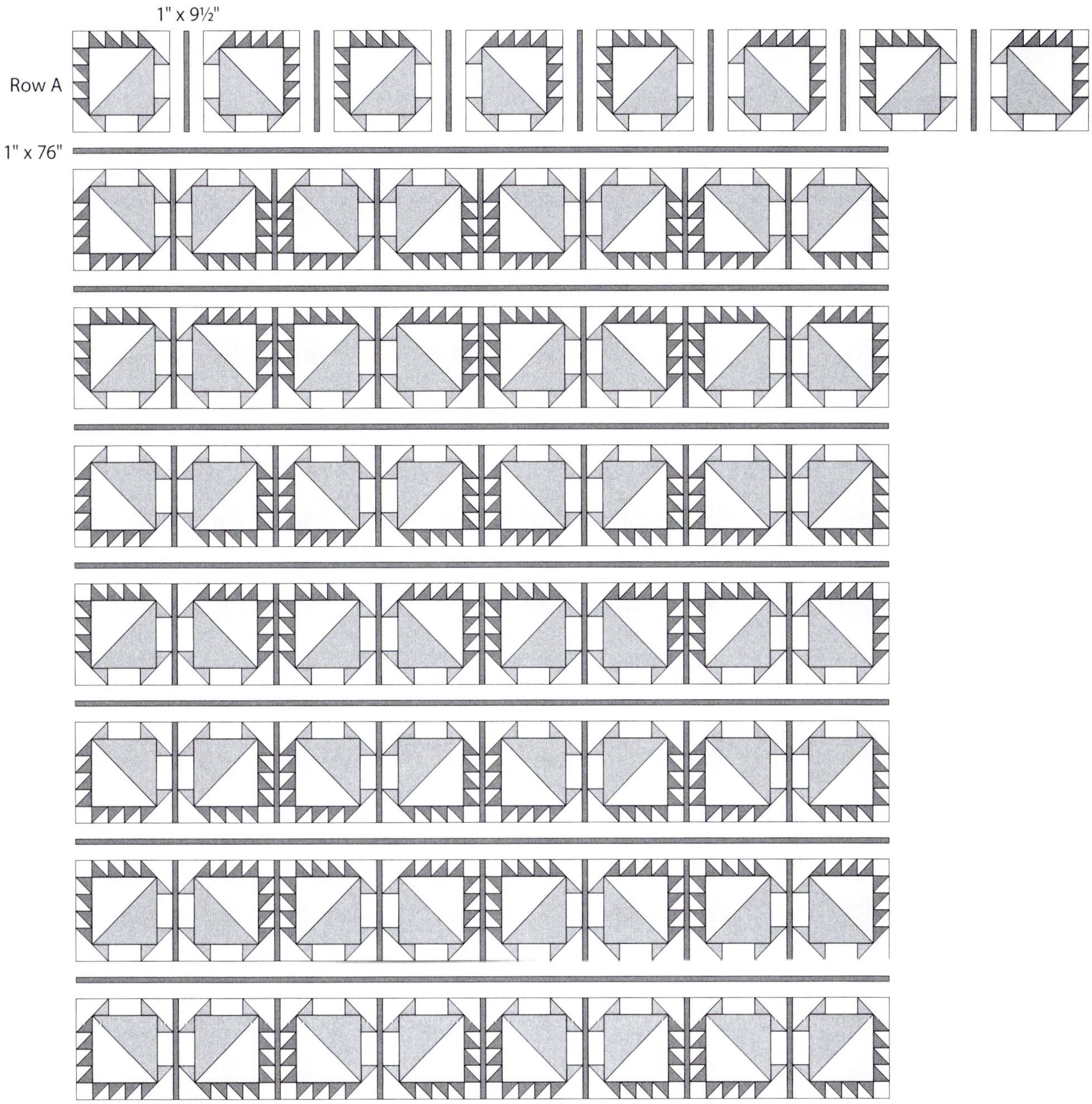

1" x 9½"

Row A

1" x 76"

Unfinished quilt top without border is 76" x 76".

Alternative to using the triangle paper:

1. Cut 1 light and 1 dark 2⅜" square. Cut the squares once on the diagonal.
2. Layer one dark and one light triangle right sides together. Sew together along diagonal using a ¼" seam allowance.
3. Press your triangles open and trim the bunny ears. Makes 2 half-square triangle units.

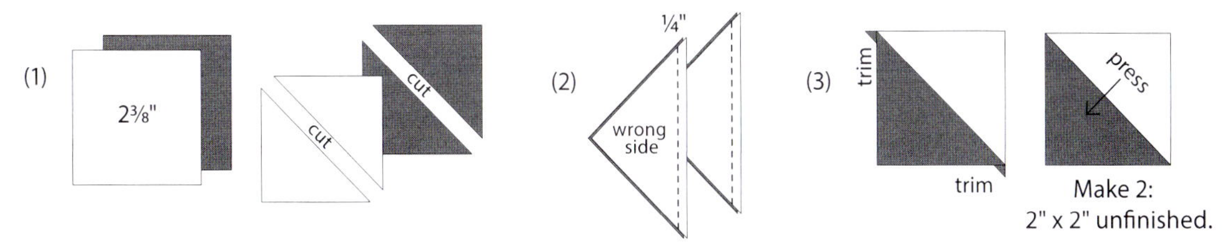

4 Add Quilt Border:

Sew the 2½" x 76" strips to the quilt sides. Add the 2½" x 80½" strips to the top and bottom as shown below. Push your seam allowances toward the border.

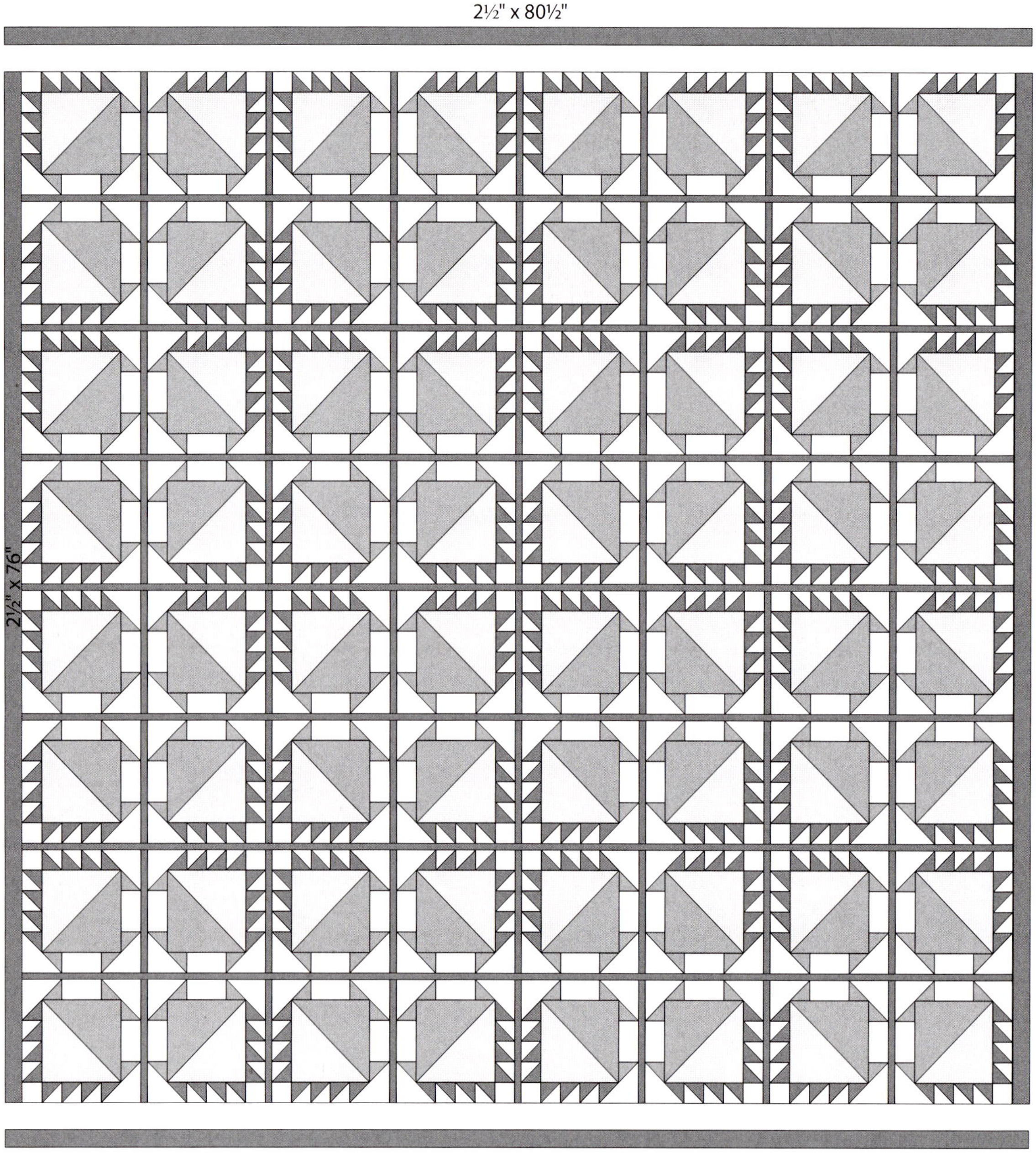

2½" x 80½"

2½" x 76"

Unfinished quilt top is 80½" x 80½".

5 Quilting:

1. Layer quilt in the following order:
   a) Quilt back, right side down, 84½" x 84½".
   b) Batting 84½" x 84½". (I prefer Hobbs for best results.)
   c) Quilt top, right side up, 80½" x 80½".
2. Baste layers together.
3. Quilt by hand or machine. I custom-quilted with stitch-in-the-ditch and a feather design for each block and used a simple braid for the border.

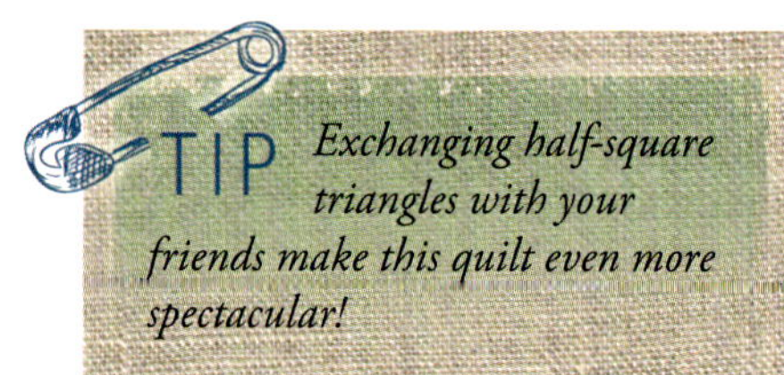

6 Binding:

Refer to My Sewing Basket on page 48 for binding directions.

SUPER-SIMPLE FOUR PATCH

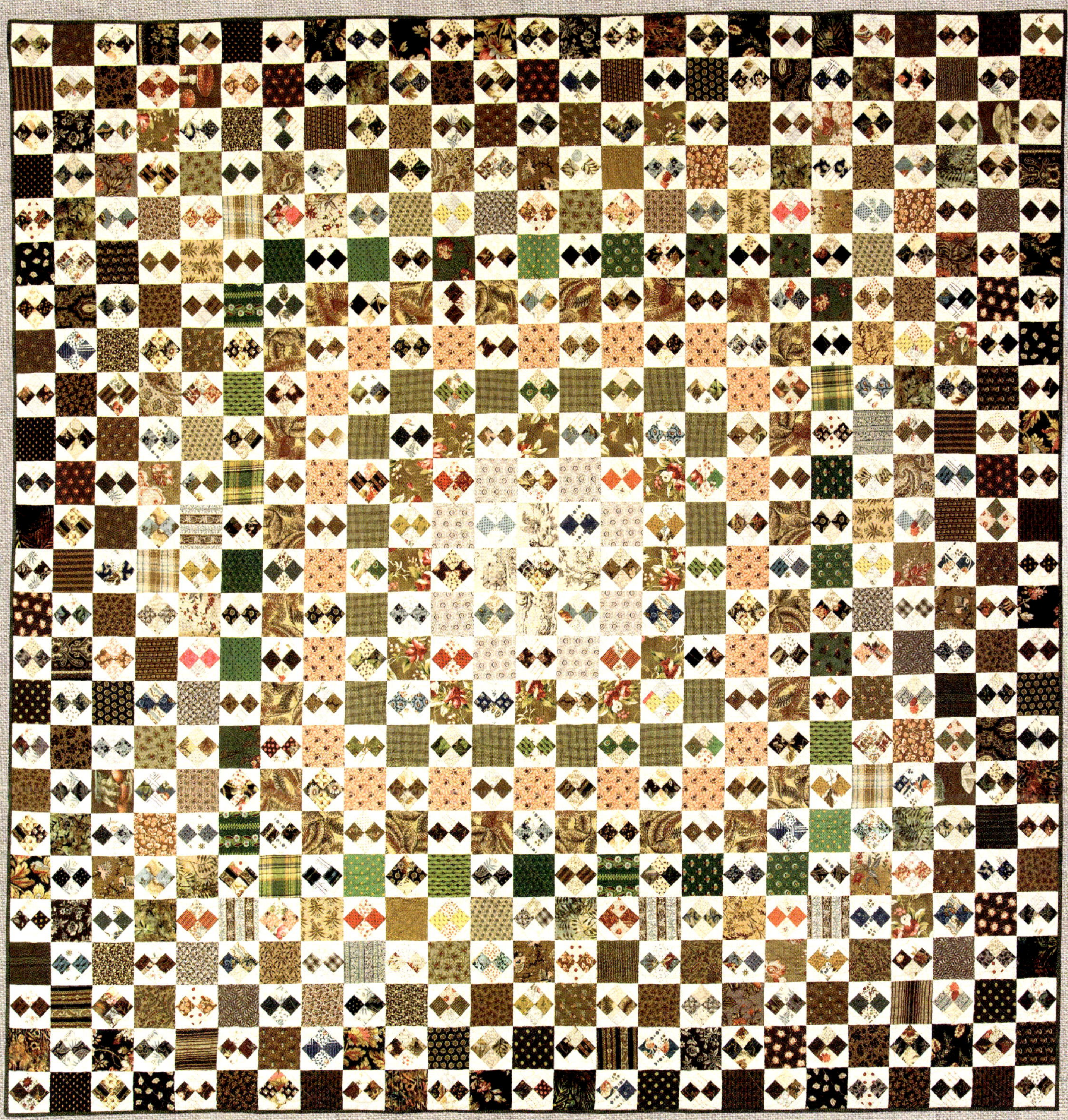

Make a dent in your scrappy basket with this big, easy beauty of four-patch blocks set in a light background. The design is based on one of my favorite antique quilts. All pieces are scrappy except the light setting triangles. Arrange the background squares to create a Trip Around the World.

SUPER-SIMPLE FOUR PATCH

Finished quilt size: 87½" x 87½".

Fabric Requirements

Four Patches:
14 fat eighths (9" x 21") multi-color dark
14 fat eighths (9" x 21") multi-color light
Setting Triangles: 3¼ yards light
Sashing Squares: 3⅞ yards total
4" x WOF light
4" x WOF medium
8" x WOF olive green
8" x WOF olive brown
8" x WOF pink
12" x WOF light brown
12" x WOF medium brown
20 strips 4" x WOF in variety of browns
Binding: ¾ yards
Backing: 2¾ yards of 108" wide fabric

Fabric Cutting

Four Patches:
From EACH of the 14 fat eighths multi-color dark, cut 4-1¾" x 21" strips (53 total)
From EACH of the 14 fat eighths multi-color light, cut 4-1¾" x 21" strips (53 total)

Setting Triangles:
42-2⅝" x width of fabric strips
From the strips, cut 626-2⅝" squares cut once on the diagonal to make 1,252 half-square triangles

Sashing Squares:
Cut 312-4" squares total:
4 light squares
8 medium squares
12 olive green squares
16 olive brown squares
20 pink squares
24 light brown squares
28 medium brown squares
200 dark brown squares

Binding: 9-2½" x width of fabric strips

Use a ¼" seam allowance. Press in the direction of the arrows.

1 **Pieced Blocks:**

(A) Sew 1-1¾" x 21" light and 1-1¾" x 21" dark strip together as shown. Make 53 strip sets. Cut 12-1¾" wide units from each strip set. Join 2 matching units to make one block. Make 313 blocks total.

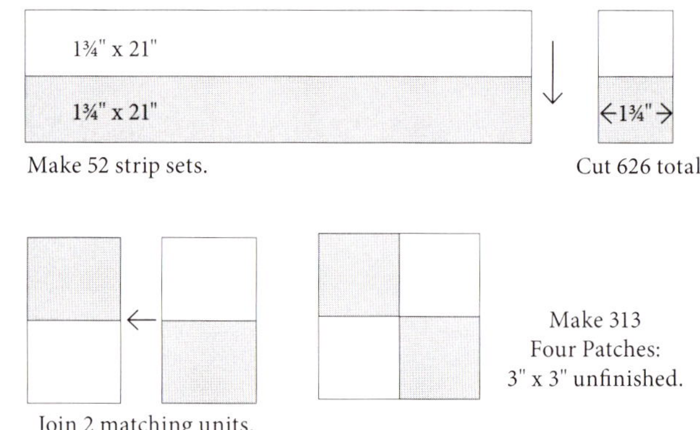

(B) Sew 4-2⅝" light triangles to each side of the block. Make 313 total.

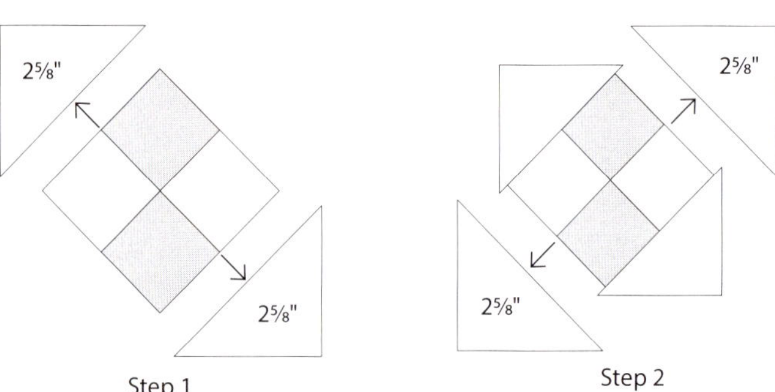

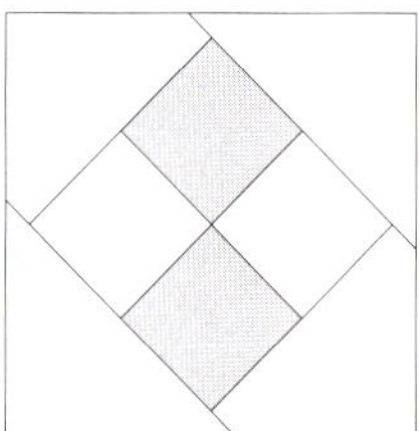

Make 313
Pieced Blocks:
4" x 4" unfinished.

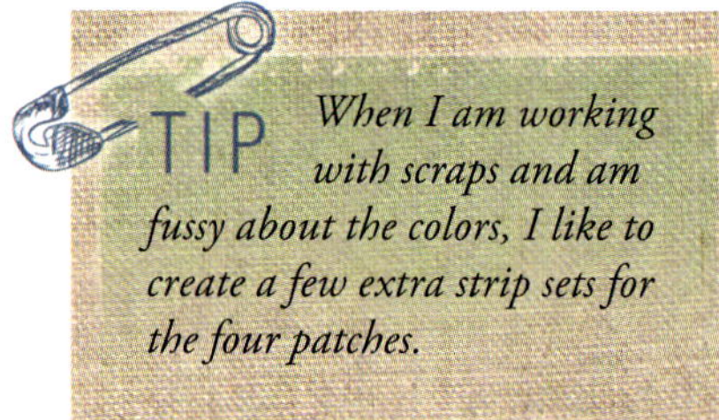

2 Assemble Quilt Center:

Sew the quilt center together in rounds. The solid blocks in each round are the same print.

Block Type	Round 1	Round 2	Round 3	Round 4	Round 5	Round 6	Round 7
Pieced blocks	5	8	12	16	20	24	28
Solid blocks	4	8	12	16	20	24	28

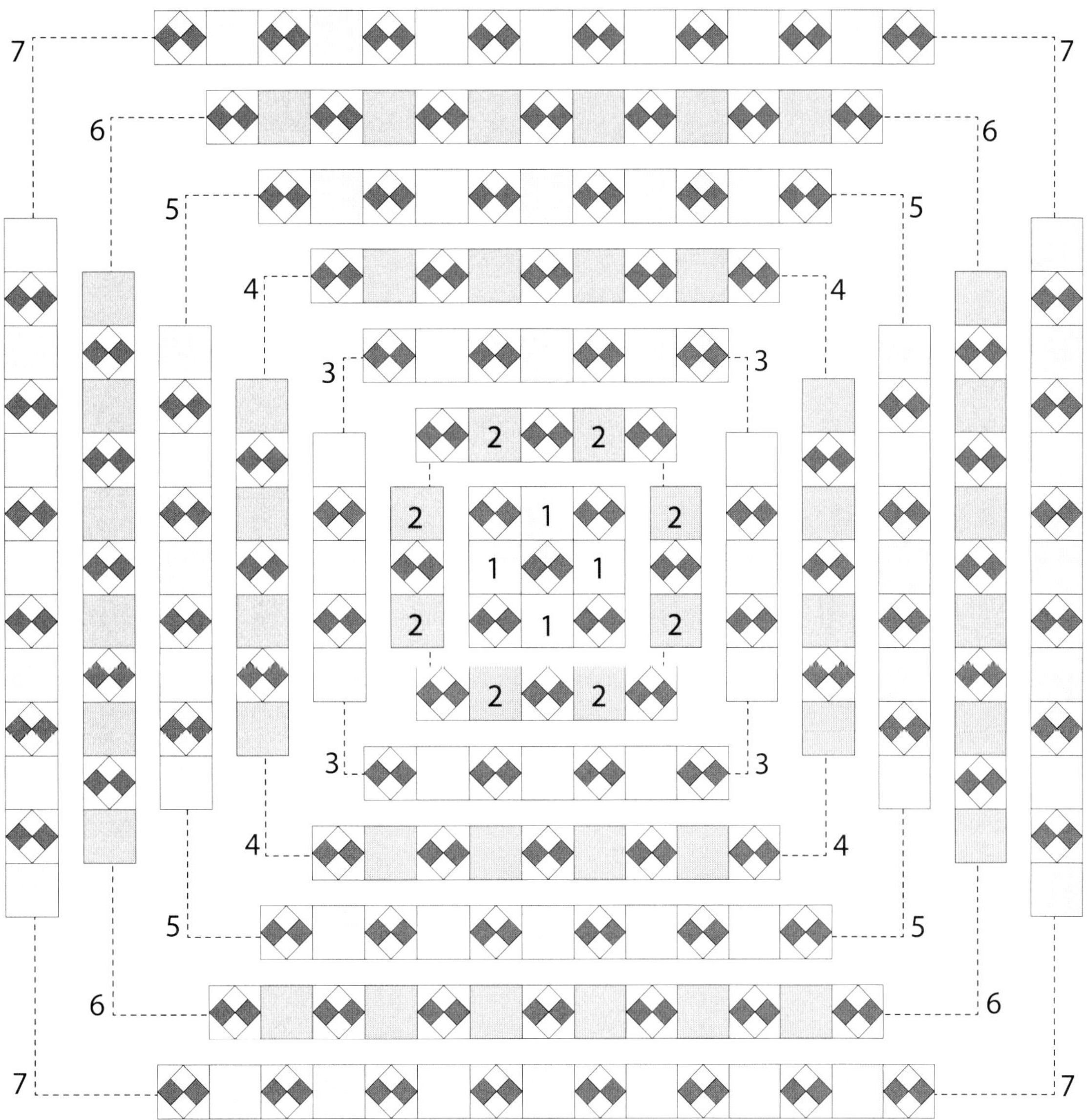

3 Sew the rows as shown in the chart. Sew the quilt center and rows together as shown.

Block Type	Row A Make 6.	Row B Make 4.	Row C Make 16.	Row D Make 14.
Pieced blocks per row	13	12	2	3
Solid blocks per row	12	13	3	2

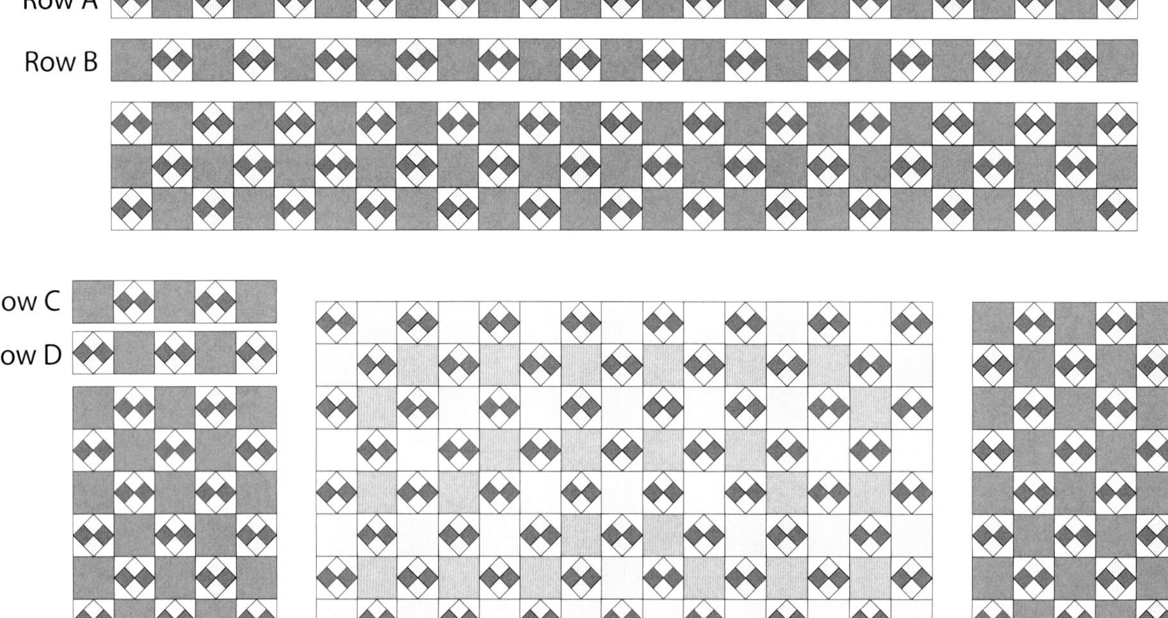

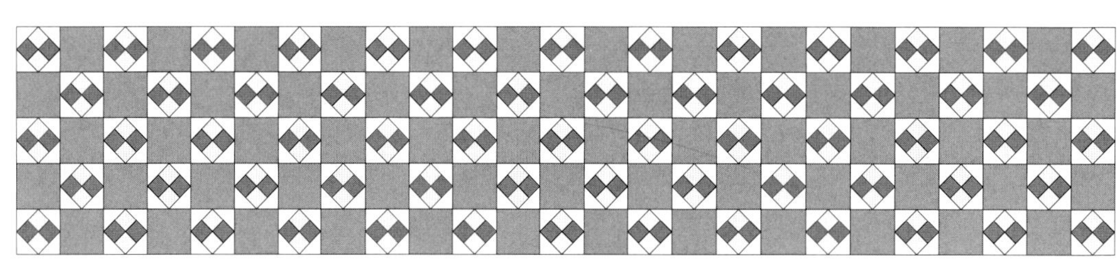

Unfinished quilt top is 87½" x 87½".

4 **Quilting:**

1. Layer quilt in the following order:
   a) Quilt back, right side down, 91½" x 91½".
   b) Batting 91½" x 91½". (I prefer Hobbs for best results.)
   c) Quilt top, right side up, 87½" x 87½".
2. Baste layers together.
3. Quilt by hand or machine. I chose a Baptist Fan overall quilting design for this quilt.

5 **Binding:**

Refer to My Sewing Basket on page 48 for binding instructions.

FLOWER GARDEN

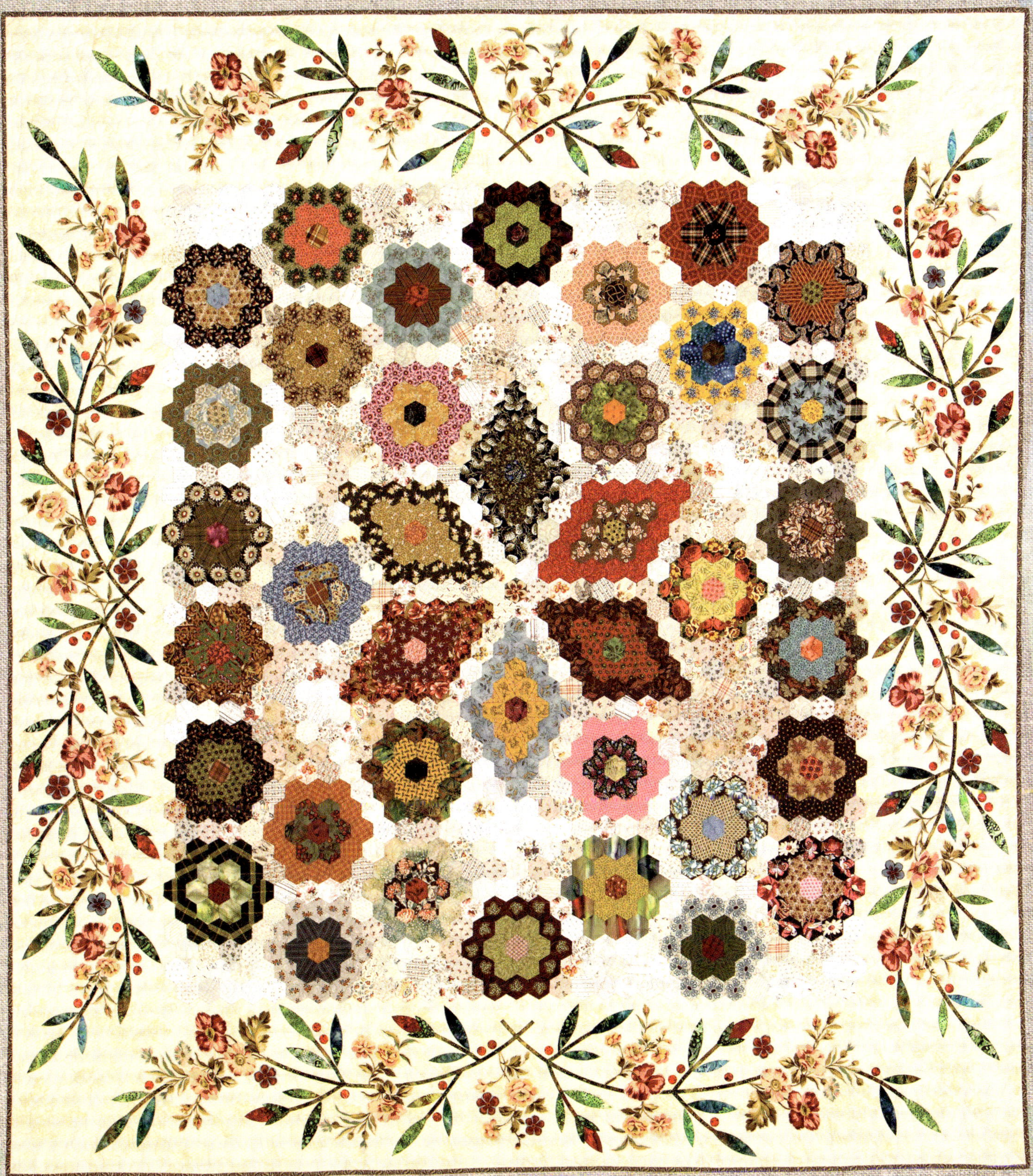

Plant yourself in quilter's Eden with this addicting hand-pieced, English piecing project that is all the more beautiful using all your little scraps. Grandmother's Garden is in full bloom, as an appliquéd or flower print border lines the fence. Try your hand at broderie appliqué to grow your hand-embellishing skills.

FLOWER GARDEN

Finished quilt size: 70½" x 76½".

Fabric Requirements

Hexagons:

13 packages ⅞" Hexagon Charms (LBQ-0453-C)
38 multi-color 2½" x width of fabric (WOF) strips
38 multi-color 2½" x 21" strips
34 light color 2½" x WOF strips

Appliqué:

8 brown fat eighths (9" x 21")
8 green fat eighths (9" x 21")
8 red squares 10"
2 yards of Large Print Floral for flower cutouts

Border: 4½ yards light fabric

Binding: ⅔ yard

Backing: 5 yards

Fabric Cutting

Flower Blocks:

From EACH of 32 multi-color 2½" x WOF strips, cut:
12-⅞" hexagons using Charm template for 2nd ring
1-⅞" hexagon using Charm template for center
From EACH of 32 multi-color 2½" x 21" strips, cut:
6-⅞" hexagons using Charm template for 1st ring

Diamond Blocks:

From EACH of 6 multi-color 2½" x WOF strips, cut:
16-⅞" hexagons using Charm template for 2nd ring
1-⅞" hexagon using Charm template for center
From EACH of 6 multi-color 2½" x 21" strips, cut:
8-⅞" hexagons using Charm template for 1st ring

Sashing:

From EACH of 34 light 2½" x WOF strips cut:
16-⅞" hexagons using Charm template for sashing

Border:

2-12½" x 76½" strip from border fabric
2-12½" x 70½" strip from border fabric

Binding and Quilt Center Hexagon:

7-2½" x width of fabric strips
1-⅞" hexagon using Charm template for center

Appliqué:

See appliqué cutting table on page 108 and appliqué templates on page 50.

Use a ¼" seam allowance. Press in the direction of the arrows.

1 **English Paper Piecing:**

English paper piecing is so much fun! I made my quilt all by hand during my free time or while I was traveling. You will need a few supplies to make this an enjoyable project.

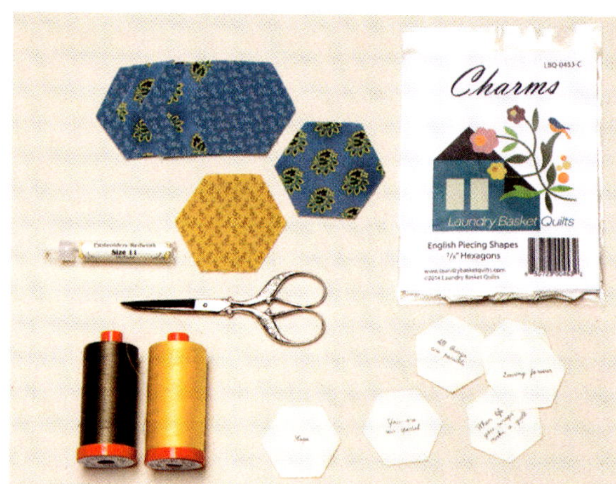

- **Fabric:** I cut my fabrics into hexagon shapes using the Charm Fabric Template on page 108. The template includes a ¼" seam allowance. Acrylic Charm cutting templates are available from Laundry Basket Quilts.
- **Thread:** 2 colors: One for hand stitching, Aurifil 2370 wt-50, and one for basting; I chose bright yellow.
- **Charm Hexagon ⅞" Shapes (LBQ-0453-C):** They are easy to use and full of delightful messages, or you can cut your own using the Hexagon Paper Template on page 108.
- **Needles:** I use hand embroidery needles size 11; I like the bigger eye, as it threads easier.
- **Small Scissors**

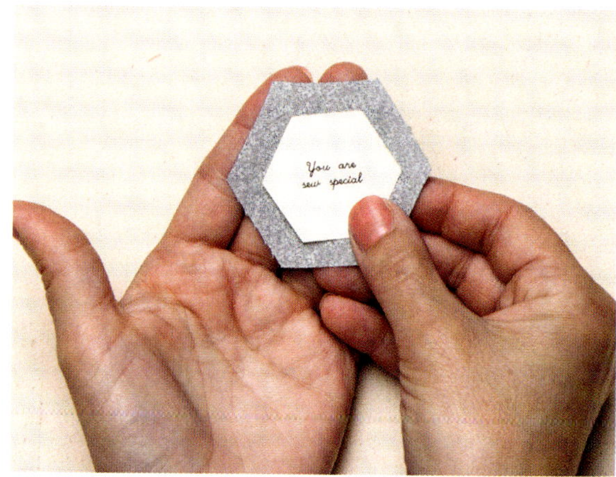

(A) Place your paper Charm hexagon in the center of the wrong side of your fabric hexagon.

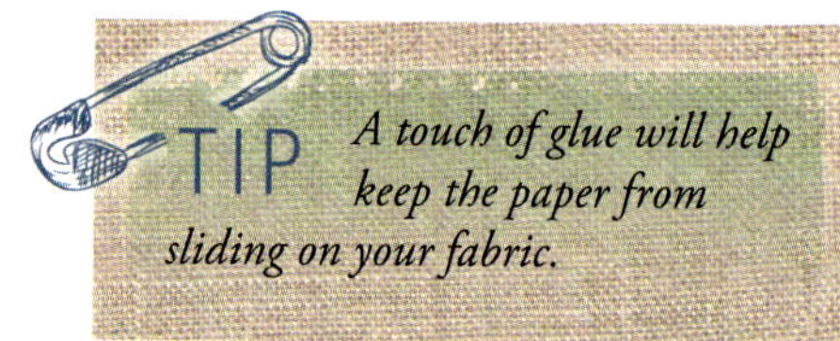

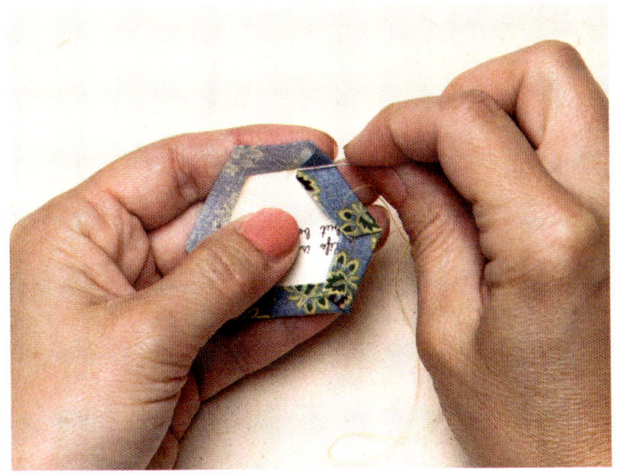

(B) Fold fabric around the edge of paper template. I like to use my needle to crease the folds and make a nice corner.

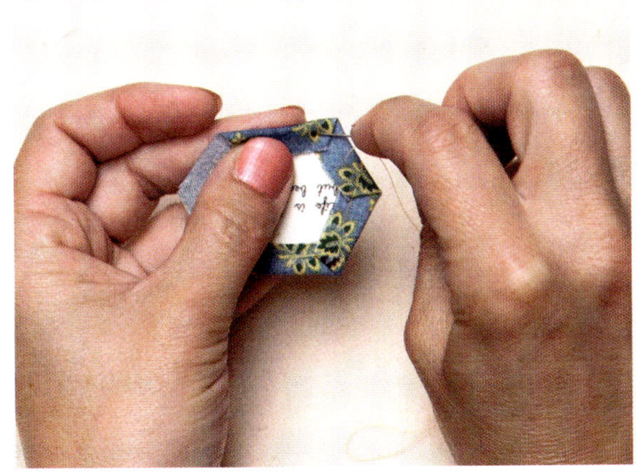

(C) Secure fabric to paper template with a needle and yellow thread using a basting stitch. You can also use glue. NOTE: All edges of paper template need to be covered.

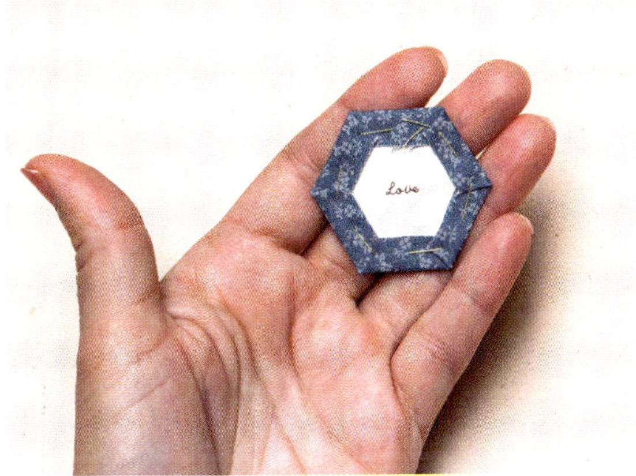

(D) Stitch twice at the end to lock your stitch, and remember not to make it too tight, as you will be removing your basting stitches later.

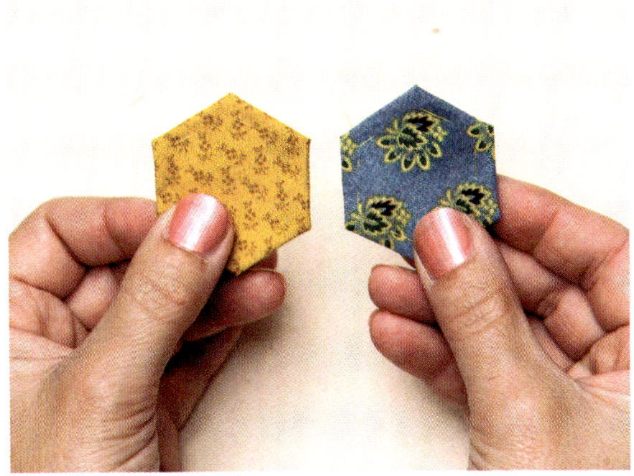

(E) Take two fabric shapes and place them fabric sides together.

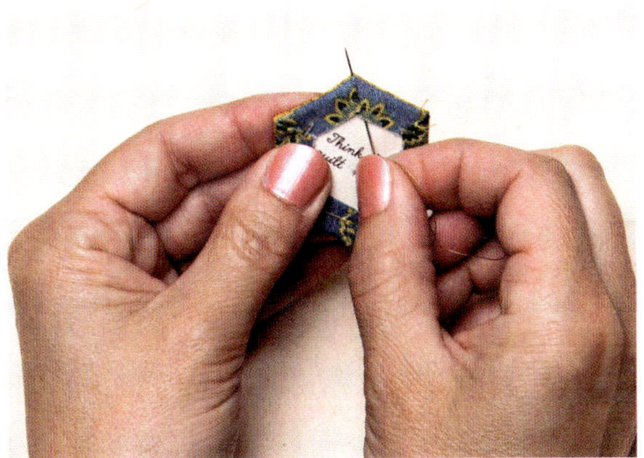

(F) Use piecing thread in your needle. Shorter thread is easier to work with. Remember to put a knot in the end. Slip your needle under the seam allowance into the corner.

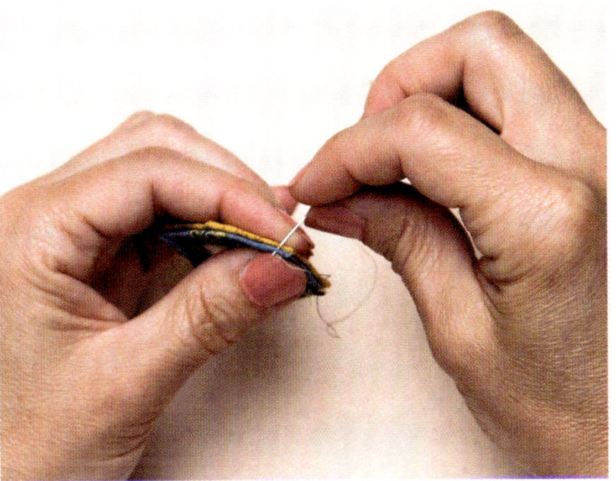

(G) Start with a double stitch at the point to lock the stitches. Stitch along one edge with whip stitch. Remember to stitch only through fabric, not the paper.

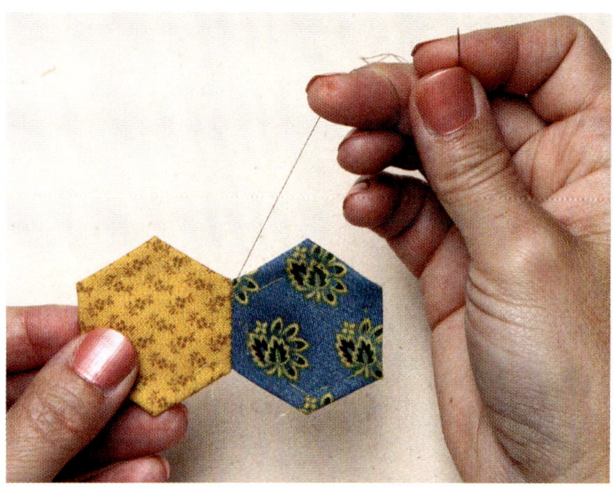

(H) Finish the seam with double stitch and do not cut your thread. Open the shapes.

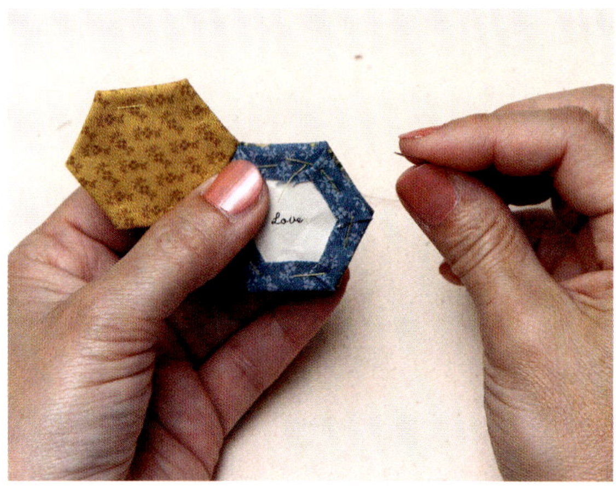

(I) Take another fabric shape and place it fabric sides together with your previously sewn set.

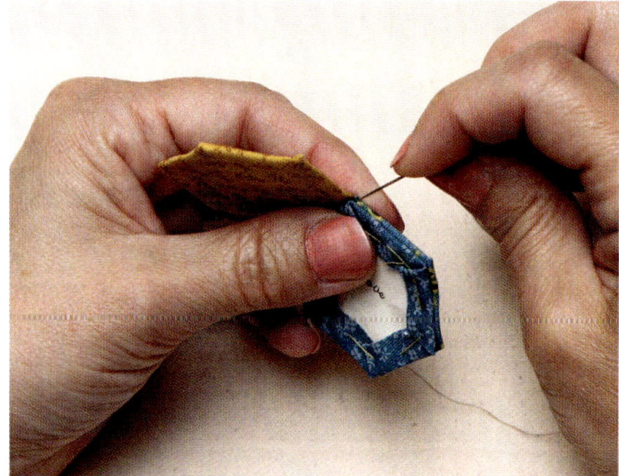

(J) Start with a double stitch at the point to lock the stitches. Stitch along one edge of the additional shape with a whip stitch.

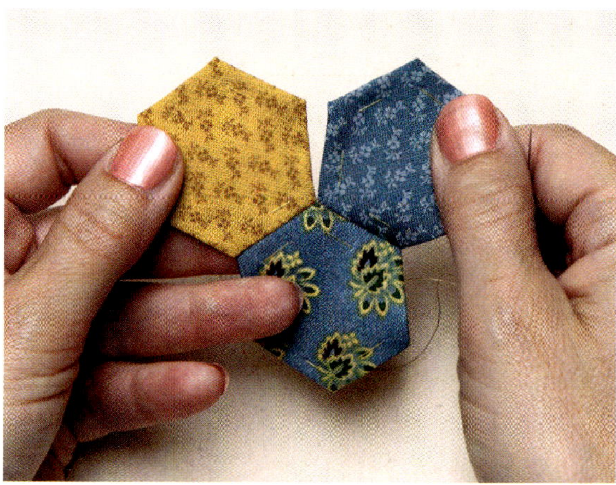

(K) Finish seam with double stitch and do not cut your thread. Open shapes then move on to stitching the next open seam.

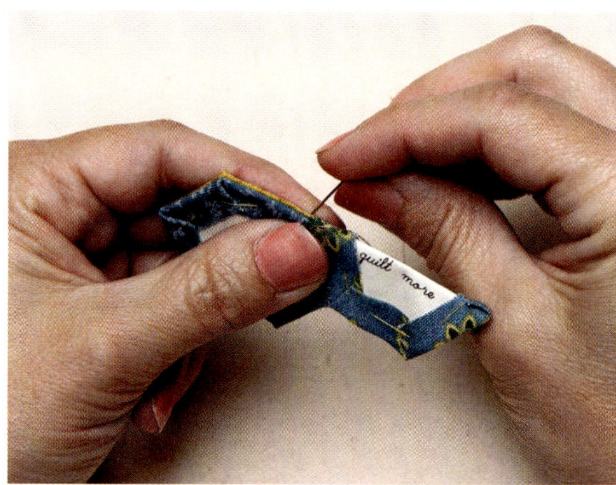

(L) Fold previously sewn shapes in half if necessary while sewing the next seam. Once the first ring of the block is finished, proceed to adding the second ring to complete your block.

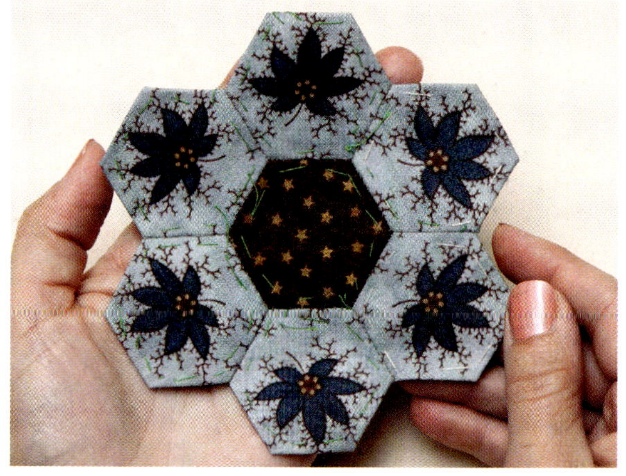

(M) Remember you can be fussy with your fabrics; it adds a nice touch to the look of each flower.

2 Blocks:

Make 32 hexagon flowers and 6 diamond blocks. Be sure to leave the paper in your shapes until the quilt top is complete.

	Flower	Diamond
Center	1	1
Ring 1	6	8
Ring 2	12	16

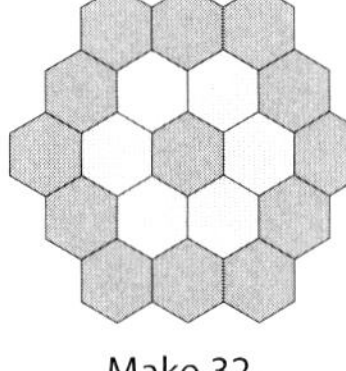

Make 32.

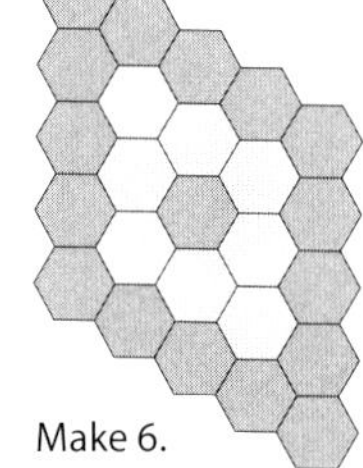

Make 6.

3 Sashings:

Make 1 dark hexagon for the quilt center and 532 light hexagons for sashings.

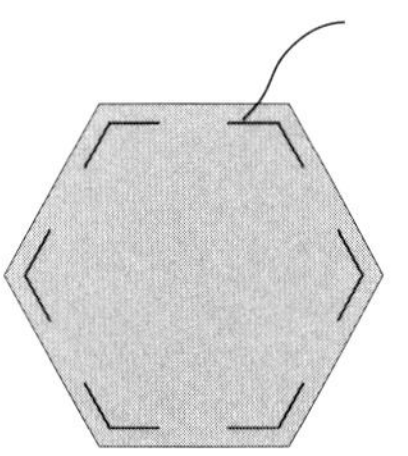

Make 1.

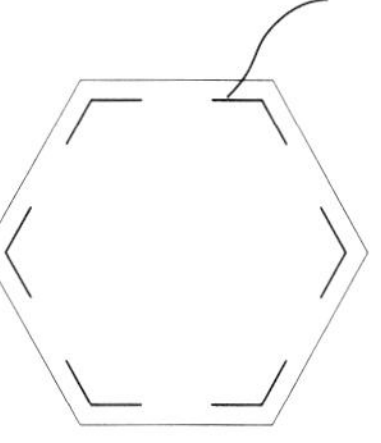

Make 532.

4 Assemble Quilt Center:

Once all flowers, diamonds, and sashing hexagons are complete, stitch them together to create a finished quilt center following the diagram below. Start your assembly with the center star, and then add flowers around the star, filling the background with sashing hexagons. Keep the Charm paper in your shapes; the added stiffness will be beneficial when appliquéing the quilt center to the border. Make a copy of the layout below to mark your progress during assembly. I also numbered each of my blocks (on the layout sheet and the back of the Charm paper) to keep my quilt top organized.

5 Appliqué:

Choose your appliqué method from My Sewing Basket on page 48. Appliqué branches and flowers to your borders following the layouts. Templates for appliqué shapes are on page 50 and directions for broderie appliqué are on page 49.

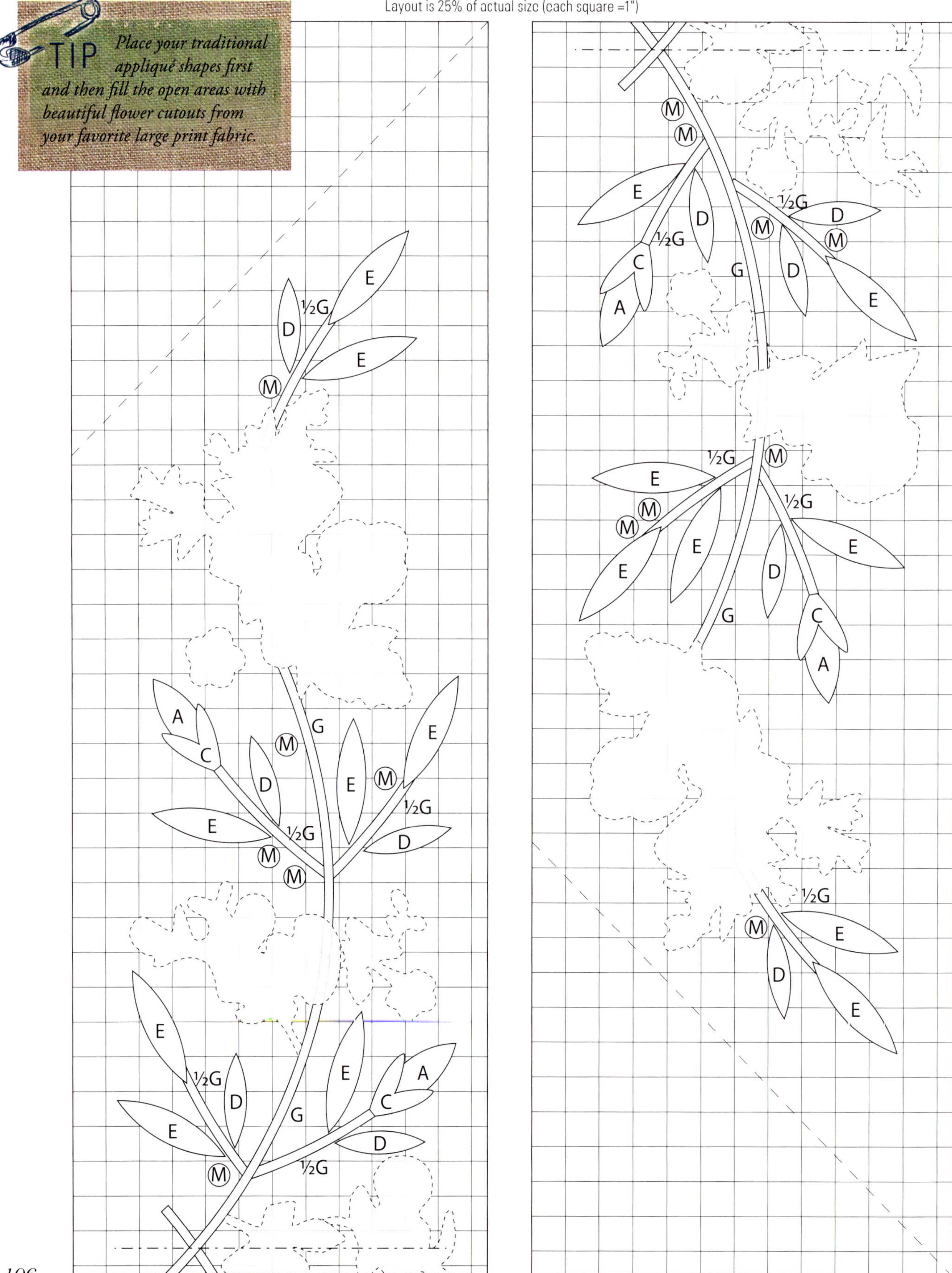

TIP *Broderie appliqué can also be done by hand. Cut fabric, staying approximately 1/4" away from the design. Needle-turn edges and secure cutout in place with a slip stitch.*

Side Border Appliqué Layout

Layout is 25% of actual size (each square =1")

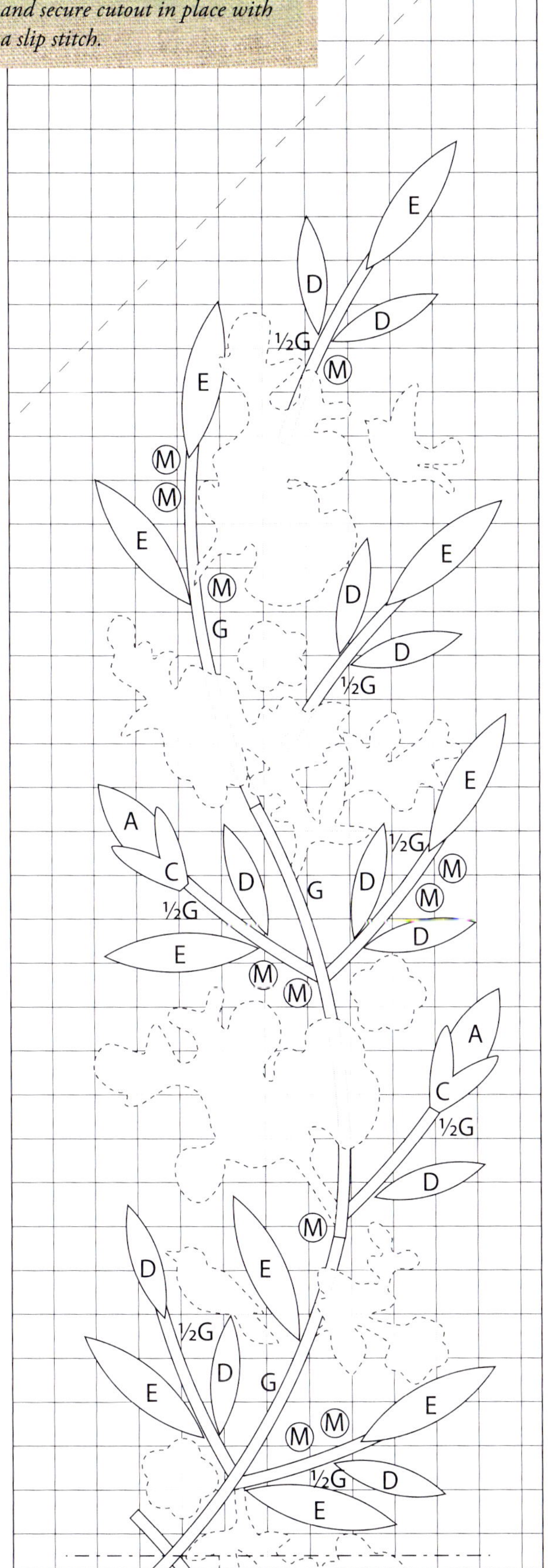

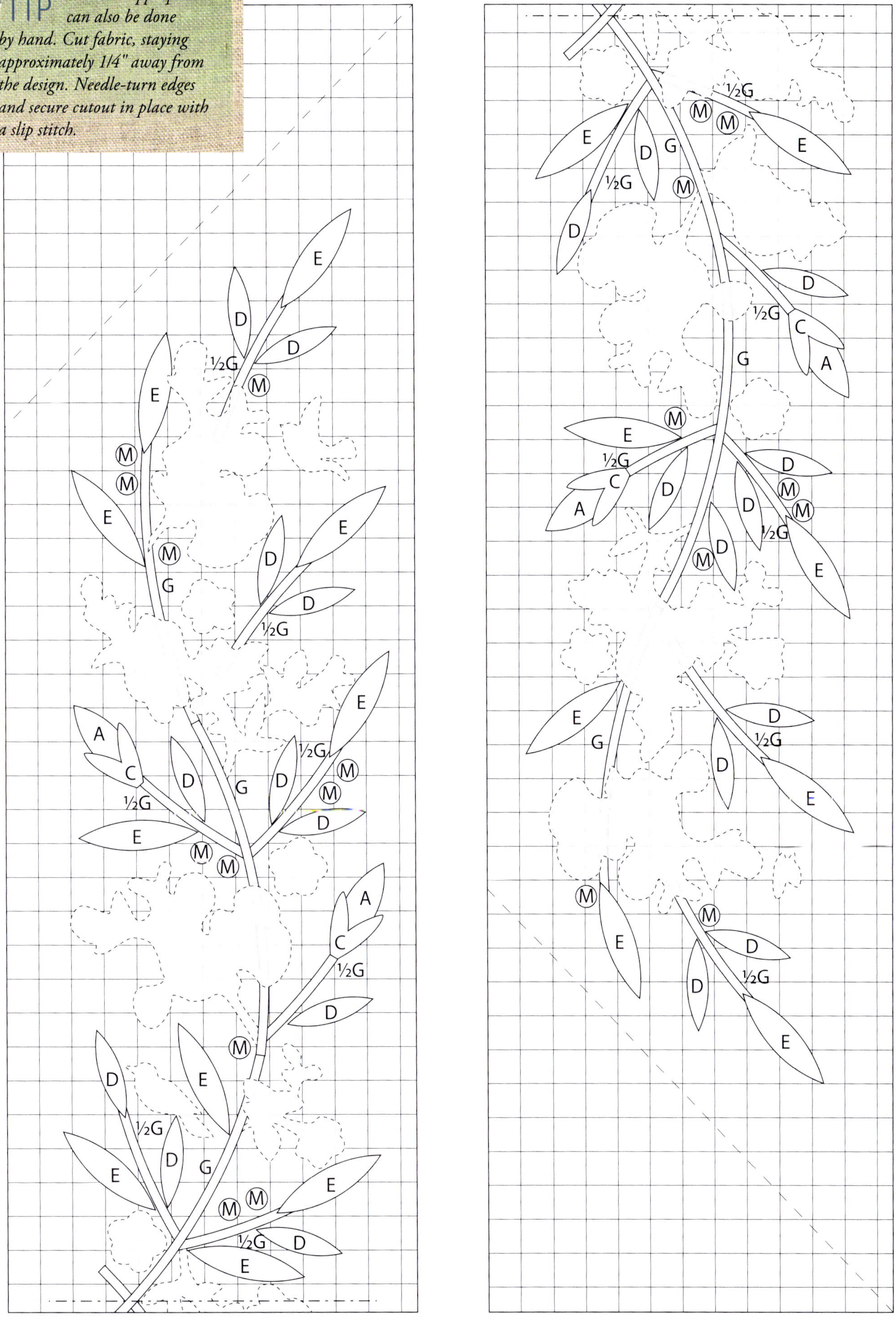

Appliqué Shape Cutting:

Template	Description	Cut	Color
A	Bud	16	Red
C	Bud Base	16	Red
D	Leaf	62	Green
E	Leaf	66	Green
G	Stem	20	Brown
½ G	Half Stem	48	Brown
M	Circle	68	Red

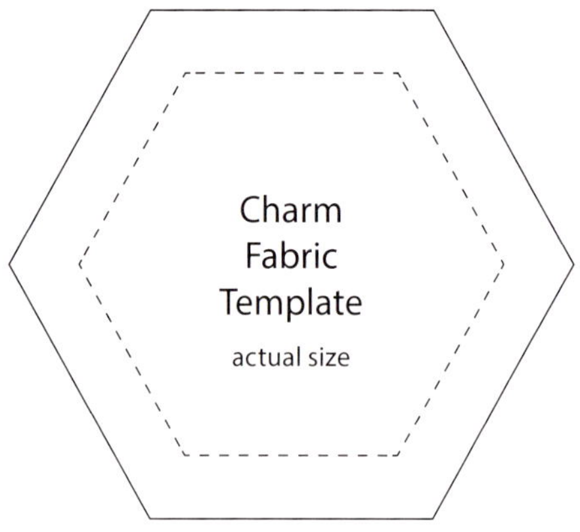

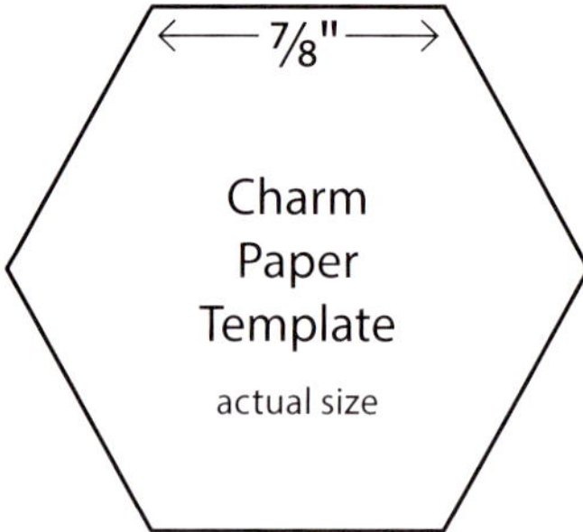

What is English Paper Piecing?

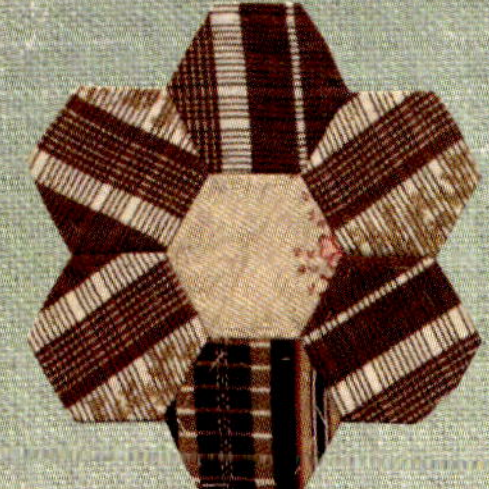

English paper piecing is a hand-piecing method that lends well to using scraps. Often associated with hexagons (and other intricate shapes), English paper piecing involves basting fabric around precut paper, and then stitching the fabric shapes together. With careful assembly and depending on the pattern's durability, the paper shapes can be reused for other projects.

Quilters love the portability of this method, as they can cut and carry their pieces anywhere. With accurate cutting and stitching, the resulting designs are also quite precise. Both beginners and seasoned quilters find success in creating elaborate, finely detailed quilt designs.

6 Border:

We need to create a border to which we will appliqué our hexagon top. I chose a 12½" border with mitered corners, which becomes the perfect canvas for the appliqué on this quilt.

(A) Layout appliquéd border pieces as shown below.

(B) Place top border piece directly on top of side border piece, right sides together, and align the edges on 3 sides.

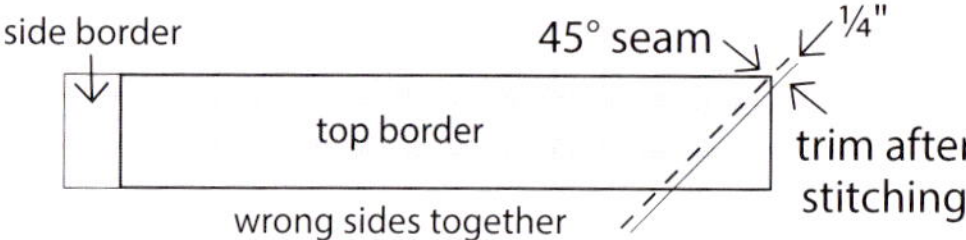

(C) Using a 12" square ruler, mark a 45° line from the outside aligned corner as shown. Sew along this line.

(D) Press seam open. Align 45° angle line of square ruler on seam line to check accuracy. If the corner is flat and square, trim the excess fabric to ¼" seam allowance.

(E) Repeat procedure for each corner to complete border frame as shown below.

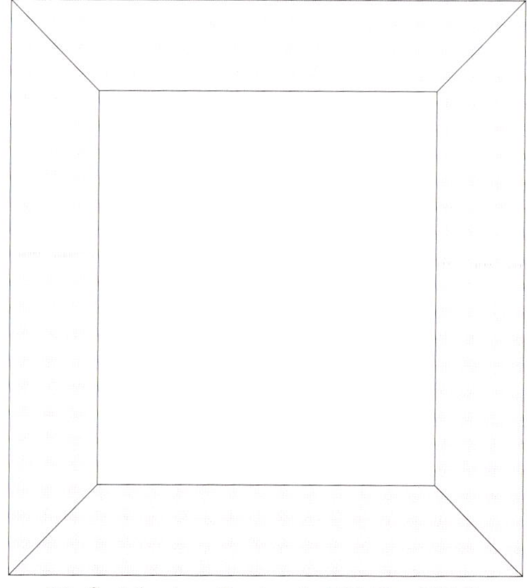

Unfinished quilt size is 70½" x 76½".

7 Assemble Quilt Top:

Place completed border frame right side up, and place quilt center right side up on top of your border frame. Align middle of border frames with the middle of the quilt center and pin in place. (I pinned each hexagon edge to my border.) Using machine or hand appliqué, stitch quilt center to the border frame. Now it's time to remove papers from hexagons.

Unfinished quilt size is 70½" x 76½".

8 Quilting:

1. Layer quilt in the following order:
   a) Quilt back, right side down, 74½" x 80½".
   b) Batting 74½" x 80½" (I prefer Hobbs for best results.)
   c) Quilt top, right side up, 70½" x 76½".
2. Baste layers together.
3. Quilt by hand or machine. This quilt was custom-quilted on a long-arm quilting machine with overall quilting on the hexagons; feathers and crackle designs were used on the border.

9 Binding:

Refer to My Sewing Basket on page 48 for binding instructions.

GATHER 'ROUND

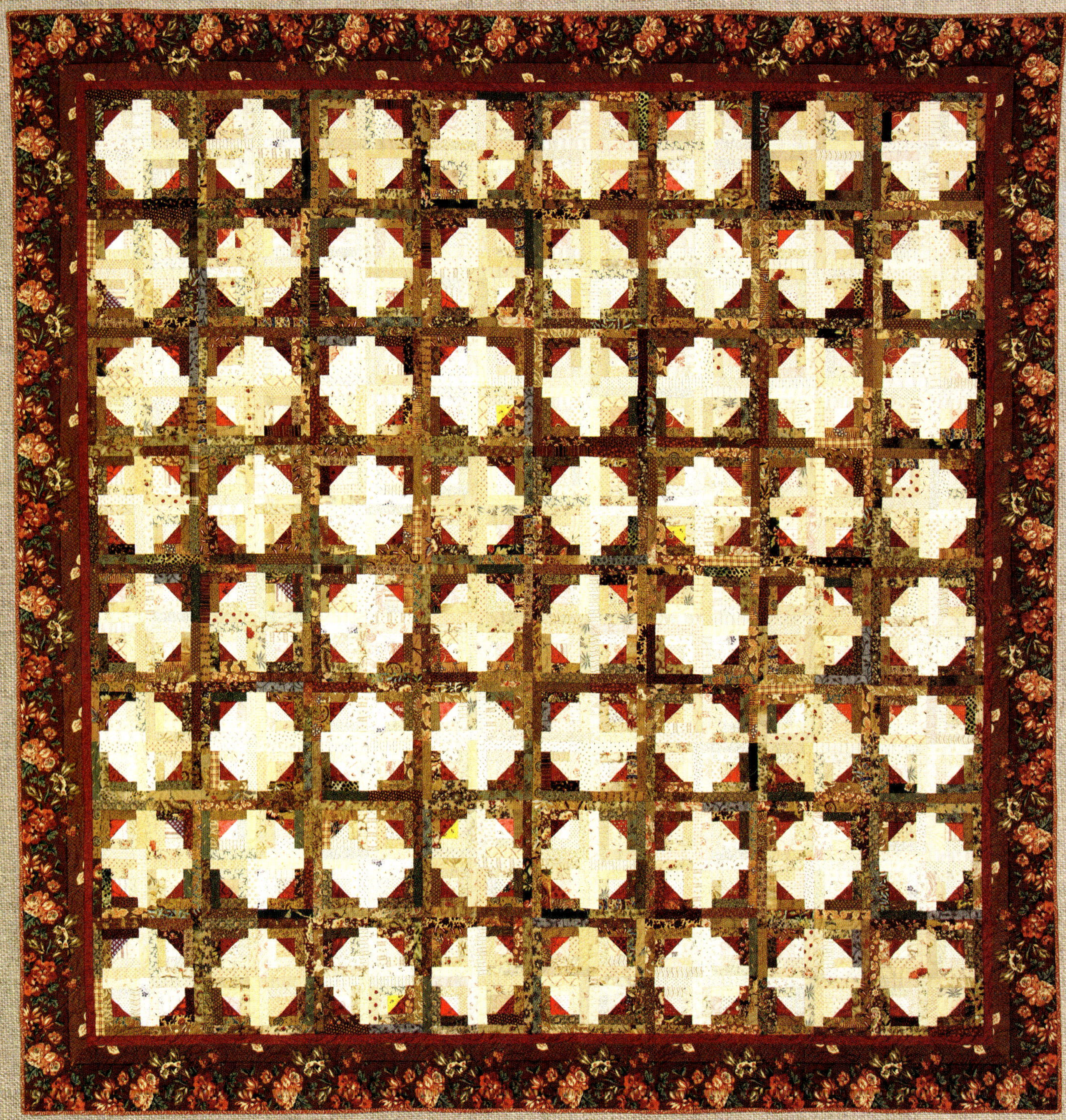

Warm tones and red corner scraps open the door to a new Log Cabin look. Pieced around a center square, light and dark strips with a hint of dusty blue create a collection of almost-round shapes: See them as snowballs, ornaments, or globes, depending on the fabrics and colors you choose.

GATHER 'ROUND

Finished quilt size: 84½" x 84½".

Fabric Requirements

Half-square triangles units for block centers:
For more variety, exchange triangles with your friends or section paper and use on a variety of fabrics.

8-6" x 21" red strips
8-6" x 21" light strips

Log Cabin Strips:

light prints: 25-9" x 21" (fat eighths)
dark prints: 30-9" x 21" (fat eighths)

Border: 2½ yards
Binding: ¾ yard
Backing: 5 yards
LBQ 1½" Exchange Triangle Paper - 8 sheets

Fabric Cutting

Log Cabin Strips:
Be careful cutting and trimming.
From EACH of the light and dark strips, cut:
7-1¼" x 22" strips

From the light strips, cut:

256-1¼" x 2" rectangles
256-1¼" x 2¾" rectangles
256-1¼" x 3½" rectangles
256-1¼" x 4¼" rectangles

From the dark strips, cut:

256-1¼" x 2¾" rectangles
256-1¼" x 3½" rectangles
256-1¼" x 4¼" rectangles
256-1¼" x 5" rectangles

Border: cut lengthwise; parallel to the selvage
2-6½" x 84½" borders
2-6½" x 72½" borders

Binding:
9-2½" x width of fabric strips

TIP *This quilt might start with special fabrics like half-square triangles from an exchange with your friends using LBQ triangle paper. It's a perfect way to gather a great variety of fabrics for the centers.*

Use a ¼" seam allowance. Press in the direction of the arrows.

1 **Half Square Triangle Units:**
(*See page 112 for an alternative to using triangle paper.*)
Select one dark and one light 6" x 21" rectangle.

(A) Layer the dark and light rectangles, right sides together, light print on the top. Press.

Following the LBQ Exchange Triangle paper directions, place the paper on top of the fabrics and pin. Sew the triangles following the dashed lines as guides. Remember to use a 50-wt thread and a smaller stitch length.

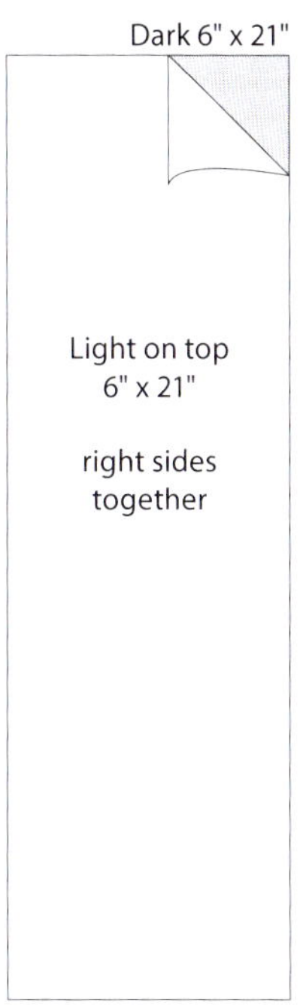

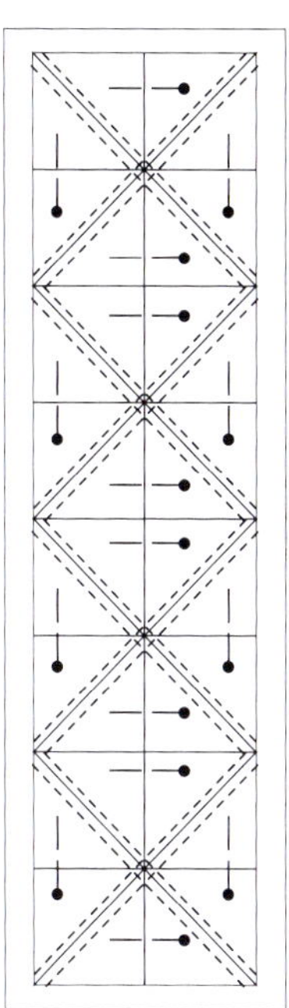

(B) Cut the triangles apart, using the solid lines as guides. *Do not remove the paper.*

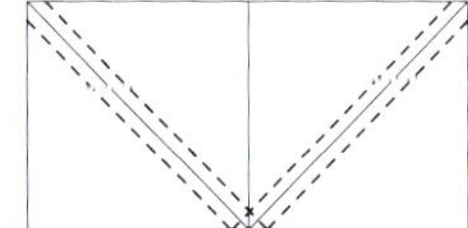
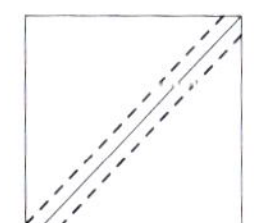
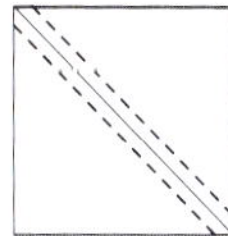
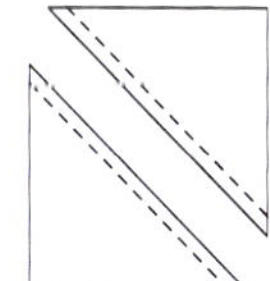

(C) Flip the triangle over so that the dark print is on the top. Press the half-square triangle unit open. Trim the "dog ears" and remove the paper. One LBQ 1½" Exchange Triangle paper makes 32 half-square triangle units.

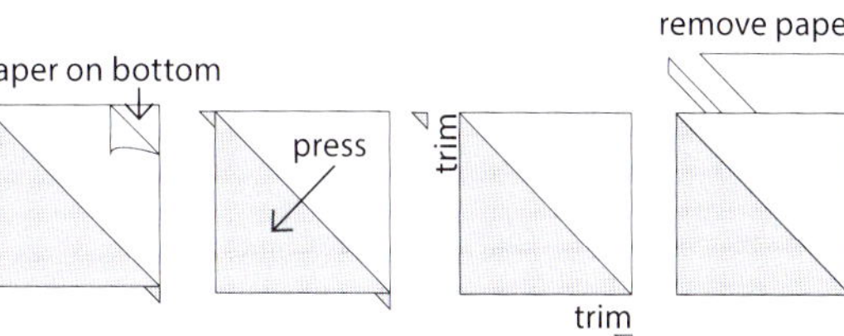

Repeat step 1 to make 8 sets of 32 half-square triangle units. Make 256 total.

2 Blocks:

(A) Diagrams show the cutting sizes of the light and dark prints and the order for stitching them together to make a block

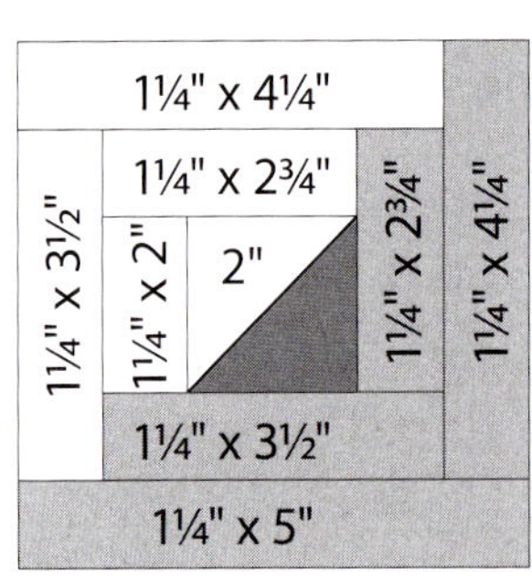

Cutting sizes.

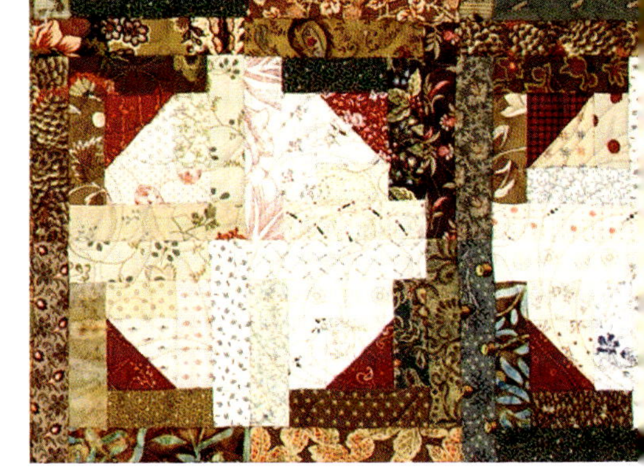

(B) Assemble the blocks as shown. Press in the direction of the arrows. Make 256 blocks total.

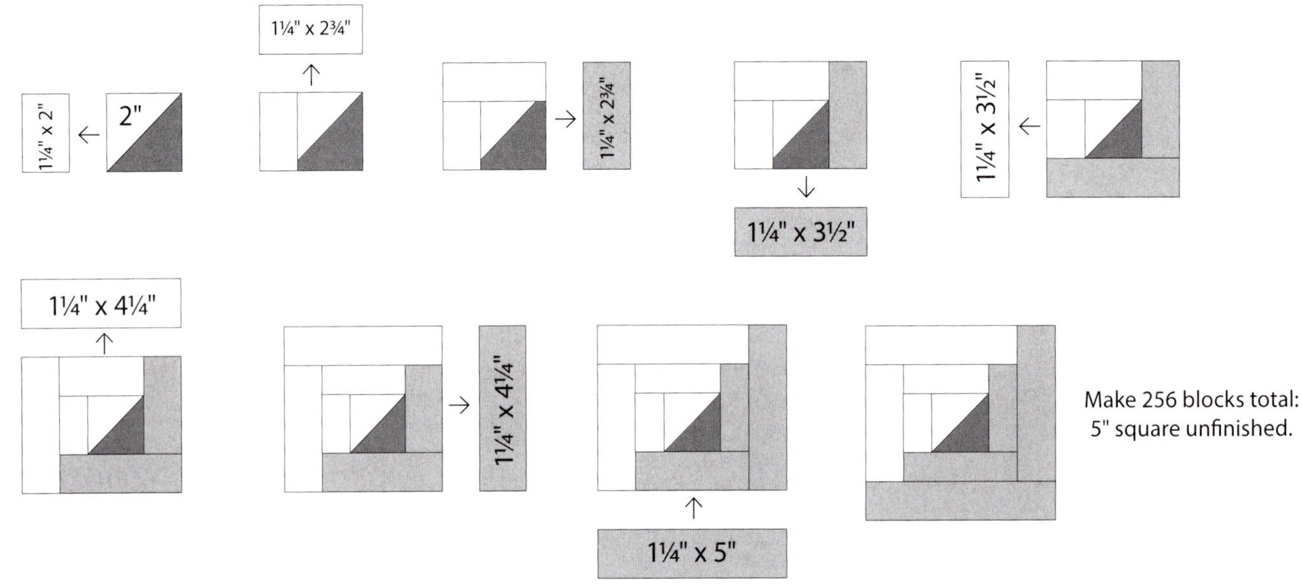

Make 256 blocks total:
5" square unfinished.

(C) Arrange 4 blocks as shown to make one main block. Make 64 blocks total.

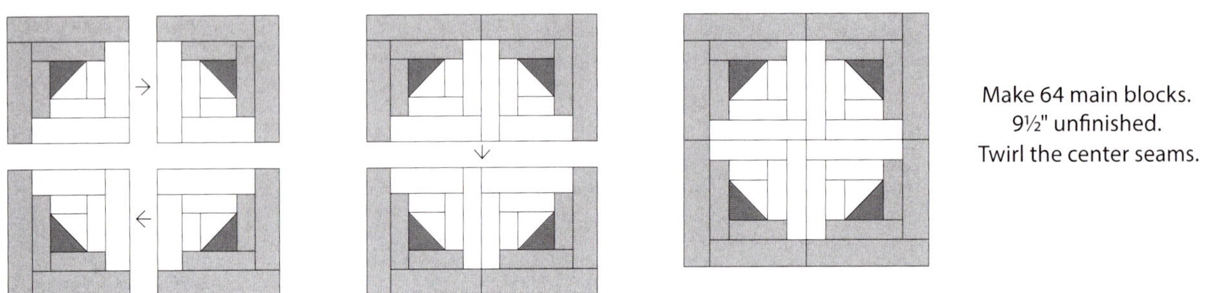

Make 64 main blocks.
9½" unfinished.
Twirl the center seams.

Alternative to using the triangle paper:

1. Cut 1 light and 1 dark 2 ⅜" square. Cut the squares once on the diagonal.
2. Layer one dark and one light triangle right sides together. Sew using a ¼" seam allowance.
3. Press your triangles open and trim the bunny ears. This makes 2 half-square triangle units.

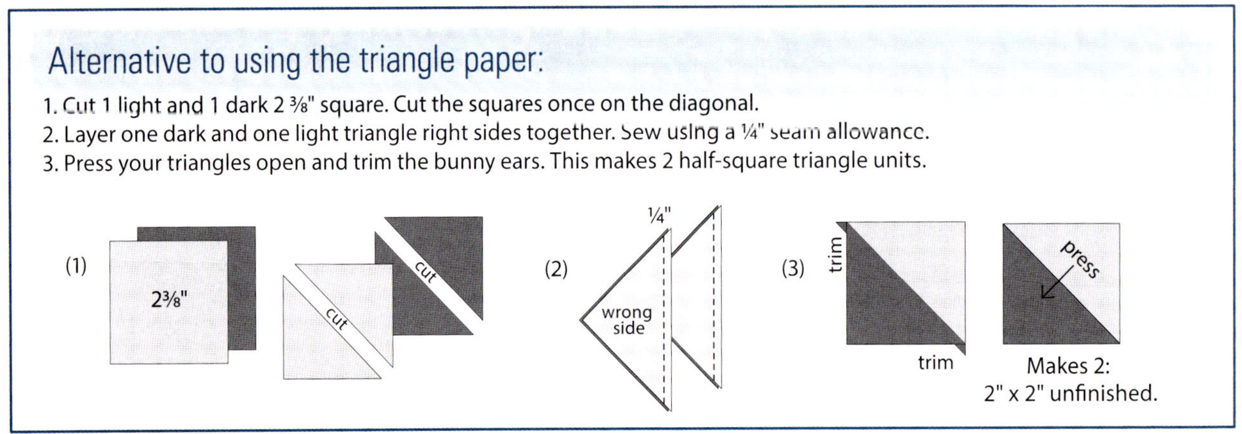

Makes 2:
2" x 2" unfinished.

3 Arrange 8 main blocks as shown to make one row; sew together. Press in one direction. Make 8 total. Rotate the even rows 180° so the seam allowance face the opposite direction. Sew the rows together. Add the 6½" x 72½" borders to the quilt sides. Add the 6½" x 84½" borders to the quilt top and bottom.

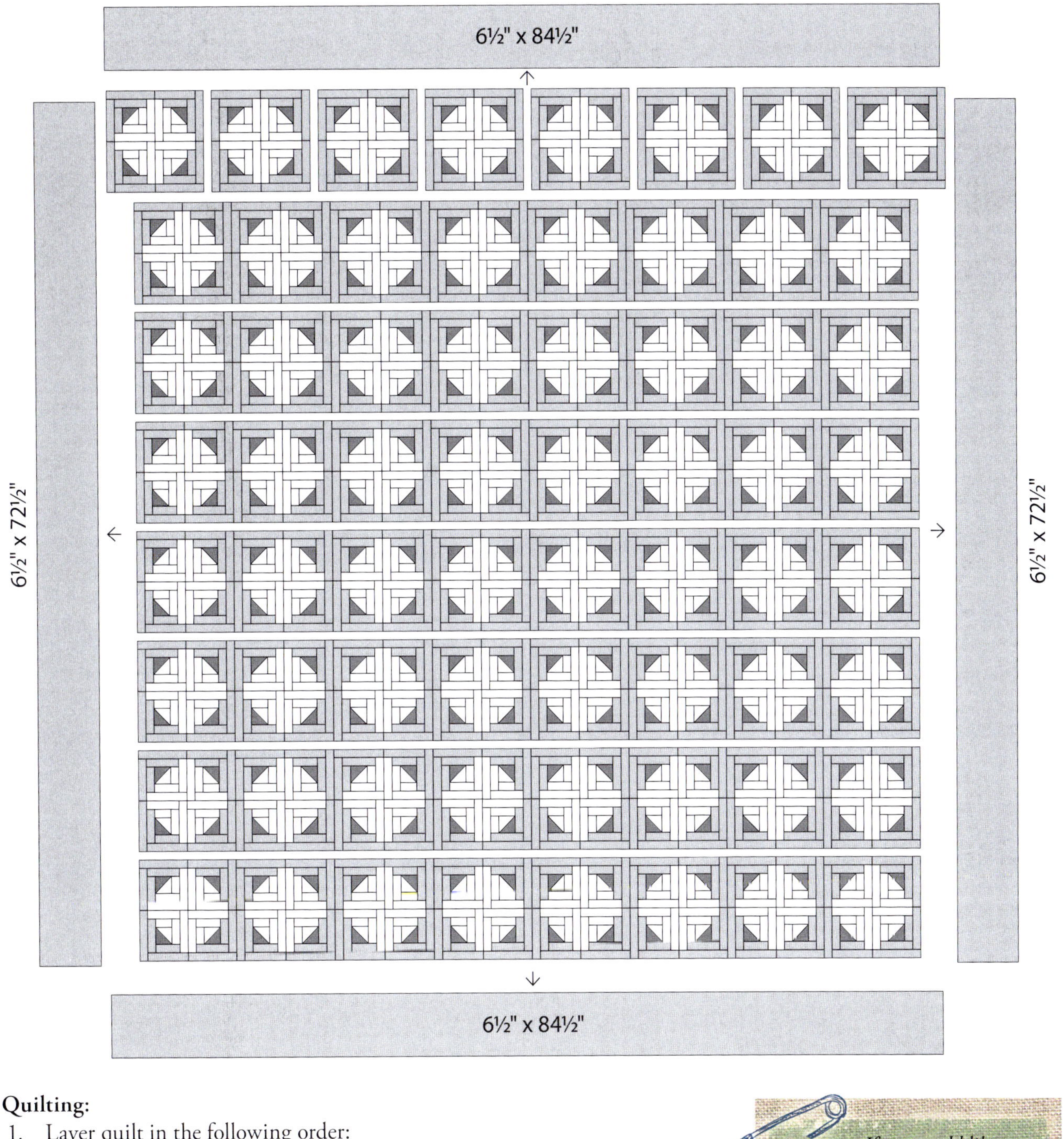

6½" x 84½"

6½" x 72½"

6½" x 72½"

6½" x 84½"

4 **Quilting:**

1. Layer quilt in the following order:
   a) Quilt back, right side down, 90" x 90".
   b) Batting 90" x 90" (I prefer Hobbs for best results.)
   c) Quilt top, right side up, 84½" x 84½".
2. Baste layers together.
3. Quilt by hand or machine. This quilt was quilted with an overall design on a long-arm quilting machine.

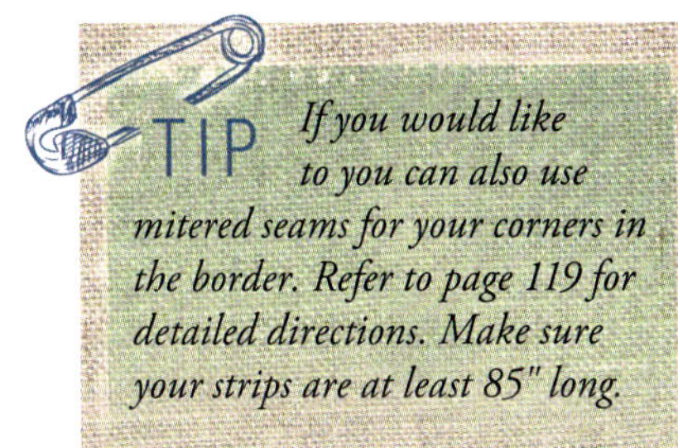

5 **Binding:**

Refer to My Sewing Basket on page 48 for binding directions.

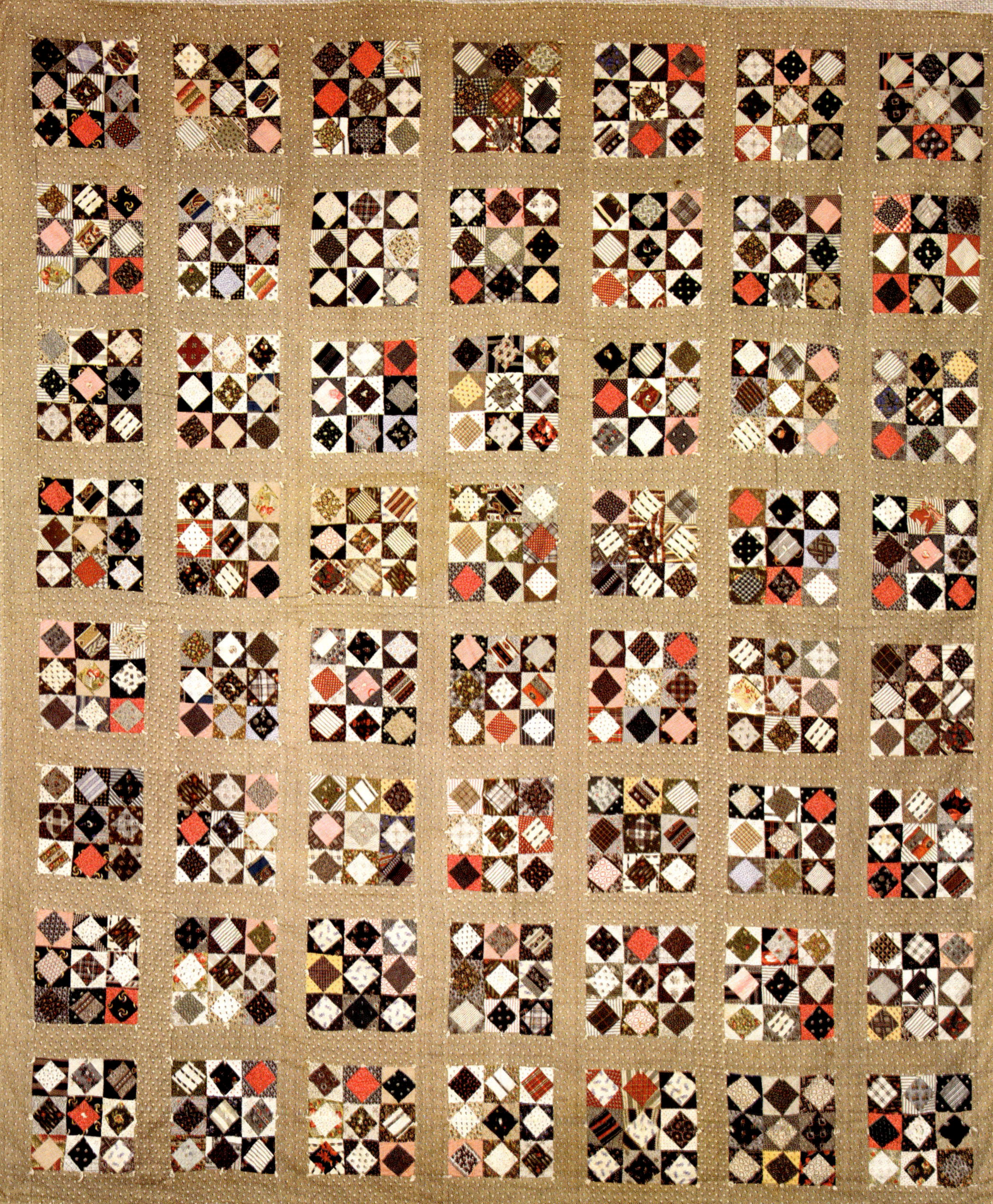

Pioneer women sometimes preserved the threads of their favorite fading quilts by sandwiching them in between a new quilt top and backing. This square-in-a-square pattern pays tribute to these keepers. Neutral sashing calls attention to each square, and tying the layers (instead of quilting them) protects the treasure inside.

SURPRISE INSIDE

Finished quilt size: 73" x 83".

Fabric Requirements

Blocks:

56-light 10" squares in a variety of colors

56-dark 10" squares in a variety of colors

Sashing: 2⅔ yards

Binding: ⅔ yard

Backing: 4½ yards

Fabric Cutting

Blocks:
From EACH of the 56-10" light squares, cut:
5-2¼" squares
8-2⅛" squares, cut in half once on the diagonal to make 16 half-square triangles

From EACH of the 56-10" dark squares, cut:
4-2¼" squares
10-2⅛" squares, cut in half once on the diagonal to make 20 half-square triangles

Sashing:
29-3" x width of fabric strips
From 13 strips, cut 63-3" x 8" rectangles
Sew 2 strips end to end. From this long strip, cut 1-3" x 83" strip. Repeat to create a total of 8-3" x 83" strips.

Binding:
8-2½" x width of fabric strips

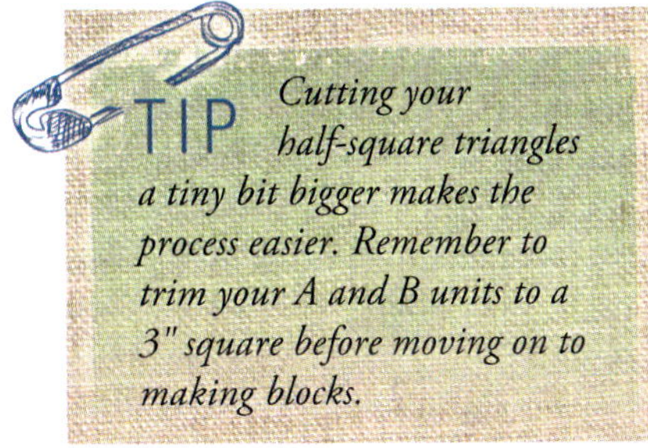

Use a ¼" seam allowance. Press in the direction of the arrows.

1 **Blocks:**
(A) Sew a 2⅛" dark half-square triangle to each side of a 2¼" light square. Repeat to make 280 unit As.

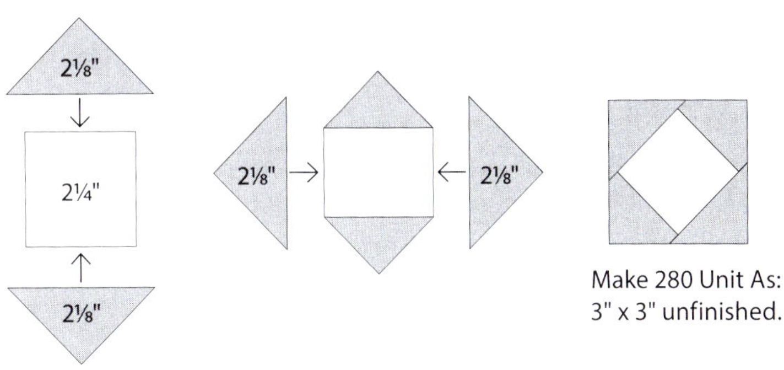

Make 280 Unit As:
3" x 3" unfinished.

(B) Sew a 2⅛" light half-square triangle to each side of a 2¼" dark square. Repeat to make 224 unit Bs.

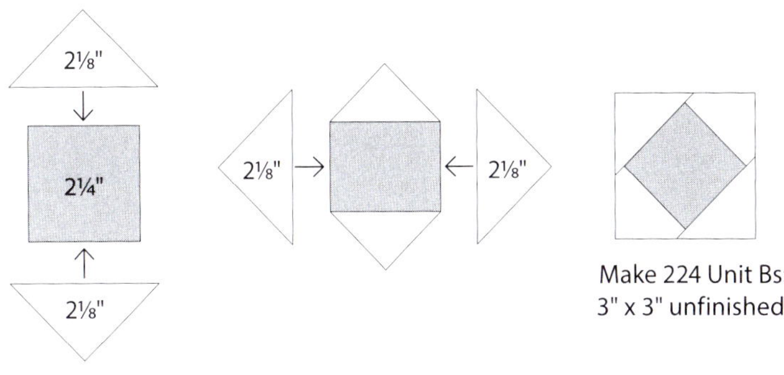

Make 224 Unit Bs:
3" x 3" unfinished.

(C) Arrange and sew 5 unit As and 4 units Bs in 3 rows as shown. Join the rows to make 1 block. Repeat to make 56 blocks.

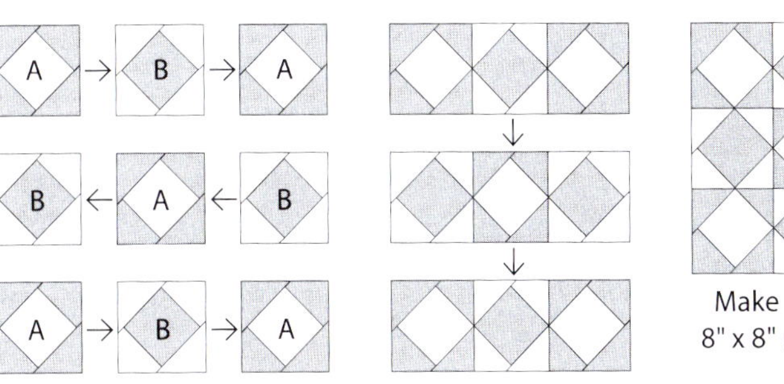

Make 56 Blocks:
8" x 8" unfinished.

2 **Assembly:**

(A) Arrange and sew 8 blocks and 9-8" x 3" sashing rectangles in 1 column as shown. Repeat to make 7 rows.

(B) Join the 7 columns and 8-3" x 83" sashing strips as shown.

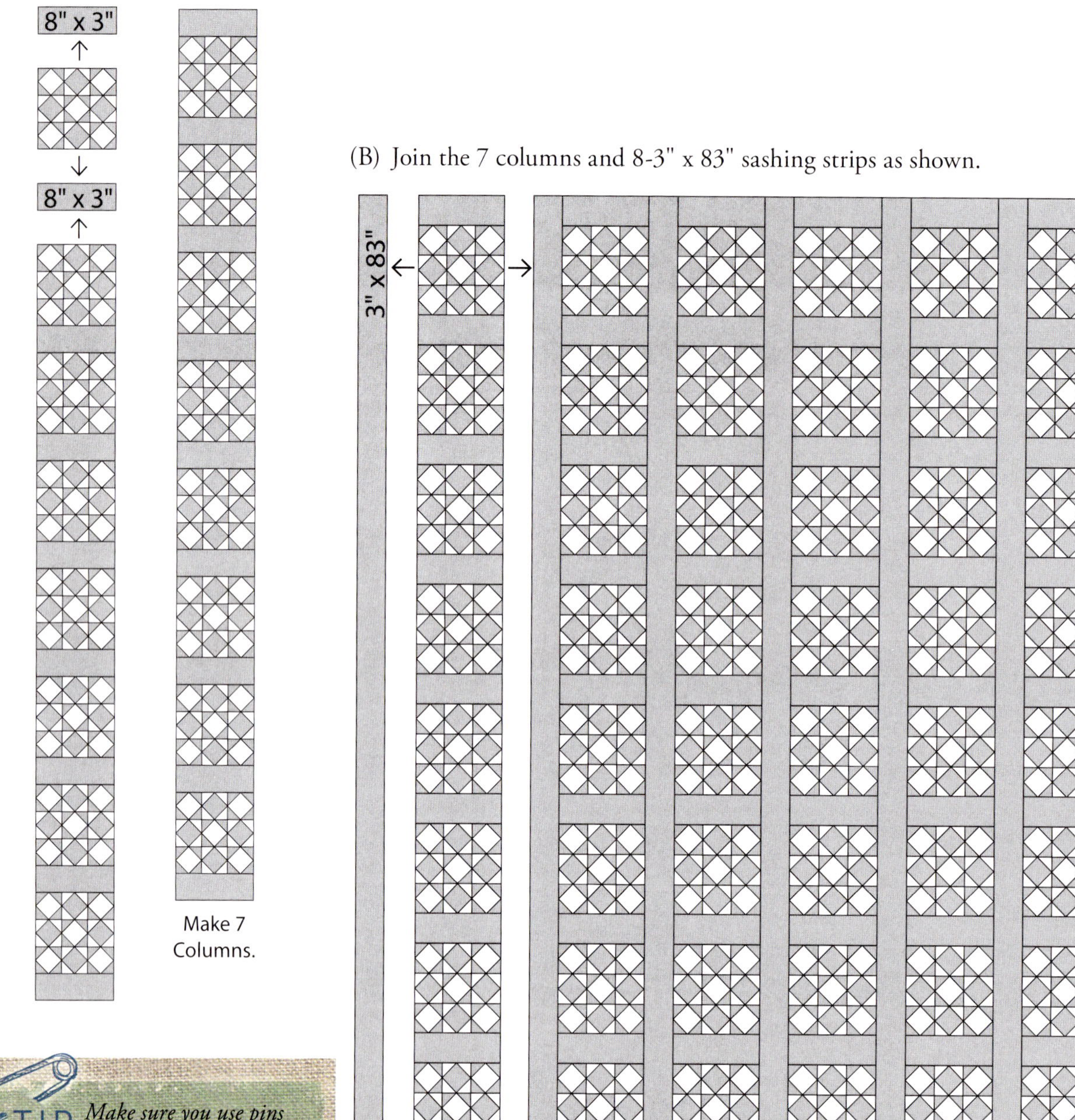

TIP *Make sure you use pins to keep columns aligned when assembling the quilt top.*

3 **Quilting:**

1. Layer quilt in the following order:
   a) Quilt back, right side down, 77" x 87".
   b) Batting 77" x 87" (I prefer Hobbs for best results.)
   c) Quilt top, right side up, 73" x 83".
2. Baste layers together.
3. Quilt by hand or machine. I chose a meandered feather overall design for this quilt.

4 **Binding:**

Refer to My Sewing Basket on page 48 for binding directions.

WILD GOOSE CHASE

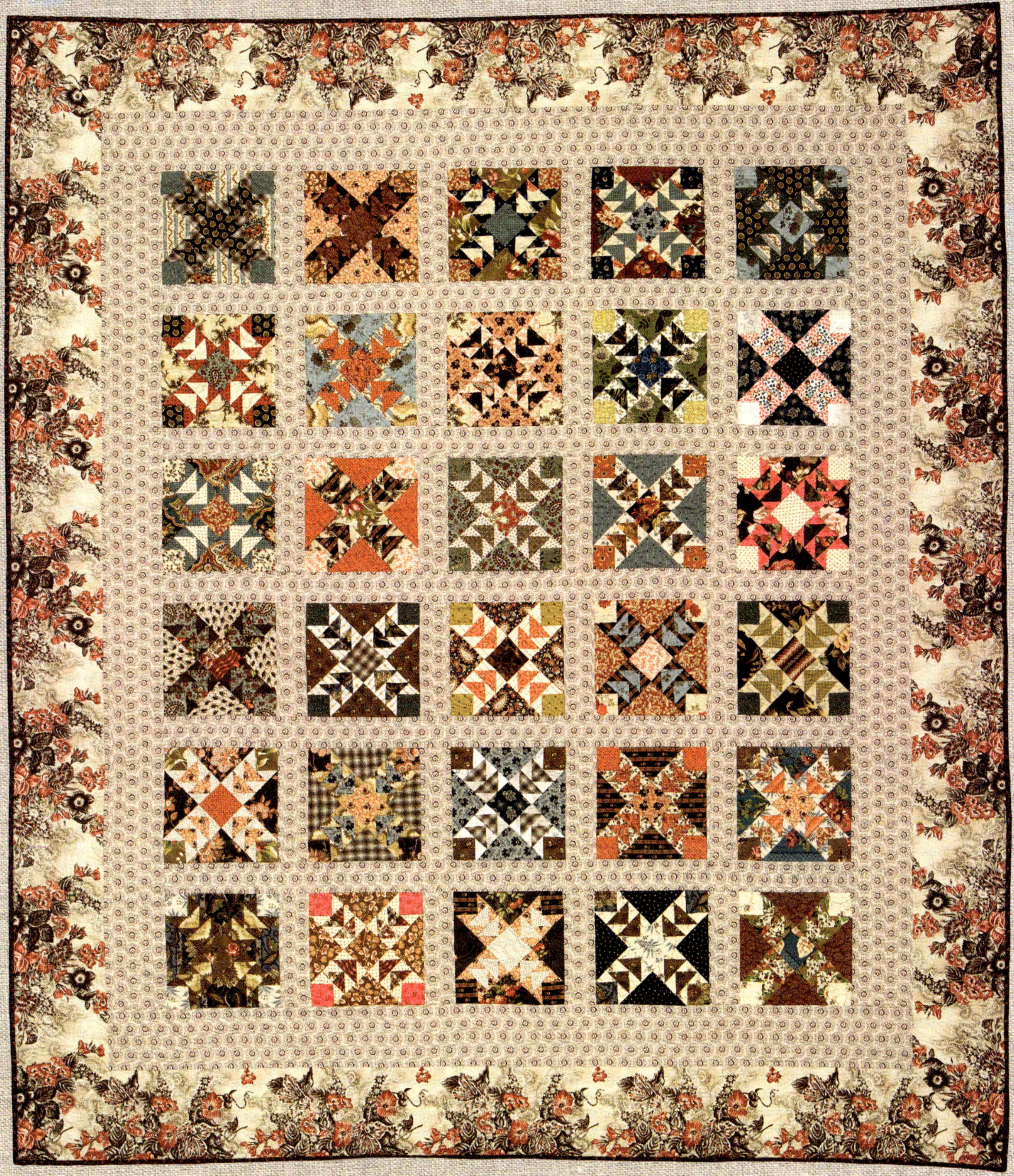

Let your scraps take flight in this variation of a Cross Flying Geese pattern that began in upstate New York in the early 1900s. Historically, these patterns pointed the way, which is fitting for a pattern that takes your piecing in new directions. No worries about matching the scraps: Just cut 30 different fabrics for 30 blocks and shuffle them to coordinate.

WILD GOOSE CHASE

Finished Quilt Size: 66" x 75½".

Fabric Requirements

Blocks:
30 assorted light to dark fat eighths (9" x 21")

Sashing and Inner Border: 1⅔ yards medium print

Border: 2¼ yards large print

Binding: ⅝ yard brown

Backing: 4 yards

TIP *A handful of light scraps for small triangles in the blocks will add a glow to this quilt.*

Fabric Cutting

Blocks: (see diagram)
From EACH fat eighth, cut:
4-2" squares for corners
1-2⅝" square for center
1-5¾" square cut in half twice on the diagonal to make 4 quarter-square triangles for setting triangles
12-1⅞" squares cut in half once on the diagonal to make 24 half-square triangles
2-3⅜" squares cut in half twice on the diagonal to make 8 quarter-square triangles

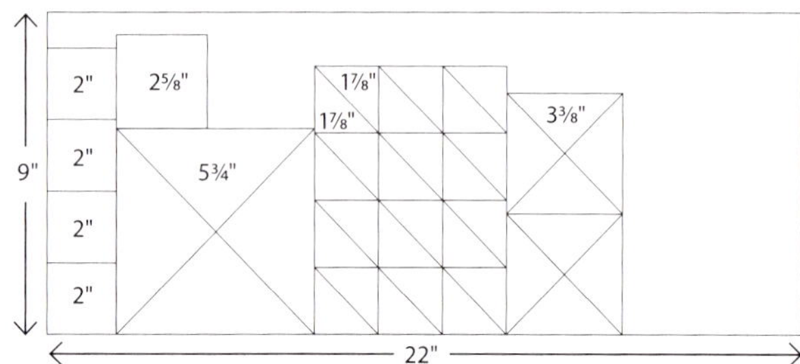

Sashing and Inner Border:
(cut lengthwise, parallel to selvage)
4-4½" x 56" strips
From the strips, cut 2-4½" x 55½", 2-4½" x 54"
9 2½" x 56" strips,
From the strips, cut 5-2½" x 46" and 24-2½" x 8"

Border: (cut lengthwise, parallel to selvage)
4-6½" x 81" strips (I cut full lengths to accommodate the large floral and mitered corners)

Binding:
7-2½" x width of fabric strips

Use a ¼" seam allowance. Press in the direction of the arrows.

You will be making 30 blocks that are 8" x 8" unfinished.

1 **Blocks:** To make 1 block, assemble:
Center: 1-2⅝" square
Corners: 4-2" squares
Setting triangles: 4-5¾" quarter-square triangles
Half-square triangles: 24-1⅞" triangles
Quarter-square triangles: 8-3⅜" triangles

(A) Join 2-1⅞" half square-triangles and 1-3⅜ quarter-square triangle. Make 8 units. Join 2 units to make 4.

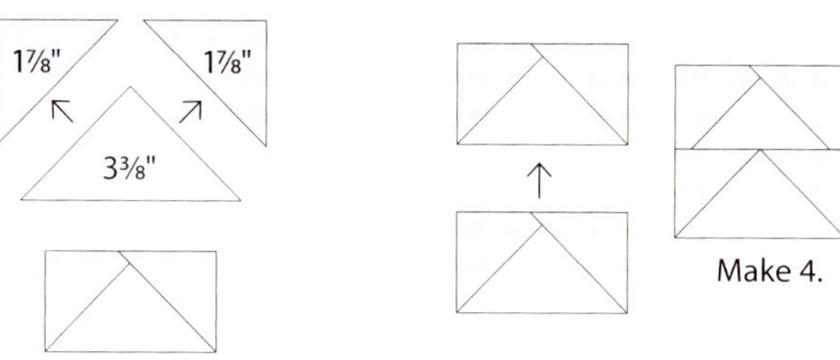

(B) Join 2-1⅞" half-square triangles and 1-2" corner square. Make 4. Join this unit and the previous unit. Make 4.

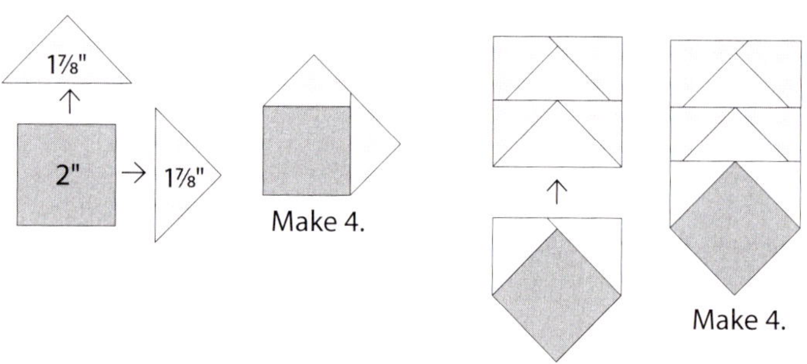

(C) Assemble the block as shown. Make 30 blocks.

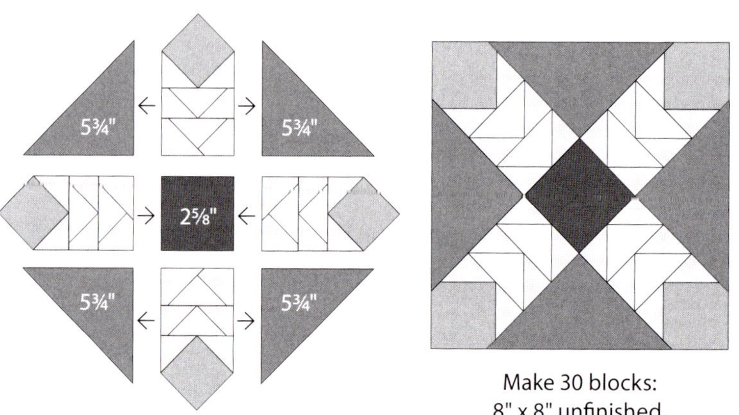

Make 30 blocks:
8" x 8" unfinished.

2 Arrange 5 blocks and 4-2½" x 8" sashing strips as shown; sew together. Make 6 rows total. Join rows and 5-2½" x 46" strips together as shown. Add the 4½" x 55½" inner border strips to the quilt sides, then add the 4½" x 54" inner border strips to the top and bottom.

4½" x 54"

2½" x 8"

2½" x 8"

2½" x 8"

2½" x 8"

2½" x 46"

4½" x 55½"

4½" x 55½"

4½" x 54"

Unfinished size is 54" x 63½".

3 Add the 6½" border strips to the quilt center using mitered seams.

(A) Center and pin left- and right-side border strips in place. Start and end seams ¼" from raw edges; backstitch to secure. Press seams toward quilt top.

(B) Repeat step A to secure top and bottom borders to quilt top.

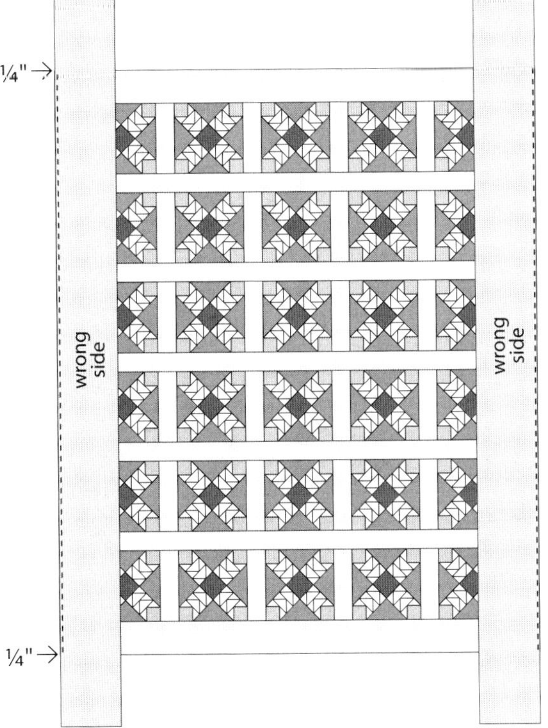

(C) Lay quilt top, wrong side up, on ironing board and fold each border end flat back onto itself, right sides together, forming a 45° angle at the quilt's corner. Press to form a sharp crease.

(D) Fold quilt on diagonal, right sides together. Align border strip raw edges, border seams at the ¼" backstitched point, and creases; pin in place. Stitch along crease, backstitching at ¼" border seam.

(E) Press seam open. With quilt right side up, align 45° angle line of square ruler on seam line to check accuracy. If the corner is flat and square, trim the excess fabric to ¼" seam allowance.

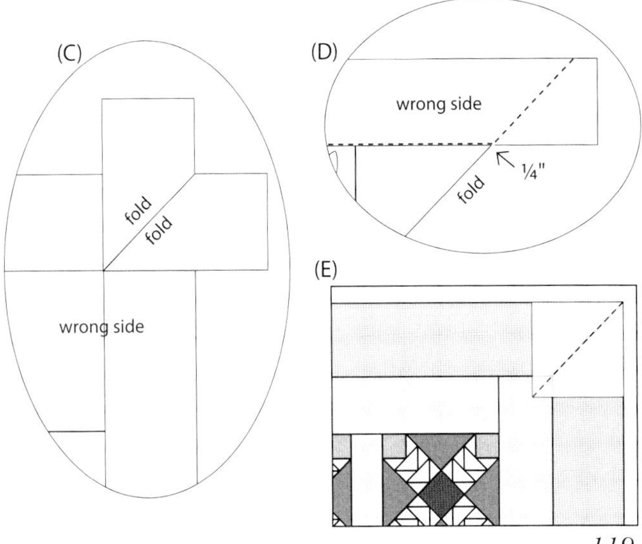

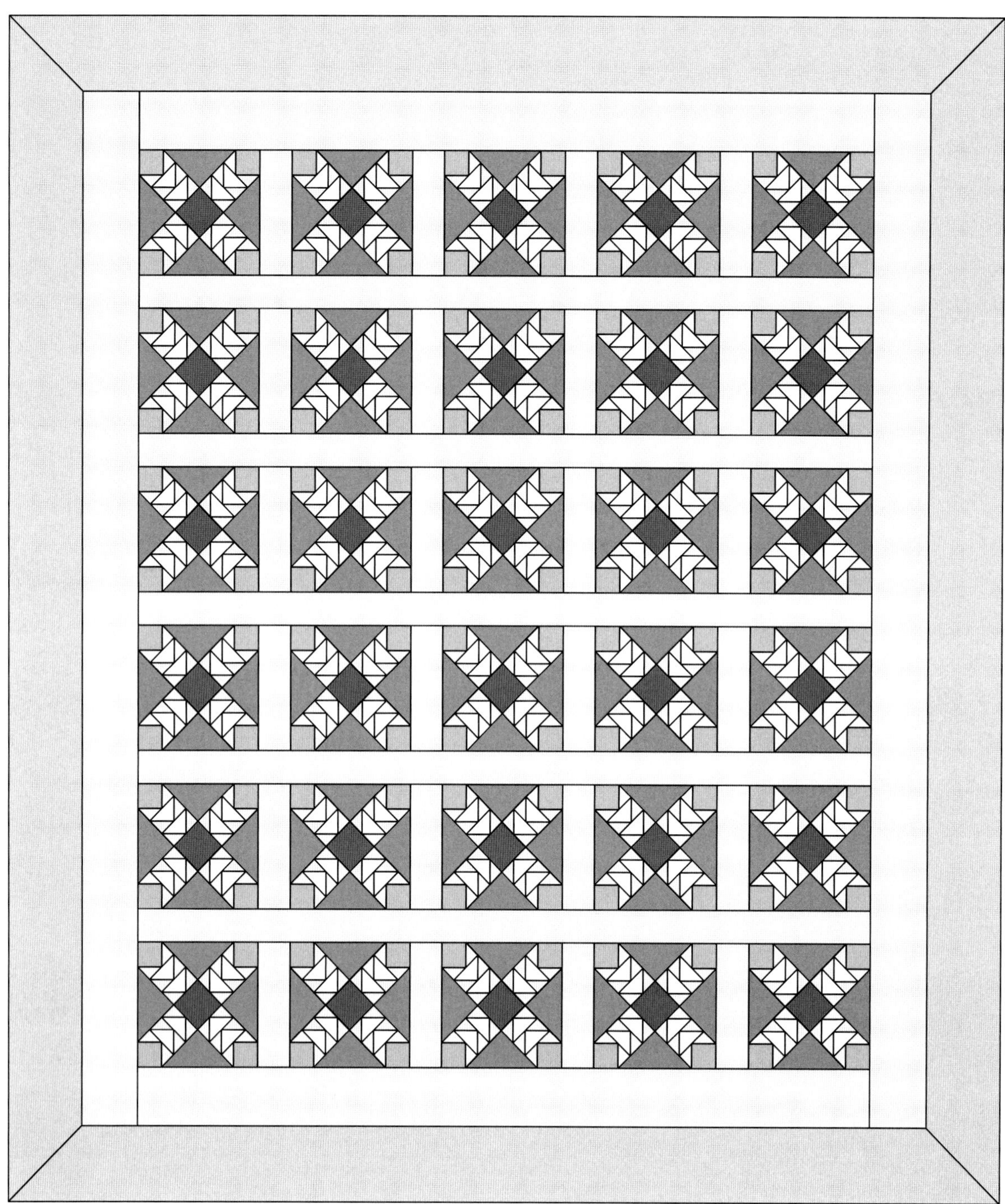

Unfinished quilt top is 66" x 75½".

4 Quilting:

1. Layer quilt in the following order:
   a) Quilt back, right side down, 70" x 79½".
   b) Batting 70" x 79½" (I prefer Hobbs for best results.)
   c) Quilt top, right side up, 66" x 75½".
2. Baste layers together.
3. Quilt by hand or machine. I used an overall machine-quilted design for this quilt.

5 Binding:

Refer to My Sewing Basket on page 48 for binding directions.

CARD BOX

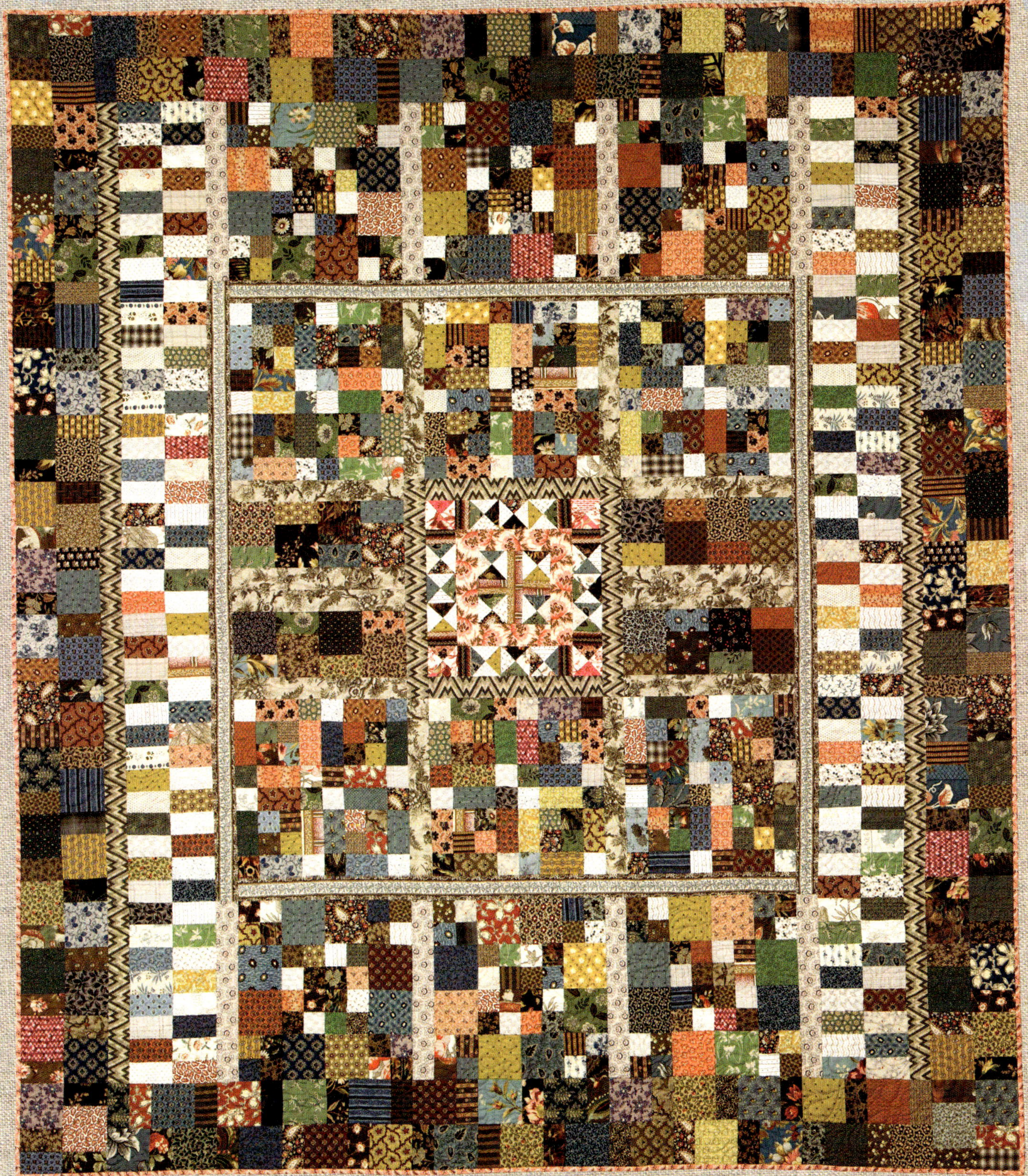

Celebrate those scraps every way but loose! Like a box of miscellaneous greeting cards, this quilt is a gathering of your sentimental fabrics. Place your postage stamps in one corner; sweep your broken dishes to another; and even add nonchalant leftover sashing to tie the busy patterns together. Put your best quilting foot forward to finish with a medallion center, and make room under the bed to start saving once again.

CARD BOX

Finished quilt size: 69½" x 78½".

Fabric Requirements

Assorted Light prints:
12 squares 10½" x 10½"

Assorted Medium and Dark prints:
42 squares 10½" x 10½"

Assorted Very Dark prints:
12 squares 10½" x 10½"

Sashings: 1¼ yards total accent fabric

Binding: ⅔ yard

Backing: 4¾ yards

Fabric Cutting

Assorted Light prints:
88-2" x 3½" rectangles
96-2" x 2" squares
10-3¼" x 3¼" squares
cut twice diagonally to 40 quarter-square triangles

Assorted Medium and Dark prints:
184-2" x 3½" rectangles
182-3½" x 3½" squares
144-2" x 2" squares
10-3¼" x 3¼" squares
cut twice diagonally to 40 quarter-square triangles

Assorted Very Dark prints:
140-2" x 3½" rectangles
144-2" x 2" squares
8-1½" x 2½" rectangles

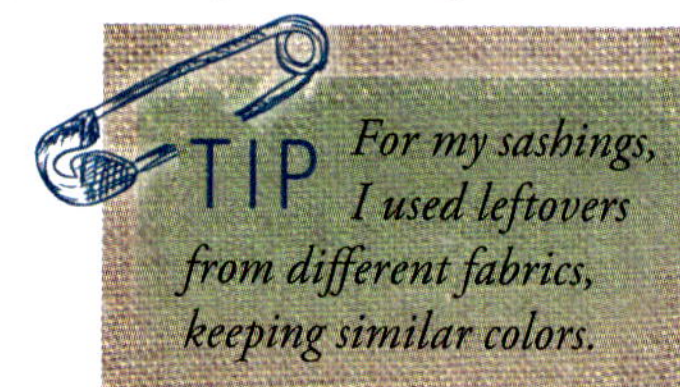

Sashings: (starting from center of quilt)
2-1½" x 2½" and 1-1½" x 5½" rectangles
2-2" x 5½" and 2-2" x 8½" rectangles
2-2" x 12½ and 2-2" x 15½" rectangles
12-2" x 12½" rectangles
8-2" x 12½" rectangles
2-2" x 39½" and 2-2" x 42½" rectangles
cut 4 strips 2" x width of fabric;
sew into 2 sets of 2" x 66½" rectangles

Binding: 8-2½" x width of fabric strips

Use a ¼" seam allowance. Press in the direction of the arrows.

1 **Section A:**

(A) Join 2-3¼" Light and 2-3¼" Dark quarter-square triangles as shown. Make 20.

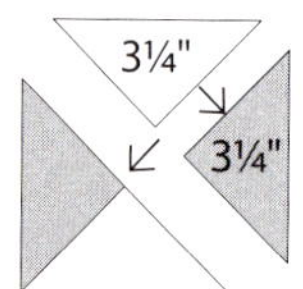

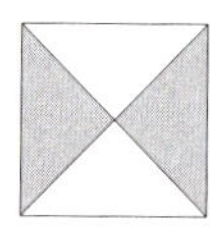

Make 20 units:
2½" x 2½" unfinished.

(B) Join 2 of the previous units and 1-1½" x 2½" sashing rectangle. Make 2. Add 1-1½" x 5½" sashing rectangle.

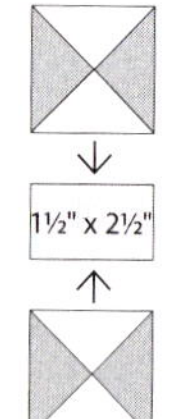

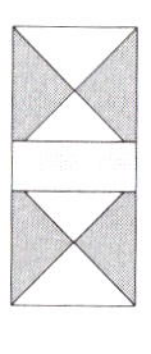

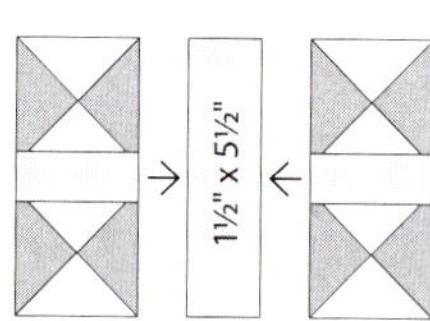

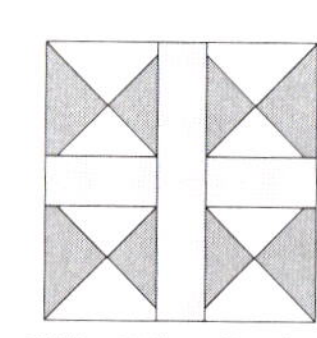

5½" x 5½" unfinished

(C) Sew a 2" x 5½" strip to each side of the block. Sew a 2" x 8½" sashing strip to the top and bottom of the block. Make 1.

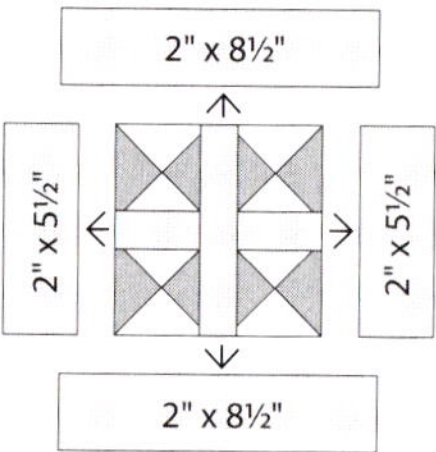

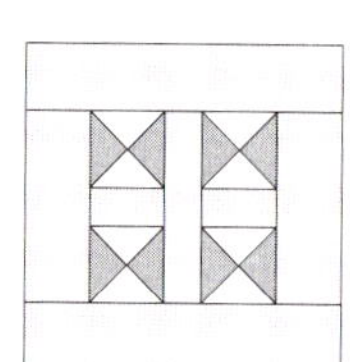

8½" x 8½" unfinished

(D) Join 2-1½" x 2½" Very Dark rectangles and 3 quarter-square triangle units as shown. Make 4.

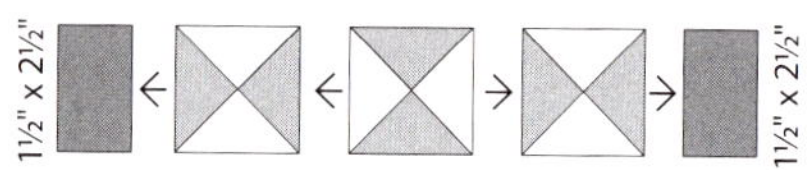

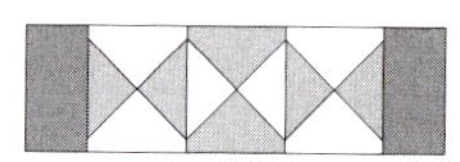

Make 4:
2½" x 8½" unfinished.

(E) Join the previous units.

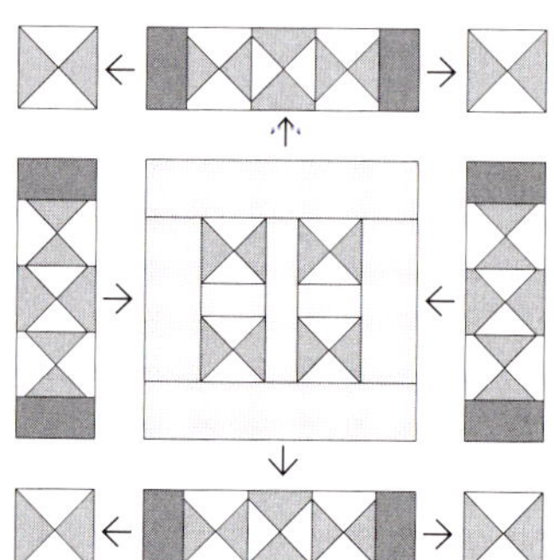

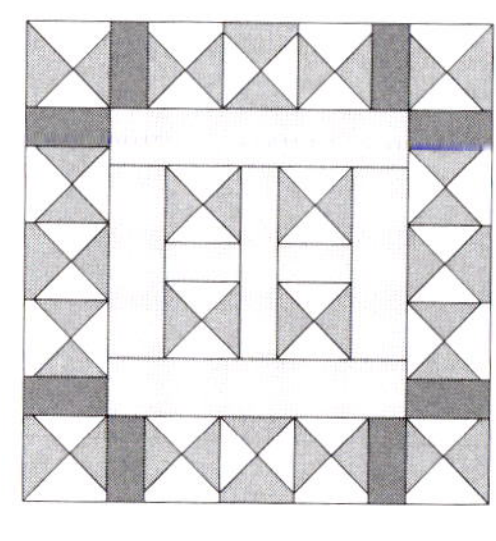

Make 1:
12½" x 12½" unfinished.

(F) Sew a 2" x 12½" sashing rectangle to the top and bottom of the block. Sew a 2" x 15½" sashing rectangle to each side of the block. Make 1.

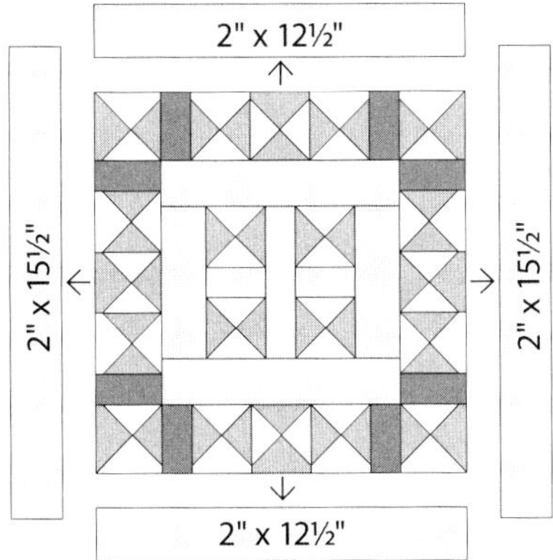

Section A is 15½" x 15½" unfinished.

2 Section B:

(A) Sew 1-2" x 3½" Very Dark and 1-3½" Dark square together. Make 132. Set aside 116 to use in step 7.

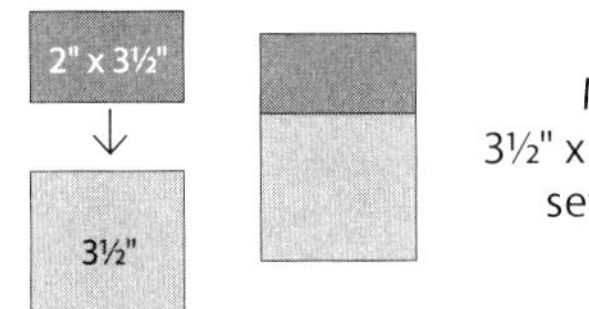

Make 132
3½" x 5" unfinished,
set aside 116.

(B) Sew 4 units together as shown. Make 4.

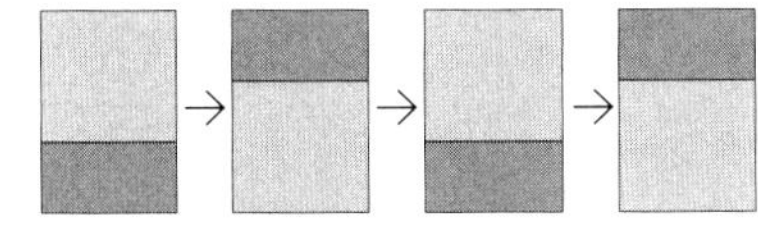

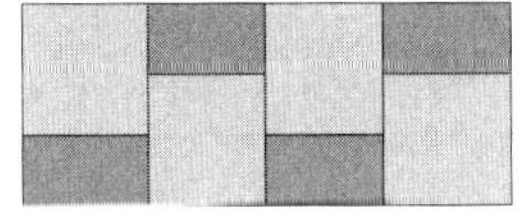

Make 4:
12½" x 5" unfinished.

(C) Sew 4-2" x 12½" sashing rectangles and 2 of the previous units in rows together as shown. Sew the rows together. Make 2.

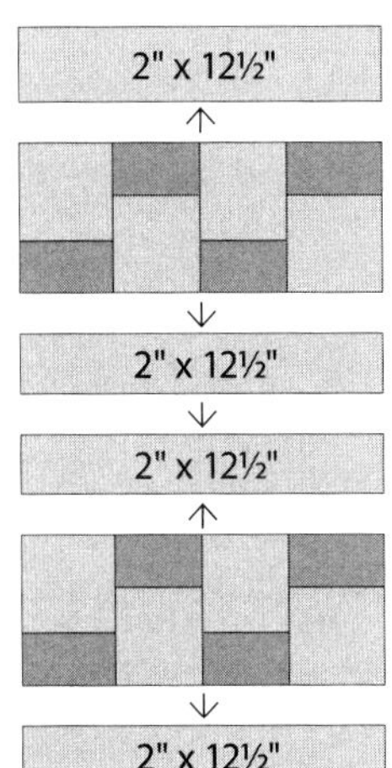

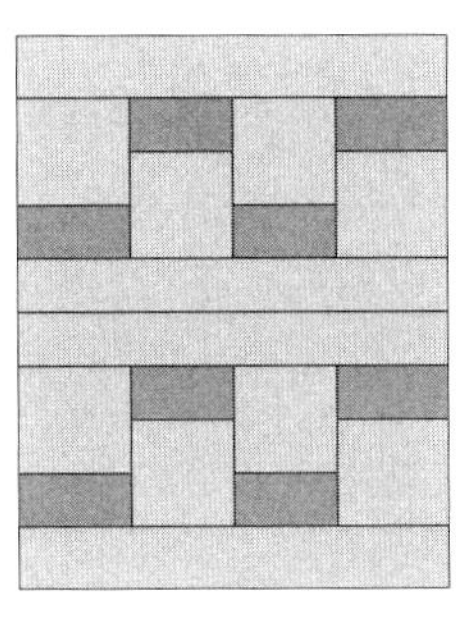

Make 2 of Section B:
12½" x 15½" unfinished.

3 Section C:

(A) Sew 2-2" Dark and 2-2" Very Dark squares in rows. Sew the rows together as shown. Make 24.

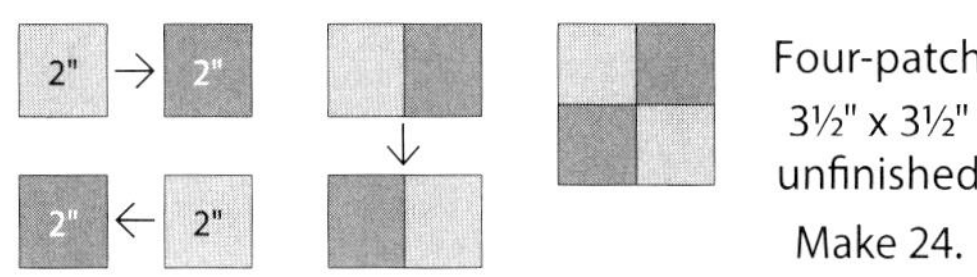

Four-patch
3½" x 3½"
unfinished
Make 24.

(B) Arrange 2-2" Light squares, 2-2" Dark squares, 4-2" x 3½" Medium rectangles, and 1 four patch in rows. Sew together as shown. Make 24.

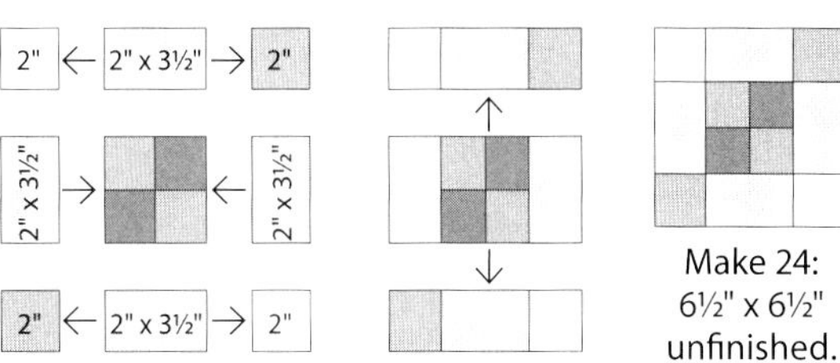

Make 24:
6½" x 6½"
unfinished.

(C) Sew 4 of the previous units in rows as shown. Sew the rows together. Make 6.

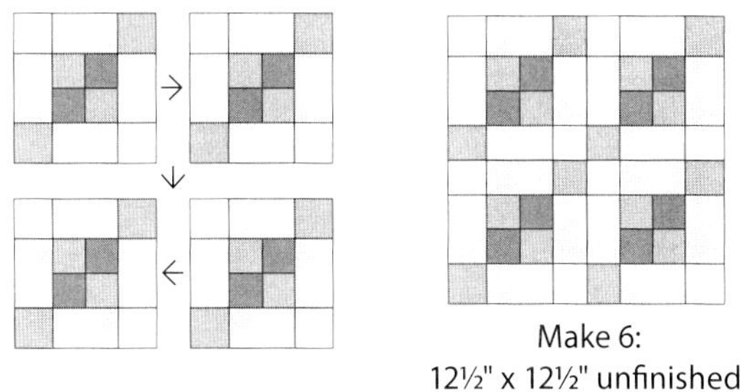

Make 6:
12½" x 12½" unfinished.

(D) Arrange 2-2½" x 12½" sashing rectangles and 3 of the previous units in rows as shown. Sew together. Make 2.

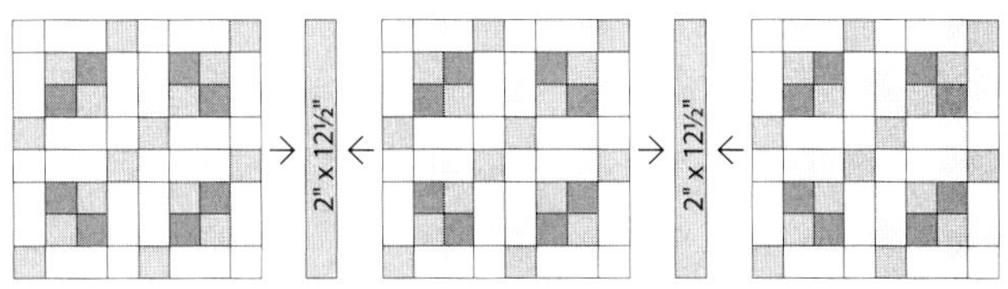

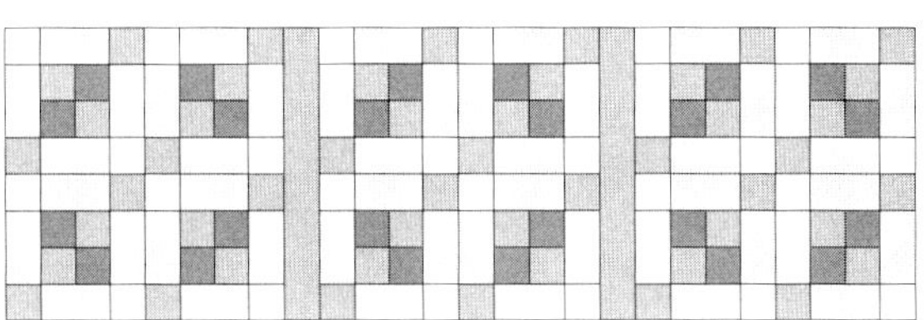

Make 2 of Section C:
12½" x 39½" unfinished.

4 Section D:

(A) Sew 2-2" Very Dark, 1-2" Light, and 1-2" Medium square in rows as shown. Sew the rows together. Make 48.

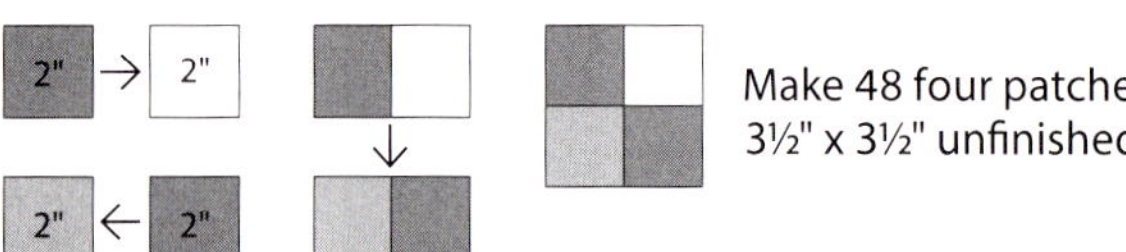

Make 48 four patches 3½" x 3½" unfinished.

(B) Arrange 2-3½" Medium squares and 2-3½" four patches in rows. Sew together as shown. Make 24.

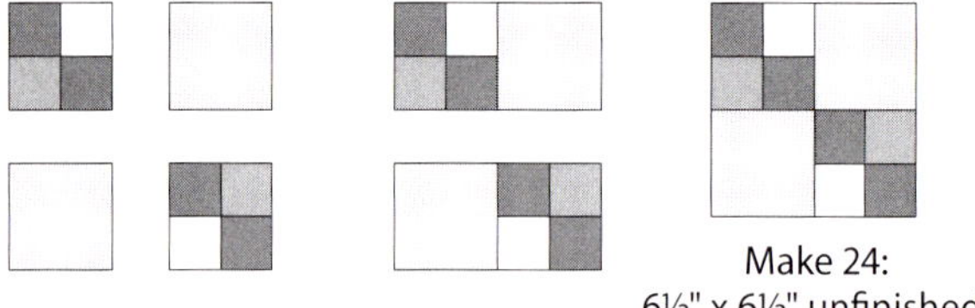

Make 24: 6½" x 6½" unfinished.

(C) Sew 4 of the previous units in rows as shown. Sew the rows together. Make 6.

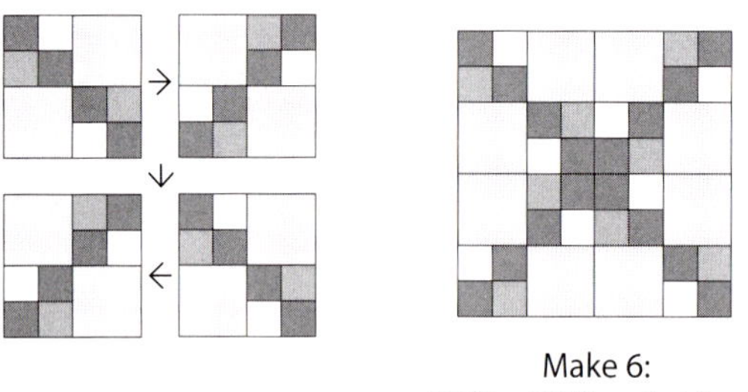

Make 6: 12½" x 12½" unfinished.

(D) Arrange 4-2½" x 12½" sashing rectangles and 3 of the previous units in rows as shown. Sew together. Make 2.

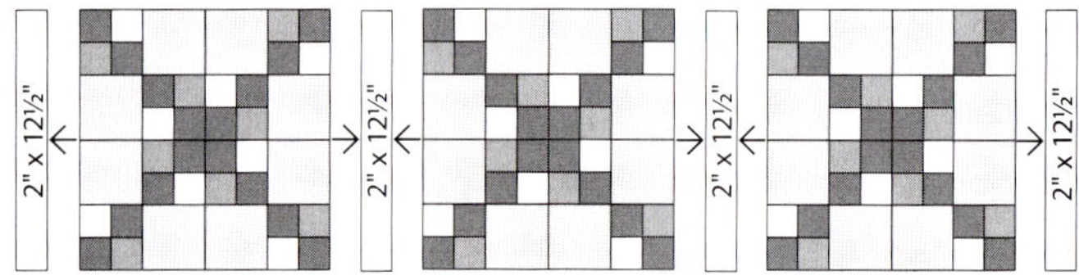

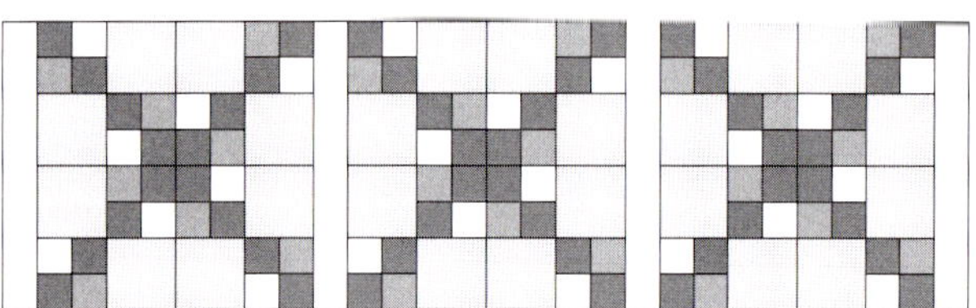

Make 2 of Section D: 12½" x 42½" unfinished.

5 Assemble Sections A - D:

(A) Join sections B and A. Add sections C. Sew a 2" x 39½" sashing rectangle to the top and bottom. Sew a 2" x 42½" sashing rectangle to each side of the block. Add sections D to top and bottom of assembly, and push seam allowance toward the sashings.

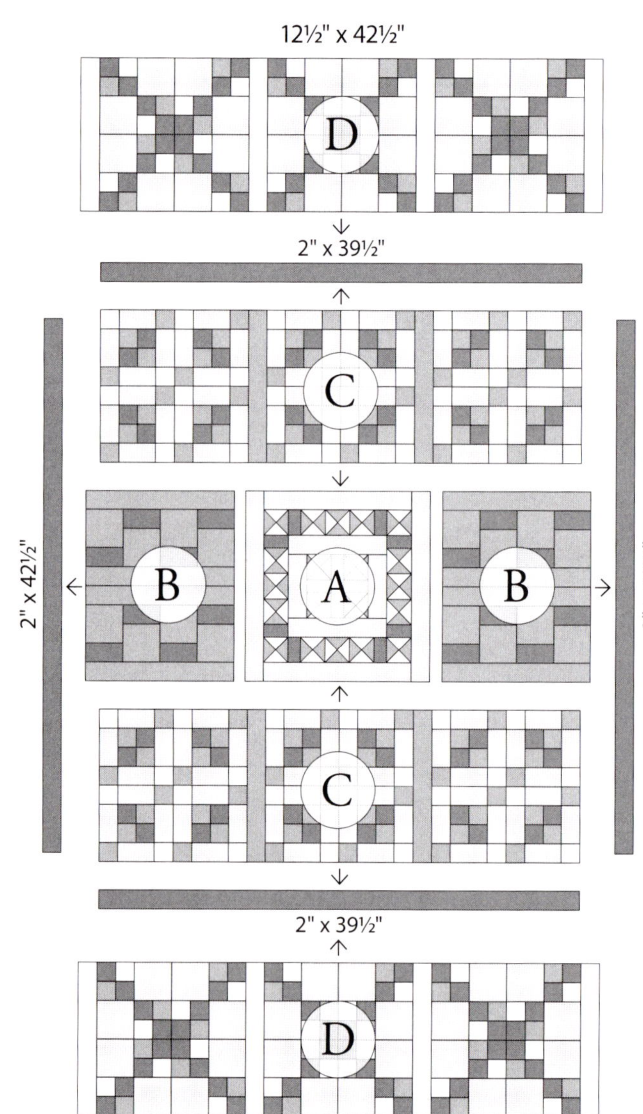

Quilt center is now 42½" x 66½" unfinished.

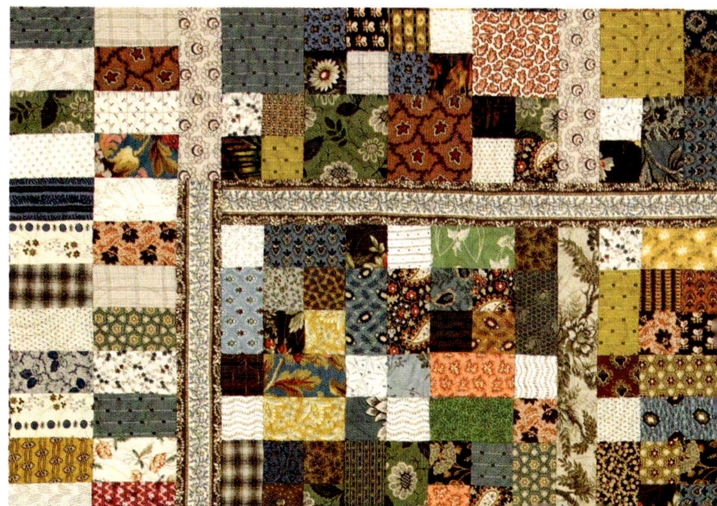

6 **Section E:**
Join 22-2" x 3½" light and 22-2" x 3½" medium rectangles as shown. Make 4. Sew 2 together.

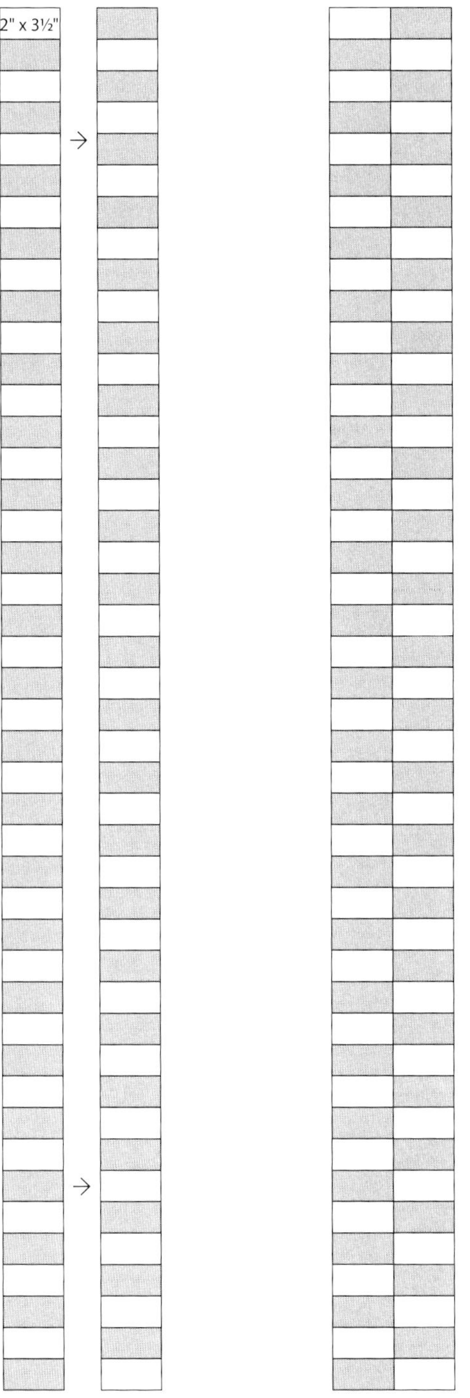

Make 2 of Section E: 6½" x 66½" unfinished.

7 **Sections F, FF, G and GG:**
Join 12 blocks from step 2 and 2-2" x 3½" Very Dark rectangles to make section F. Repeat to make 2.
Join 12 blocks from step 2 and 1-3½" Dark square to make section FF. Repeat to make 2.
Join 17 blocks from step 2 and 1-2" x 3½" Very Dark rectangle to make section G. Repeat to make 2.
Join 17 blocks from step 2 and 1-2" x 3½" Very Dark rectangle to make section GG. Repeat to make 2.

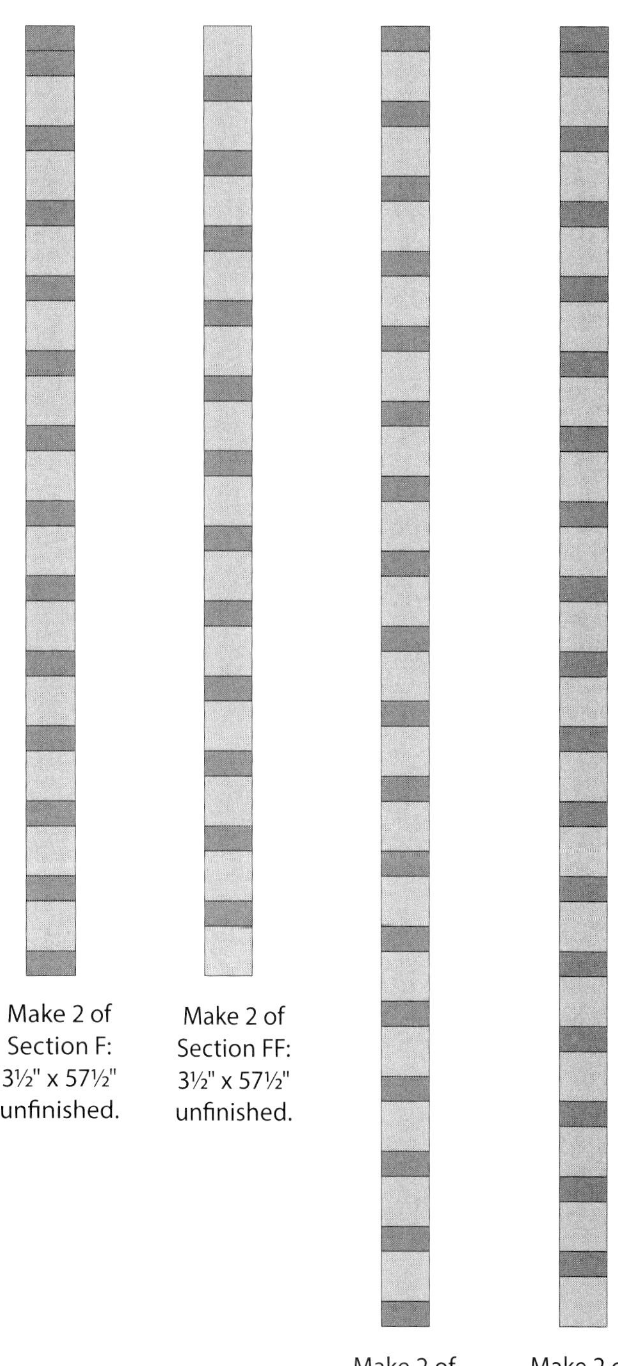

Make 2 of Section F: 3½" x 57½" unfinished.

Make 2 of Section FF: 3½" x 57½" unfinished.

Make 2 of Section G: 3½" x 78½" unfinished.

Make 2 of Section GG: 3½" x 78½" unfinished.

8 Assemble Quilt Top:

Join section E to each side of the center assembly. Next, add 1-2" x 66½" sashing rectangle to each side. Add sections F and FF to the top and bottom of the quilt. Add sections G and GG to each side.

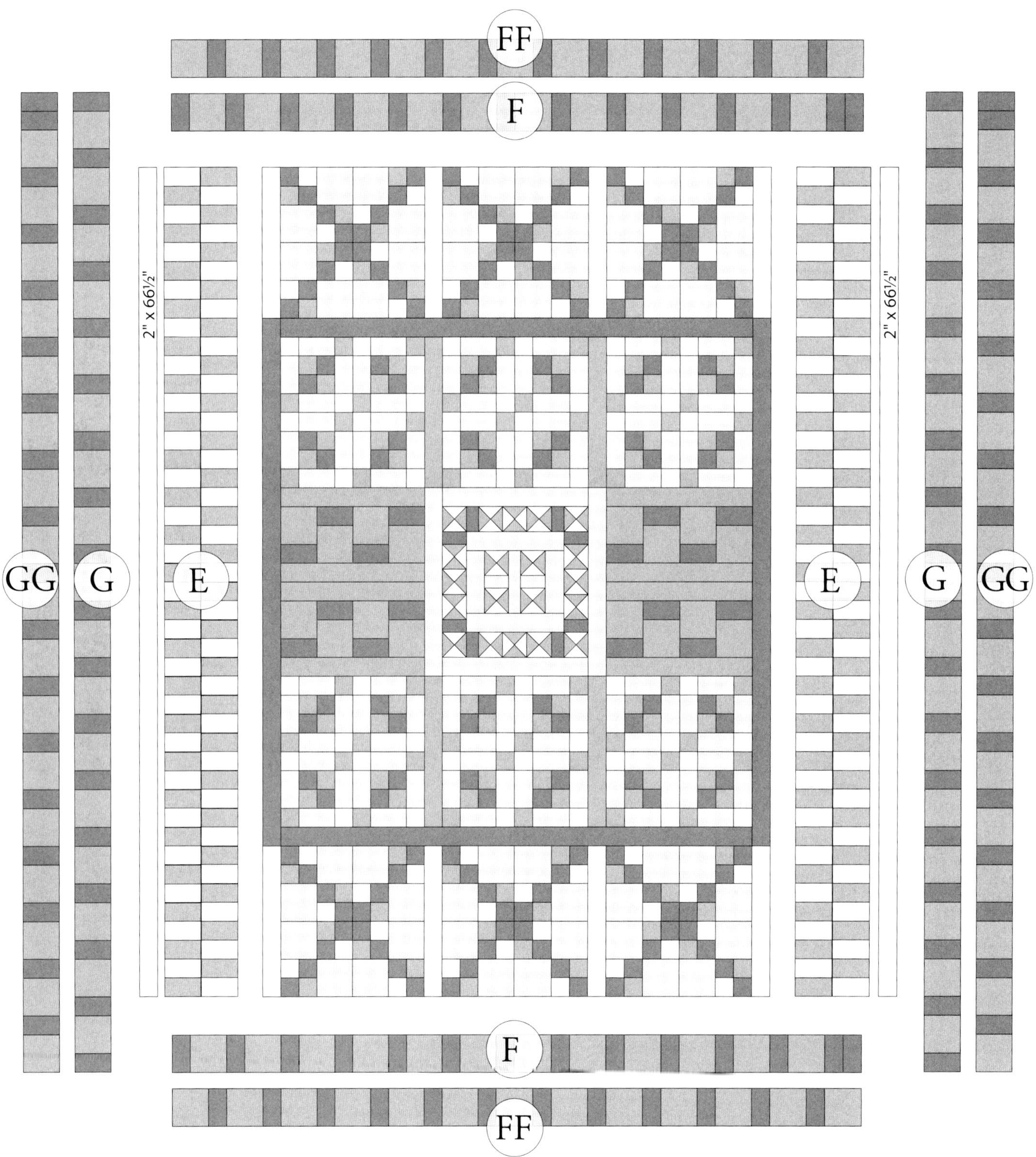

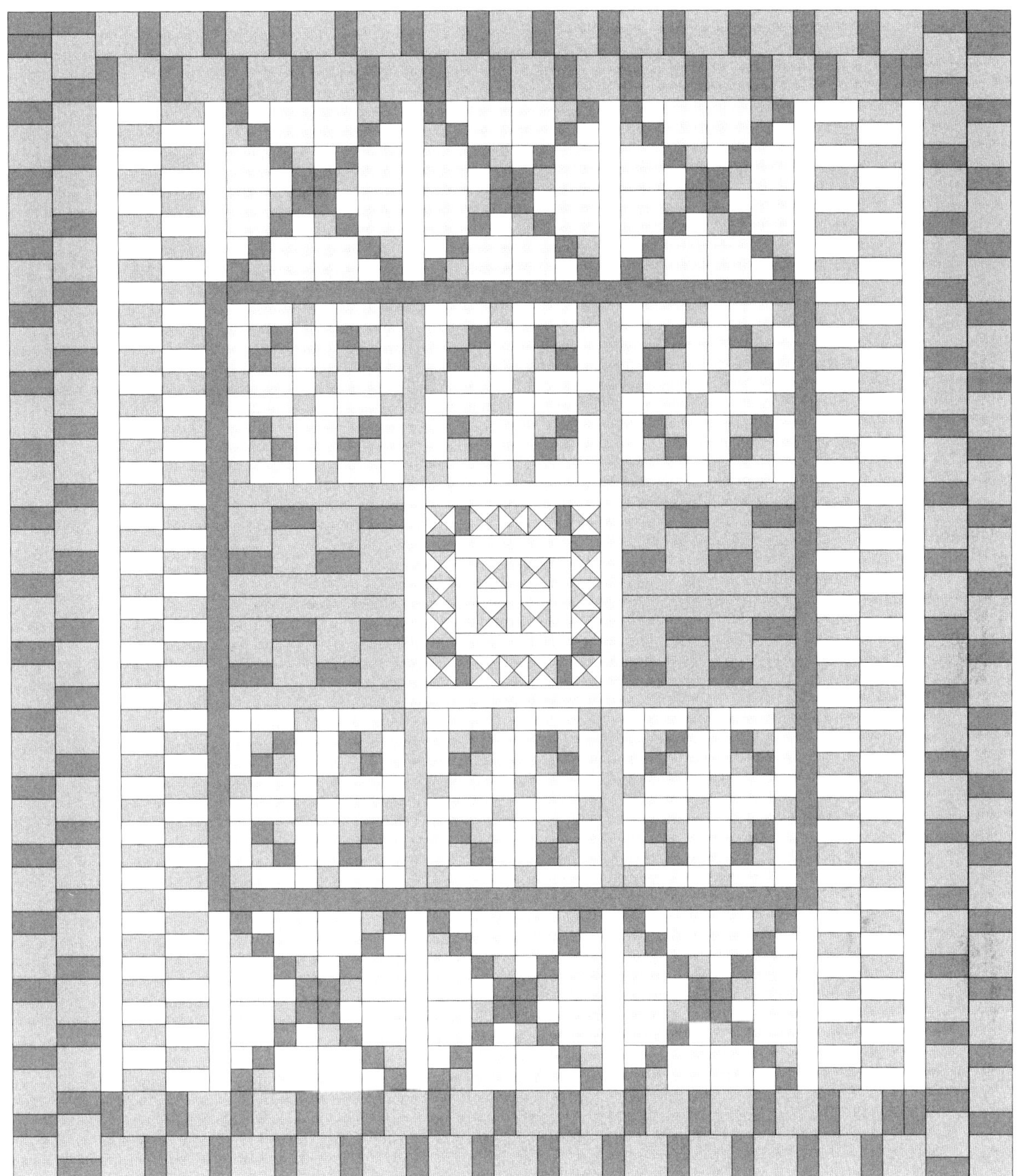

Unfinished quilt top is 69½" x 78½".

9 Quilting:

1. Layer quilt in the following order:
    a) Quilt back, right side down, 73½" x 82½".
    b) Batting 73½" x 82½" (I prefer Hobbs for best results.)
    c) Quilt top, right side up, 69½" x 78½".
2. Baste layers together.
3. Quilt by hand or machine. This quilt was quilted with an overall design on a long-arm quilting machine.

10 Binding:

Refer to My Sewing Basket on page 48 for binding directions.

ABOUT *the* AUTHOR

Meet Edyta...

Edyta's lifelong relationship with fabric began in Poland at a very young age, when she cut her mother's drapes to design her first project. Fortunately, for all of us, Edyta's mother recognized her passion for fabric that would later unfold into a consummate gift.

One of Edyta's dearest blessings is her marriage to her husband, Michael—and connection to the Sitar family quilting tradition. Both her mother-in-law, Carol, and grandmother-in-law, Anna, sat with Edyta over the quilt frame to teach her the ins and outs of quilting—and the ups and downs of life. With the help of two generations of Sitar women, Edyta found her confidence in this cottage craft, not only as a boundless creative outlet, but also as a means to filter her passion.

In observing the beauty of things around her, experiencing the thrills and challenges of being a woman, and reflecting profoundly on the human condition, Edyta expresses her existence through quilts. "My children and my husband are my greatest motivation," she says. "This is a Cinderella dream for me. Being able to do what I love and share this love with others is the greatest feeling and reward I could imagine!"

Edyta's intuitive feel for fabric, keen eye for color, and family teachings all contribute to her amazing quilts and natural evolution to pattern and fabric designing. Now working as owner and co-founder of Laundry Basket Quilts (www.laundrybasketquilts.com), Edyta has created close to 150 quilt patterns, traditional and batik fabrics with Moda, and threads, stencils, and templates for quilting. Her most recent innovations include ready-to-appliqué, fusible, laser-cut fabric shapes, ideal for quilting and handwork.

Edyta has documented her quilting stories in her 2011 book *Reasons for Quilts*. She has been published in national magazines and books, and has been featured on *The Quilt Show*. She spreads her quilter's spirit through ongoing workshops, presentations, and classes, including the popular *Craftsy* online creative forum (craftsy.com).

She enjoys gardening and small-town living in Michigan with her husband Michael and three children. Edyta connects with quilters everywhere through inspiring stories about the quilts she makes. Her artistry is evident even in the smallest bits of fabric, which debut here in *Handfuls of Scraps*.

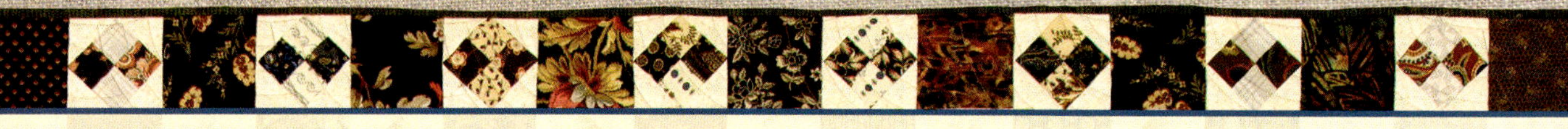

Other books by Edyta Sitar:

Hop To It! (Landauer, 2009), winner of the "2009 Midwest Book Award" in Crafts, Hobbies, and How-To by the Midwest Independent Publishers Association (MIPA); and winner of a silver award for "2009 Book of the Year" in Crafts and Hobbies by ForeWord Reviews

Friendship Triangles (Landauer, 2009)

Friendship Strips and Scraps (Landauer, 2010)

Reasons for Quilts (Laundry Basket Quilts, 2011)

Scrappy Fireworks (Landauer, 2012)

Seasonal Silhouettes (Landauer, 2013)

Rainbow Nest (Landauer, 2014)

Resources:

Laundry Basket Quilts .... www.laundrybasketquilts.com
Moda Fabrics .... www.unitednotions.com

Accuquilt .... www.accuquilt.com
Aurifil™ Threads .... www.aurifil.com
Bernina USA .... www.bernina.com
Quilting Creations International ... www.quiltingcreations.com

Judith Stern Friedman .... jsfcom@ameritech.net
Hardy Design Studio .... kayleen@hardydesignstudio.com